THE ENVIRONMENT OF INTERNATIONAL BANKING

CHARLES W. HULTMAN
University of Kentucky
Lexington, Kentucky

Prentice Hall, Englewood Cliffs, New Jersey 07632

Library of Congress Cataloging-in-Publication Data

Hultman, Charles W.
  The environment of international banking / Charles W. Hultman.
    p. cm.
  Bibliography: p.
  Includes index.
  ISBN 0-13-282856-1
  1. Banks and banking, International. 2. Banks and and banking—United
States. I. Title.
HG3881.H837 1990
332.1'5—dc20

89-8681
CIP

Editorial/production supervision
  and interior design: NANCY HAVAS FARRELL
Cover design: DIANE SAXE
Manufacturing buyer: ED O'DOUGHERTY

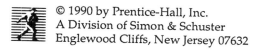

© 1990 by Prentice-Hall, Inc.
A Division of Simon & Schuster
Englewood Cliffs, New Jersey 07632

Printed in the United States of America
10 9 8 7 6 5 4 3 2 1

ISBN   0-13-282856-1

PRENTICE-HALL INTERNATIONAL (UK) LIMITED, *London*
PRENTICE-HALL OF AUSTRALIA PTY. LIMITED, *Sydney*
PRENTICE-HALL CANADA INC., *Toronto*
PRENTICE-HALL HISPANOAMERICANA, S.A., *Mexico*
PRENTICE-HALL OF INDIA PRIVATE LIMITED, *New Delhi*
PRENTICE-HALL OF JAPAN, INC., *Tokyo*
SIMON & SCHUSTER ASIA PTE. LTD., *Singapore*
EDITORA PRENTICE-HALL DO BRASIL, LTDA., *Rio de Janeiro*

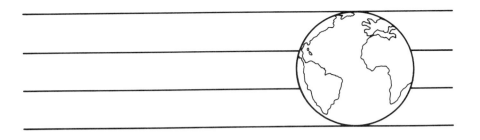

CONTENTS

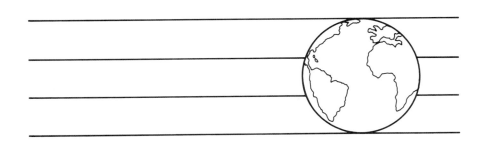

PREFACE

Dramatic and far-reaching changes have occurred in international financial activity in recent years. The movement away from rigidly pegged exchange rates, the establishment and early success of OPEC, the rapid expansion of the Eurodollar market, advances in communications technology, and the growth in commercial bank lending and subsequent debt servicing problems are among the major factors that have greatly affected the nature and extent of financial and banking activities among countries. From the perspective of the United States, international commercial banking has been altered with the development and growth of multinational corporations, the continuing expansion of international trade in goods and services, balance of payments, problems of many low income, debtor countries, and unprecedented capital flows across national boundaries. The passage of the International Banking Act of 1978 and subsequent legislation continues to have a significant and widespread impact on foreign banking activity in the U.S. and U.S. commercial banking activity abroad.

International banking is intertwined in a most extensive way with world trade, finance, and investments, and the allocation of resources among nations of the world. In addition, the flow of world capital has increased more rapidly than the flow of goods and services and has come to be a major factor influencing exchange rates. The leading commercial banks of the world play a key role in the purchase and sale of foreign exchange, the elimination of certain types of risks in international transactions of private traders, and the extension of credit for exports, imports, and medium- and long-term investment projects. In many instances, banks have found it advantageous to set up some type of operation in markets outside the country in order to better service domestic clients with overseas facilities and to secure new clients of a foreign nationality. Furthermore, banks are sometimes permitted to engage in a broader range of activities when performing outside of the boundaries of their respective domestic markets.

Developments in international banking are even more significant when juxtaposed against the related range of developments occurring in domestic U.S. banking. The major changes include deregulation of the financial sector while increasing the effectiveness of monetary policy, both reflected particularly in the Depository Institutions Deregulation and Monetary Control Act of 1980. This act increased the range of services that may be offered by nonbank financial institutions. As a result, competition has become more intense among suppliers of financial services as a greater variety of customer demands are satisfied by more institutions, as the geographical scope of any given institution's market expands, and as interest rates on time and savings deposits became more responsive to market conditions. In addition, the establishment of broader and more uniform reserve requirements for commercial banks and thrift institutions has enhanced implementation of monetary policy. Improvements in communications and technological change have also contributed to "nonlocal" competition and increased the number of suppliers available to users of financial services.

A basic theme of this book is that international commercial banking is an integral part of a system that is undergoing change—change that is more dynamic and dramatic than that ever experienced in the history of commerce among nations. These developments are manifested in new conditions in the foreign exchange market and the legal framework within which banking occurs as well as by new sources of medium- and long-term credit, and by a shift in attitudes toward external debt obligations. The change is the result not only of developments within banking itself, but also the result of developments that are essentially exogenous to the system.

Equally important is that the change occurring as old attitudes and institutions give way to new ones is not simply transitory from one relatively stable period to a second. Rather, it gives the appearance of an unending, shifting, evolving process, the outcome of which is neither in sight nor predictable.

The rapid increase in the volume of international lending and other financial activity has forced the United States to reevaluate policies regarding operations of foreign banks in this country and of U.S. banks abroad. To what extent should offices of foreign banks in the U.S. be regulated and controlled? Do U.S. banks operating abroad have the opportunity to compete on an equitable basis? To what extent should their actions be supervised and controlled to avoid financial losses or instability in world money and capital markets? Are the Federal Reserve and the central banks of other countries in a position to exercise effective monetary restraint given the large amount of offshore lending? Can the private lending institutions adequately supply the demands of the borrowing countries without jeopardizing their own liquidity and solvency? Can the debt problems of major debtor countries be resolved or at least alleviated without threat to the U.S. and world financial systems? To what extent has financial innovation rendered existing national and international supervision obsolete?

The purpose of this volume is to provide a basis for an understanding of international commercial banking and the framework within which it occurs, particularly in terms of the U.S. interest in such activity in recent years. Coverage of the volume begins with a description of the nature of commercial banking and lending, and a brief review of the international financial system within which commercial banks operate. This includes an examination of the basis for international lending, an analysis of the role of the International Monetary Fund, the shift to floating exchange rates, the nature of the Eurocurrency market and the role of international reserves.

Against this background, the evolving nature of foreign commercial banking activity in the U.S. through different forms of offices is considered (Part II). The American reaction is also analyzed, particularly as this activity has led to, and is affected by, the International Banking Act of 1978. In addition, the concern over foreign acquisitions of U.S. banks is explored. Finally, because of the nature of the dual banking system in the U.S., the financial environment in the various states is analyzed.

In the next section, Part III, the role played by U.S. banks abroad is examined. This includes the nature and volume of such activities, and the nature and treatment of commercial banks in external markets. The function and implications of International Banking Facilities, a relatively new development in American banking, is also considered. A major portion of Part III relates to the international debt problem and the response of American commercial banks, the U.S. government, and international institutions. Coordination of bank regulation and supervision is also examined as reflected in the Basle Concordat and the U.S.-U.K. and G-10 proposals.

Although Part II (foreign banking in the U.S.) and Part III (the activity of U.S. institutions abroad) reflect separate treatments of bank operations, it must be recognized that, given the nature of international banking and capital flows, this is an artificial separation. Such a division is helpful for descriptive and analytical purposes, but the artificiality becomes apparent in a discussion of Edge Act Corporations, International Banking Facilities, capital adequacy guidelines, and even the Eurocurrency market. These topics can be covered either in the analysis of foreign banking in the U.S. or the analysis of U.S. banking abroad. This situation reflects the essence of international commercial banking—an activity that transcends national boundaries and yet occurs in both a national and international framework.

Part IV provides a concluding analysis of developments in banking markets in the U.S. and abroad. An effort is also made to provide some projections regarding the future of international banking and the environment within which it occurs.

Although the organization of the book was designed to provide some logic to the complex study of international commercial banking, other arrangements of topic coverage may prove satisfactory for pedagogical purposes. For example, Chapter 3 on the structure of international banking might be used as an introductory chapter. The analysis of International Banking Facilities in Chapter 10 could be included as part of Chapter 3. And, finally, Chapter 14 on international banking supervision could be included in those sections of Part II that focus on legislation and regulation.

Although a substantial amount has been written about international commercial banking in the last several years, the literature is included in such a variety of sources that it is not always readily available, even if the interested reader is aware of it existence. This publication is designed to make some of the relevant information conveniently available to those interested in the rapidly changing area of international finance and business.

While the objective is to provide a relatively comprehensive outline of international commercial banking activity from a U.S. prospective, a complete and detailed treatment would require several volumes of material. As suggested by the title, the environment of international banking is given special emphasis on the assumption that banking activity is influenced by the conditions and framework within which it occurs. No effort is made to duplicate the detail pertaining to such topics as the mechanism of the foreign exchange markets, the shipping and collection documents of international trade, detailed items included in the balance of payments, and the basics of bank management, all of which are covered in many standard references. In order to supplement the overview, extensive footnotes and a bibliography are provided to facilitate access to additional reading material. Much of the early data and information on international commercial banking comes from official sources—central banks, the Bank for International Settlements, and the International Monetary Fund. However, a growing share of information and analysis is available in academic and trade journals and other publications.

Although the material may be most useful to the person with an undergraduate course in Money and Banking or International Trade, much of it will be readily understood by anyone with a general background in business and economics. The book is intended to supplement the standard textbooks in these and related courses where additional emphasis on international banking is desired. When included with designated reading material on an extensive basis, it could provide the foundation for a course in International Commercial Banking or International Financial Institutions. The material is also intended to give the general reader an overview of the international financial system with a major focus on the private U.S. banking system and how it affects and is being affected by international economic and political developments.

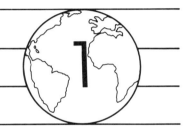

STRUCTURE OF
INTERNATIONAL BANKING

International banking can be defined to include a wide variety of financial activities of commercial banks that range from the purchase and sale of foreign currencies to the participation with other banks in a consortium to extend a project loan to a foreign government. For the individual bank, it may reflect the simple establishment of an international department with a limited involvement in foreign currency purchases and sales, participation with other lenders in a loan to a foreign government, or a physical presence in a foreign country through the establishment of a branch or subsidiary.

Depending upon the type of operation, international commercial banking activity has much in common with domestic banking in terms of involvement in financial transactions, provision of financial advice, the creation and holding of checking accounts and savings deposits, and extension of loans of varying maturity dates to a wide range of borrowers. But international banking is more complex and varied because it involves two or more currencies, differing sets of legal institutions and banking arrangements, and coping with political risk and the possibility of interruptions in servicing of external debts.

1

One of the more apparent characteristics of international commercial banking in recent years is the change that is occurring not only in the number and nature of financial institutions themselves but also in the framework within which they operate. This change is perhaps more dynamic and dramatic than that ever experienced in the history of international commerce. The developments include new practices that have served to integrate the U.S. money and capital markets more completely and closely with overseas markets. They include a significant shift in the source of medium- and long-term credit for use in borrowing countries. They are reflected in a shift in attitudes regarding external debt obligations; coping with repayment problems has led to renegotiation and rescheduling of debt that in part has become a somewhat common procedure for many countries. Other changes include the growth in fee-income activities of commercial banks in response to new conditions in the financial markets.

The changes in commercial banking and the environment in which banking takes place are pervasive. Equally important is that these developments, occurring as attitudes, institutions, procedures, and practices alter, cannot be characterized as a transitory phase leading from one relatively stable period to another. Rather, they give the appearance of an unending, shifting, evolving process, the outcome of which cannot yet be determined.

This pervasive change along with the unprecedented growth in international commercial banking activities has forced U.S. bankers and the U.S. government to reevaluate their practices and policies. New financial legislation has been enacted in Congress and more is under consideration, all of which will continue to have a major impact on the financial community. Commercial banks in turn find that the once relatively stable and predictable nature of financial activity has been altered not only by new legislation, bank regulations, and competition from the thrift institutions but also by new profit opportunities, new types of risk, and innovative methods of dealing with these risks.

The purpose of this chapter is to provide an overview of the structure of international commercial banking. It outlines the general nature of banking across national boundaries as well as the types of organizations used in performance of their activities. In addition, the importance of banks from different countries in global finance is considered.

ENTERING INTERNATIONAL COMMERCE

For a given bank, entry into international commercial activity is usually a gradual process that commences with the provision of financial assistance to local firms interested in exporting or importing. The establishment of an international department may also be considered by the bank. These, in turn, lead to the issuance of various instruments and procedures to help exporters and importers finance international trade.

Efforts may also extend to the provision of a variety of foreign services including the purchase and sale of foreign currencies (deposits in foreign banks) to assist exporters, importers, and investors; issuance of traveler's checks to persons traveling abroad; the provision of foreign drafts for payments abroad; and direct bank transfers through foreign wires and cables. Foreign exchange services provided by banks for their customers include transactions for immediate delivery (the spot market) and the accommodation of foreign currency exchanges in the anticipation of movements in the price of such currencies (the forward market). Commercial banks serve an intermediary role in the exchange market; they are prepared to both buy and sell foreign currencies at appropriate prices to cover the demands of customers, and they also trade in foreign currencies for their own account. A further expansion of banks into international activities may occur in a variety of ways, each of which is described briefly in the following sections.

TYPES OF OFFICES AND RELATIONSHIPS WITH FOREIGN BANKS

Depending upon the bank's size, location, and desire to expand, it may establish a close relationship with one or more foreign banks, which as a minimum involves creating an account relationship between firms. The banks provide services on a reciprocal basis including the exchange of information and advice, acceptance of instruments used in financing of trade, the collection of items for the bank depositor, and the provision of other related types of services. However, the firms remain separate institutions.

An approach to international commerce on a limited basis is also possible through participation with other banks in the extension of loans to both bank and nonbank institutions. Many small- and medium-sized banks are able to become involved in international lending through these arrangements.

The expansion of activities beyond the home office requires a major decision. If the decision is made by a U.S. bank to concentrate primarily on transactions involving international commerce, the establishment of a limited service type of office may be adequate. A physical presence in a foreign country that includes only a limited number of functions can be established most easily.

An extensive overseas involvement is most likely to characterize the large money center banks—those located in the financial capitals of the world. The larger regional banks—those situated in major cities away from the financial centers—are also likely to be involved internationally, especially to the extent that local commercial and industrial activity is tied to foreign trade.

The more extensive foreign activities require the establishment of a full service type of operation capable of performing all of the usual banking functions. Banking becomes truly international when an institution establishes offices in more than one foreign country. International banking includes an increased involvement in new forms of financing to accommodate changes in the patterns of borrowing.

The international dimension of financial activities is related to the growth of services provided to multinational corporations, and to the opportunities provided by the expansion and integration of international money and capital markets. The major international banks generally maintain a network of overseas offices and frequently participate in types of financial transactions, such as security purchases, not regularly open to U.S. banks in the domestic market. By the end of 1987, about 260 U.S. banks maintained offices in foreign countries, Puerto Rico, and U.S. territories and possessions.

NATURE OF OFFICES AND RELATIONSHIPS

United States banks may have a *correspondent* relationship with foreign banks. They may also establish a physical presence in a foreign market with a *representative office* or an *agency* in order to perform a limited number of banking services. Full banking services are provided overseas with either a *branch*, a *subsidiary*, or an *affiliate*. Frequently, a subsidiary or affiliate is set up under a United States-based *Edge Act* or *Agreement Corporation* or through the use of a *holding company*. Finally, U.S. banks may participate with other banks to undertake international commercial activities through *joint ventures, consortia,* or *syndicates*. Foreign banks establish offices in the United States in many of the same ways as U.S. banks participate in foreign markets. They may also establish *New York Investment Companies*.

Correspondent Banking

Correspondent banking describes the use of a bank native to the foreign market (Bank 2) to act as an agent for a nonnative bank (Bank 1) typically on a reciprocating basis. The relationship is developed to facilitate export and import trade particularly relating to the instruments and financial documentation of trade. Correspondent banking is also evolving to accommodate innovative techniques and instruments relating to foreign exchange operations and custodial services for securities. Compensation for services is accomplished either through the maintenance of correspondent balances or on the basis of service fees.

This approach does not involve Bank 1's physical presence in the foreign market. For some large U.S. banks, the holding of foreign correspondent balances and the provision of correspondent services has grown to become a major component of their overseas efforts.[1]

Representative Office

A representative office is designed primarily to solicit business for the parent bank and its other affiliates; the arrangement involves a limited physical presence in the foreign market. The office does not accept deposits or make loans but rather serves a liaison function for the parent bank. Representative offices may be set up rather freely in the United States but registration with the Secretary of the Treasury is required. United States banks are limited to the use of representative offices in several foreign countries that do not allow full service commercial banks but which desire some type of arrangement to facilitate American trade.

Agency

Agencies are used primarily to accommodate international commerce; they are usually also an integral part of the parent company but can perform more functions than a representative office. A major difference is that agencies are allowed to accept foreign demand deposits. While they are not authorized to accept domestic demand deposits, they are permitted to hold credit balances. Unlike other depository institutions, agencies are not required to hold reserves against deposit liabilities.[2]

[1]Although correspondent banking has a long history, recent changes in this function appear to be as great as in any other component of commercial banking. See, for example, Hans W. Wolpers, "Changes in International Correspondent Banking," *The Bankers Magazine* (March-April 1982), pp. 17-20.
    A useful analysis of some of the instruments of international credit including letters of credit and bankers' acceptances is provided in Nicholas L. Deak and JoAnne Celusack, *International Banking* (New York: New York Institute of Finance, 1984), pp. 35-84.

[2]Obligations may be considered to be credit balances if they are incidental to or arise out of the exercise of lawful banking power, serve a specific purpose, are not solicited from the general public, are not used to pay routine operating expenses in the United States, and are withdrawn within a reasonable period of time. See Federal Regulation K (Section 211.22).

Foreign Branch

A foreign branch is an office of an institution located outside the country under the laws of the country in which the institution is organized. It is an integral part of the parent institution, usually not separately capitalized, which typically performs all of the traditional banking functions allowed by the host country, including accepting deposits and extending loans. For many banks, branches are the most important form of overseas office. (About 15 percent of the branches of foreign banks located in the United States are "limited" branches that do not perform full service operations. These are primarily branches located outside the designated home state of the foreign bank.)

Subsidiary

The subsidiary is an organization with a specified portion of the voting stock held directly or indirectly by the parent bank or which is otherwise capable of being controlled by the parent bank. The subsidiary is separate legally from the parent firm, is organized under the laws of the host country, and may engage in full banking activities. It may be established as a new organization (de nova), or by acquisition of an existing bank. The establishment or acquisition of a foreign bank can be accomplished directly or through an Edge Act Corporation.[3]

Affiliate

As defined in Federal Reserve Regulation Q, an affiliate of an organization is any company that is a subsidiary of the organization. The affiliate in some instances is defined as a foreign institution in which the parent company owns 20 to 50 percent of the equity stock; in general, the affiliate does not involve control by a company holding its stock.[4]

[3]As defined by 12 C.F.R., a subsidiary of a foreign banking organization is an organization 25 percent or more of whose voting shares is directly controlled by a foreign banking organization. However, 12 C.F.R. 211.2(p) defines a foreign subsidiary of a U.S. banking firm as an organization more than 50 percent of the voting stock of which is held directly or indirectly by the investor, or which is otherwise controlled or capable of being controlled by the investor or an affiliate of the investor.

[4]Several of the institutions and relationships were defined by the Federal Reserve Board in 1979 in Regulation Q and are contained in Federal Register (Washington: June 20, 1979), pp. 36005-36012. However, there are variations in usage of the terms, and some are used interchangeably by various writers. In addition, definitions may vary depending upon the applicable regulations. See "Definition of Affiliate," Federal Reserve Bulletin (Washington: November 1982), pp. 694-697. See also International Trade Commission, The Relationship of Exports in Selected U.S. Service Industries to U.S. Merchandise Exports (Washington: 1982), pp. 173-174; and Stuart Robinson, Multinational Banking (Leiden, Switzerland: A. W. Sijthoff, 1972), pp. 19-31.

For example, New York has several state-licensed, foreign-owned agencies with

Edge Act Corporations

Edge Act Corporations (Edges or EACs) are subsidiaries of banks or bank holding companies and are designed primarily to permit banks to undertake international financial transactions, but their efforts are restricted to international commerce. Edges are chartered by the Federal Reserve Board and may be owned by either U.S. or foreign interests. Most are located in New York, Florida, and Texas.

Agreement Corporations

Agreement Corporations have essentially the same powers as EACs, but are state chartered. They enter into an agreement with the Federal Reserve to operate according to its regulations.

Bank Holding Company

As defined by the Federal Reserve Board, a bank holding company is a company that holds at least 25 percent ownership of a bank. In some instances, the Board may assume effective control with less than 25 percent of the stock and presume the firm to be a holding company. Holding companies usually are established for control purposes and are not operating entities. United States and foreign bank companies employ holding companies as part of their organizational structure to accommodate the expansion of activities both in terms of lines of activity and geographical area.

Joint Ventures

Joint ventures usually reflect acquisition of a minority interest in a foreign bank in an effort to pool resources of participating institutions and to share the associated risks. They are defined by Regulation K as organizations with 20 percent or more of the voting stock held by the investor, but which are not a subsidiary of the investor. Joint ventures may last for a limited period of time, subject to renewal.

---

power to accept deposits from U.S. residents. These organizations are identified as branches by the Federal Reserve System. See Federal Reserve Board, *Foreign Investment in U.S. Banking Institutions* (Washington: 1987).

Numerical listings of subsidiaries of foreign banks in the United States may vary depending upon the definition used. For example, the Federal Reserve Board's *Annual Report* indicates the number of subsidiaries of foreign banks in terms of majority-owned banks owned by foreign banking organizations. The more inclusive *Foreign Investment in U.S. Banking Institutions* lists U.S.-chartered banks of foreigners to include all banks with some foreign ownership and regardless of type of ownership, whether by banking organizations or by individuals.

Consortium Bank

A consortium bank is sometimes defined as an entity formed by a group of banks to operate within a defined area or to perform a specified function. A consortium *of* banks may also be a group of banks that combine to perform a specified function, such as financing a loan transaction.

Syndicate

A syndicate is also represented by a group of banks that pool their resources in a cooperative effort usually for the provision of large loans. Syndications frequently imply the existence of a lead or managing bank.

New York Investment Companies

These companies are established under New York law and are permitted to conduct commercial banking operations of an international and wholesale nature, although they cannot accept deposits. They are also permitted to deal in U.S. corporate securities.

FACTORS AFFECTING TYPE OF OFFICE

Traditionally banks have initially moved into external markets with an agency or a representative office because of the relative ease with which they can be established. Most U.S. banks and bank holding companies operating abroad after a period of time create or acquire a branch, a subsidiary, or an affiliate.[5]

The type of office that is established is particularly relevant for legal, regulatory, tax, and other related purposes.[6] The most important factor affecting the choice of office is the attitude of the host country as reflected in its laws, regulations, and policies toward financial institutions. As described in Chapter 8, some countries prohibit foreign commercial branches; others prohibit foreign-held subsidiaries (or affiliates). And, of course, some governments exclude both foreign branches and subsidiaries. In other instances, entry of new firms is prohibited, but outside firms already in existence are permitted to function under grandfather provisions. Over a dozen foreign countries permit no foreign

---

[5]Information and literature on U.S. banking offices in foreign countries do not make a sharp distinction between branches and agencies. In some instances, they are simply grouped as a single category; in others, no reference is made to U.S. agencies overseas.

[6]A useful analysis of the sequence of increasing foreign participation on the part of U.S. banks is provided in James V. Houpt, *International Trends for U.S. Banks and Banking Markets* (Washington: Federal Reserve System, 1988), pp. 4-13.

commercial banking except for representative offices; only a small amount of trade is conducted with these countries.

United States laws permit foreign banks to establish offices in several states in this country; these states generally encompass major financial centers, and thus foreign firms are given substantial access to American markets. These offices are subject to the same control as U.S. banks at the federal and state level.

In some cases, the policy of the home country of the parent bank may determine or at least influence the type of office established abroad. In at least a few instances, certain types of overseas offices are not permitted by the government of the parent company.

Generally, branches are easier to establish than a subsidiary in a foreign country and they afford the parent company the greatest degree of control. Accordingly, as full service types of offices, branches play a key role in external operations. The type of office a bank establishes abroad also depends upon the extent of market participation desired by the bank, the amount that can be invested in the facility, and the availability of trained and talented staff.

The nature of the office may also depend upon the type of service to be provided. Usually commercial banking is categorized as retail, wholesale, or service banking. Retail activities include offering different types of services such as deposit holding for users other than banks, providing financing for small exporters and importers, and lending to individuals, households, small corporations, and partnerships. This type of banking usually requires a branch or a subsidiary office. Retail operations of foreign bank offices in the United States might include serving an ethnic group in a major city, but generally retail activities are not the major function of foreign offices in U.S. markets. Among the banks that have established extensive retail operations and outlets in the United States are National Westminster Bank (United Kingdom) and California First Bank (Japan), each of which has an extensive system of branch outlets. Citicorp and Chase are two of the few U.S.-owned banks that have pursued retail activities on a worldwide scale.

A bank's first overseas effort is likely to be in wholesale or service banking. Wholesale banking includes transactions principally with large corporate customers, banks, other financial institutions and governments in large loans, deposits, and related functions. Wholesale banking may be undertaken by subsidiaries, branches, and agencies. But perhaps the most important consideration is that the major international banks are engaged primarily in wholesale banking.

The wholesale and international emphasis is particularly apparent in the assets and liabilities of agencies, branches, and Edges of foreign banks operating in U.S. markets. In relative terms and as compared with domestic chartered banks, these offices hold a small volume of real estate and individual loans, but a relatively large share of commercial and industrial loans. On the liability side, offices of foreign banks hold a relatively smaller share of transactions accounts (demand and other checkable deposits) and savings deposits.

Service banking is sometimes identified as a separate type of banking. To a great extent, it consists of providing advice and information to overseas subsidiaries of a parent bank's clients. Service organizations are usually representative offices and agencies, both of which are restricted in their authority to accept demand deposits.

Tax provisions also vary depending upon the type of organization. Although U.S. tax laws and provisions are complex, a basic difference is that U.S. branches and agencies of foreign banks are not taxed as entities separate from the parent firms. The parent firm is taxed at the prevailing U.S. corporate rate on the net income earned within the United States. The net income of the subsidiary is taxed at the corporate tax rate. United States taxation of foreign branches of U.S. banks has been different from that of subsidiaries. However, as described in Chapter 8, the difference changed as a result of the Tax Reform Act of 1986 as banks are no longer able to defer the U.S. taxation of foreign income until repatriated.

Although bank facilities abroad may take any one of several forms, the two most important types in terms of performing the traditional banking functions are the branch and the subsidiary. A first approximation of the magnitude of the activity of each of the types of institutions is indicated by the value of the assets.[7] Assets of banking institutions generally include currency, deposits in other banks, bonds, and loans receivable. By 1987, the magnitudes were as follows:

Assets of major foreign branches of U.S. banks: $350 billion.

Assets of major foreign subsidiaries of U.S. banks: $132 billion.

Assets of branches and agencies of foreign banks in the United States: $463 billion.

Assets of subsidiaries and affiliates of foreign banks in the United States: $128 billion.

---

[7]Detailed statistical information is available on U.S.-chartered insured commercial banks and branches and agencies of foreign banks in the semi-annual table, *Foreign Investment in U.S. Banking Institutions*, provided by the Division of Research and Statistics, Federal Reserve Board. The information provided includes the types of charter, percentage of foreign ownership, type and country of foreign ownership, value of assets, and state in which the office is located.

Additional data are included in James V. Houpt, *International Trends for U.S. Banks and Banking Markets* (Washington: Federal Reserve System, 1988).

The form of banking organization has implications that are also essential to an understanding of the nationality of a particular institution. For example, is the foreign branch of a U.S. bank located in West Germany a U.S. or a German institution? And is the subsidiary of a British bank located in the United States a British or American institution? In practice, a given bank is identified as either a U.S. or a foreign institution depending upon the criteria used as the basis for determining its status. Thus a distinction must be made between the country in which the financial control of an office exists and the one in which the operation of the office actually occurs. From a U.S. perspective, banks may be designated as either *U.S.-owned* or *U.S.-located*. For example, focusing attention on the operation of offices or residency, U.S.-located banks include:

a. Domestic offices of U.S. banks
b. Subsidiaries, branches, and agencies of foreign banks located in the United States.

In contrast, with the focus on nationality or country of ownership of financial control, U.S.-owned banks include:

a. Domestic offices of U.S. banks
b. Foreign branches and subsidiaries of U.S. banks; i.e., branches and subsidiaries of U.S. banks located abroad.

Generally the definition based on the country of ownership or reflecting the nationality of the banks is most easily understood. However, the location criterion is frequently most meaningful—for example, when the balance of payments impact of a banking activity is considered.[8] Thus international banking statistics pertaining to lending are frequently based on the location of the bank. One illustration of the difference relates to the lending of U.S. banks. As noted in Chapter 8 (Table 8.2), by early 1988, U.S. banks held their own dollar claims against foreigners in the amount of $440 billion. However, the $440 billion claims were those of *U.S.-located* banks; in fact, more than half of the claims were held by offices of foreign banks located in the United States.

---

[8]For an analysis of the implications of the country designation, see Rodney H. Mills, Jr., "U.S. Banks are Losing Their Share of the Market," *Euromoney* (February 1980), pp. 50-62.

The significance of the difference is also apparent in lending statistics. See, for example, Net International Bank Credit (Table 2.1) in which the focus is on the location of operations, and Cross-Border Claims of U.S. Commercial Banks (Table 8.3) in which the focus is on country of ownership or financial control.

THE NETWORK OF INTERNATIONAL BANKS

The branches, subsidiaries, and other offices of parent banks are part of a global network of financial institutions that are both a result and one of the causes of the growth in world trade and investment. How extensive is the network and which countries are involved? According to one estimate reflecting the extensiveness of transnational banking organizations for the years 1978-1979, approximately 520 banks from various countries had established a total of about 6000 subsidiaries, affiliates, and branches in other countries throughout the world (Table 1.1). Banks in the United States and the United Kingdom have been major participants in the creation of global networks. In addition to these countries, banks from France, the Netherlands, Japan, West Germany, and Canada also maintain a global presence. Banks in most of the remaining countries as a minimum have external offices in the major financial centers (New York and London) or in nearby countries with which they have close commercial ties.[9]

A second and more recent source indicates that at the end of 1981, some 600 banks representing 85 different countries had established

TABLE 1.1   Commercial Banks with Foreign Offices, 1978–1979

Country of Origin	Number of Banking Institutions	Subsidiaries	Affiliates	Branches
United States	151	113	244	800
United Kingdom	25	86	54	961
France	19	37	126	228
Japan	23	29	93	127
Netherlands	6	20	25	109
Canada	8	34	39	222
Germany	21	16	115	55
All other	267	105	536	1873
Total	520	440	1232	4375

Source: Derived from Diane Page and Neal M. Soss, "Some Evidence on Transnational Banking Structure," *Staff Papers* (Washington: Comptroller of the Currency, September 1980), p. 53.

[9]Diane Page and Neal M. Soss, "Some Evidence on Transnational Banking Structure" *Staff Papers* (Washington: Comptroller of the Currency, September 1980).
The basis for international bank consortia is examined in M. Fennema, *International Networks of Banks and Industry* (The Hague: Martinus Nijhoff Publishers, 1982), pp. 149-193.

offices in a country other than that of the parent bank. The foreign offices controlled by the parent banks included about 450 subsidiaries and about 5000 branches; they also maintained over 1000 direct affiliations.[10]

CHIPS

The extensive involvement of banks in a wide range of both domestic and international financial transactions necessitates the transfer of funds estimated to exceed $1 trillion each day. This transfer requires an efficient mechanism. Historically, payments have been accomplished largely by currency exchanges and the transfer of demand deposits by checks. However, the growth in commercial activity and innovations in instruments of finance have resulted in major changes in payments procedures. The manual system, which had become too cumbersome and costly, gave way to a computerized electronic funds transfer system that reflects the latest in modern technology.

The most important component of the system, the Clearing House Interbank Payments System (CHIPS), a privately owned operation, was initiated in the early 1970s by the 12 member banks of the New York Clearing House Association. CHIPS and other networks such as the Federal Reserve's Fedwire account for about 85 percent of the payments transactions; they specialize in dollar transactions, accommodating payment for trade as well as foreign exchange and Eurodollar clearings. The systems facilitate a massive flow of funds and include performing the accounting functions needed to effect clearing and settlement.[11]

---

[10]See David Williams, "Opportunities and Constraints in International Lending," *Finance and Development* (March 1983), pp. 24-27.

[11]The volume of activity and the associated risk in the payments system are described in Barbara Bennett, "Controlling Payments System Risk," *Weekly Letter*, Federal Reserve Bank of San Francisco (August 14, 1987), pp. 1-3.

An analysis of CHIPS, Fedwire, and payments system risk is included in Robert A. Eisenbeis, "Eroding Market Imperfections: Implications for Financial Intermediaries, the Payments System, and Regulatory Reform," *Restructuring the Financial System*, Federal Reserve Bank of Kansas City (August 1987), pp. 19-54.

A summary of the payments systems of several major countries is included in Julian Walmsley, *The Foreign Exchange Handbook* (New York: John Wiley & Sons, 1983), pp. 393-402.

Electronic techniques to transfer funds internationally have developed rapidly in recent years. A legal guide to the use of such techniques is provided in United Nations Commission on International Trade Law, *UNCITRAL Legal Guide on Electronic Funds Transfer* (New York: United Nations, 1987).

THE RELATIVE U.S. POSITION

The large number of offshore branches, subsidiaries, and affiliates is an indication of the global nature of commercial banking and of commercial activity more generally. The network of international banks promotes capital movements and the flow of goods and services across national boundaries, and is the foundation for internationally integrated financial markets. A major part of the network is the U.S. banks and their foreign affiliates.

Countries that are major financial centers are usually hosts to a large number of external banks. The importance of countries as hosts to offices of foreign banks depends upon at least two key factors: (1) the role of the country in world trade and finance and (2) the receptivity of governments to a foreign banking presence within their respective economies. As indicated in Table 1.2, the United States is by far the most important host country with almost 800 foreign bank offices by mid-1985. In terms of numbers, growth has occurred in all countries since 1970 but particularly in the United States, the United Kingdom, and Germany. Growth depends upon the size as well as the number of offices. According to one estimate, the foreign banks' share of total assets of national banking systems doubled in all major industrial countries during the period 1970 through 1985.[12]

TABLE 1.2   Foreign Banking Presence by Host Country[1]

	1970	1980	1985 Second half
United States	50	579	783
United Kingdom	95	214	336
Germany	77	213	287
France	58	122	147
Switzerland	97	99	119
Japan	38	85	112
Luxembourg	23	96	106
Belgium	26	51	58
Canada	0	0	58
Netherlands	23	39	44
Italy	4	26	40

[1]Data are not fully comparable.

Source: Morgan Guarantee Trust Company of New York, *World Financial Markets*, December 1986. Used with permission of the copyright holder.

[12]G. Russell Kincaid, "Policy Implications of Structural Changes in Financial Markets," *Finance and Development* (March 1988), pp. 2-5.

The structure and size of U.S. banking facilities overseas is affected to a great extent by the large number of domestic banks, the internal product and geographical restrictions imposed upon them, and the opportunity for expansion in foreign markets. In comparison with other countries, a large number of U.S. banks have established branches and/or subsidiaries in foreign markets. But only a small *share* of U.S. commercial banks—about 260 of a total of over 14,000 banks —participates to the extent of maintaining offices abroad. In absolute terms, the magnitude of U.S. banks in international commerce is the result of participation on the part of many institutions rather than the dominance of a few U.S. banks.

In terms of size, U.S. banks no longer dominate in world finance. According to *American Banker*, on the basis of the dollar value of deposits, only one U.S. bank (Citibank, ranked at number 28) was among the top 30 banks in the world at the end of 1987. In terms of numbers, 18 of the top 30 were Japanese, two were from the United Kingdom, four from France, and three from West Germany. The largest was Japan's Dai-Ichi Kangyo, followed by nine other Japanese banks—Sumitomo Bank Ltd., Fuji, Mitsubishi Bank Ltd., Sanwa, Norinchukin, Industrial Bank of Japan, Mitsubishi Trust and Banking Corp., Tokai Bank Ltd., and Sumitomo Trust and Banking Co.[13]

United States dominance in world commerce has diminished since the 1950s. Although there are different ways of measuring bank size, including either the volume of deposits or the value of assets, the number of U.S. institutions included among the rankings of the world's largest banks has declined.

---

[13]"The Top 500 Banks in the World," *American Banker* (July 19, 1988), pp. 41-49. See also "Ranking the World's Largest Banks," *Institutional Investor* (June 1988), pp. 143-154.

In its assessment of the *national* (federally chartered) banks under its jurisdiction, the Comptroller of the Currency identifies only 12 U.S. banks of a *multinational* nature—the largest U.S. banks with significant foreign as well as national operations. About 190 are identified as *regional* with assets in excess of $1 billion. About 4730 are defined as *community* banks with assets less than $1 billion. See Comptroller of the Currency, *Quarterly Journal* (Washington: September 1986), p. 1. Community banks are also sometimes identified as independently owned banks not affiliated with a holding company.

Reference is also sometimes made to *superregional* banking organizations. These are identified as large banking firms (among the top 100 in the United States), not located in a money center, that have full commercial banking operations in more than one state. Superregionals are expected to increase in number as a result of developments in interstate banking. About 40 banks qualified as superregionals in 1986. Included are Sun Trust Banks, Inc. (Atlanta), First Bank of Boston Corp. (Boston), Banc One Corp (Columbus), NCNB Corp (Charlotte), and First Bank System, Inc. (Minneapolis). As compared with other large U.S. banks, many of the superregionals have relatively high equity capital/asset ratios.

BANK SIZE AND THE GROWING JAPANESE INFLUENCE

On the basis of a ranking of major banks throughout the world by size (measured in terms of value of deposits held), the decrease in the number of U.S. banks has been offset by an increase in the number of Japanese firms. For example, the number of U.S. banks represented in a ranking of 50 of the world's largest banks by deposit size dropped sharply from 25 in 1956 to two by the end of 1987. During the same period of time, the number of Japanese institutions increased from three to 24.

The significance of U.S. banks in international activity may be underestimated by considering only the largest firms. For example, although Japan led the list with about 110 institutions among the top 500 banks in the world in terms of deposits at the end of 1986, the United States was second with about 90.[14]

Yet there is other evidence that U.S. banks have been replaced by Japanese firms as the dominant financial power. According to estimates of the Bank for International Settlements, Japanese-owned banks hold about 35 percent of the world's international banking assets of the major industrial countries; U.S. institutions, about 15 percent.[15]

Several factors have contributed to the shift in composition of the dominance of banks in world markets. Perhaps the most important was the reconstruction and recovery of the European and Japanese economies in the post-World War II period. Initially, Japanese banks concentrated primarily on assisting the industrial reconstruction of their own economy. Even by the mid-to- late 1970s, the foreign efforts of Japanese banks were severely limited by action of their government. Because of extensive controls, the financial markets of that country were almost totally separate from the rest of the world. Japan's banks were strictly limited in external operations until the latter part of the 1970s.

During the late 1970s and early 1980s, a number of changes were introduced by the Japanese government to liberalize the monetary structure of the economy in order to tie their money and capital markets more closely to the world financial system. As a result, Japanese banks moved aggressively into world markets. The overseas expansion by Japanese

---

[14]See "The Top 500 Banks in the World," *American Banker* (July 19, 1988), pp. 41-49. Information is also provided in "The World's Largest Banks," *Institutional Investor* (June 1986), pp. 179-183.
       An analysis of bank rankings by size is provided in C. Stewart Goddin and Steven J. Weiss, "U.S. Banks' Loss of Global Standings," *Staff Papers* (Washington: Comptroller of the Currency, 1980).
       [15]See Bank for International Settlements, *Fifty-Eighth Annual Report* (Basle, Switzerland: 1988), p. 121.

manufacturing and banking firms represents an interest in an increase in the country's invisible income in the form of interest and dividends as well in a market for and source of products. With a small domestic natural resource base, the manufacturing sector has found it necessary to internationalize; Japanese banks have played a major supportive role in this process. In addition, there is a greater acceptance of Japanese direct investment in overseas markets and the resulting job creation, which is perceived as an alternative to direct imports produced by Japanese labor.[16] Japanese financial expansion has also been aided by a high rate of internal savings and a large current account surplus. Japanese banks play a major role as intermediaries in the investment of available funds, accounting for about one-fourth of all international lending.

The growth in the Japanese banking influence is associated with a development that is sometimes termed the "internationalization" of the yen. The yen is gaining some importance as a trading currency with a small but growing share of Japanese trade denominated and paid for in terms of the yen. The yen is also gaining in importance as a reserve currency; treasuries and central banks of other countries are accepting an increasing share of their official holdings of foreign exchange in the form of yen claims. And Japan has become a major source of international capital, replacing the United States as the dominant creditor country since the mid-1980s.

Legal constraints have been suggested as one important factor contributing to the relative decline in U.S. banking activity. United States banks are somewhat more restricted in domestic product and geographic diversification efforts than are the banks in many other industrial countries. However, both Japanese and Canadian banks are also restricted in the types of financial activities that may be performed.[17]

Yet it is essential to recognize that, at least in the short run, the ranking of banks and value of assets are affected significantly by statistical factors. The reason is that in the compilation of size for comparative purposes the value of bank assets are converted to one currency unit, such as the dollar. As a result, asset values are altered by movements in exchange rates, among other things. Thus, the appreciation of the U.S. dollar relative to many currencies from 1980 through early 1985 lowered the dollar value of assets of foreign banks. But the depreciation of the dollar between 1985 and 1988 (by 25 to 50 percent against the yen and

[16]See Andreas R. Prindl, *Japanese Finance: A Guide to Banking in Japan* (New York: John Wiley & Sons, 1981); and Barry Johnson, "Liberalization of Japan's Financial Markets Has Important Impact on International Transactions," *IMF Survey* (September 28, 1987), pp. 277-281.

[17]R. M. Pecchioli, "The Scope of Banking Activity," *Prudential Supervision in Banking* (Paris: Organization for Economic Cooperation and Development, 1987), pp. 57-70.

several European currencies) raised the dollar value of assets of foreign banks and accordingly resulted in a lower ranking of U.S. banks compared with those from many other countries. In addition, U.S. banks have moved more aggressively into fee-income types of activities which, unlike interest-income activities, may not involve an increase in assets and liabilities.

In addition, although Japanese banks dominate the rankings of the world's largest banks in terms of assets, their status is significantly different if ranked on the basis of equity capital/asset ratios. The equity capital/asset ratio, one measure of the financial strength of an institution, is generally lower for Japanese banks than for the banks of many other industrial countries. As noted in Chapter 14, banks from Japan and several other countries will be expected to maintain a higher ratio as a result of the adoption of minimum capital adequacy requirements by the industrial countries in 1988.

Apart from the prestige factor, there may be nothing inherently desirable about being the country with the greatest number of big banks. Economies of scale do not appear to provide a major incentive for bank expansion.[18] Size alone does not necessarily convey meaning regarding the impact on profits, resource use, or economic efficiency. Ultimately the critical factor depends upon the capability of banks in their role as financial intermediaries and the promotion of an efficient use of resources, not only for the United States but also the rest of the world.[19]

SUMMARY AND CONCLUSIONS

International commercial banking includes activities and an organizational structure that are more complex than those involved in domestic transactions. Many banks have found international transactions to be sufficiently profitable, particularly at the wholesale level, to induce the establishment of offices overseas including agencies, branches, and subsidiaries. As a result, a network of banks and their affiliates has contributed to the development of a global financial system.

---

[18]Economies of scale in banking are examined in "The Myth of Leviathan: International Banking," *The Economist* (London) (March 26-April 1, 1988), pp. 10-16.

[19]For example, Alan Greenspan, Chairman of the Federal Reserve Board, notes, "...there is no evidence that extraordinary size is necessary for successful international competition." *Testimony before the House Subcommittee on Telecommunications and Finance*, U.S. Congress, Washington, October 5, 1987.

For many years, U.S. banks dominated world finance in terms of number of overseas offices, volume of lending, and performance of other functions designed to facilitate world trade and investment. In more recent years, restrictions have been eased on Japanese banks by their government; with a large domestic savings base and current account surplus, and a strong interest in world commerce, Japanese financial institutions have gained importance in international markets.

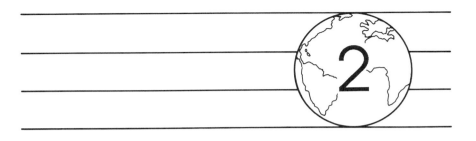

BASIC FUNCTIONS
OF INTERNATIONAL BANKS

As financial intermediaries, commercial banks perform several important functions to facilitate international trade and investment. Banks are the single most important participant in the foreign exchange market. Their role as international lenders has grown significantly since the mid-1970s although it has leveled off since about 1982. International banks also accommodate commercial traders and investors wishing to avoid exchange rate risks. They have introduced innovative products to the financial markets to facilitate what has come to be called a securitization process.

BANKS AND THE FOREIGN EXCHANGE MARKET

One of the most important activities of international banks pertains to their role in the foreign exchange market, in which they serve several distinct functions. They assist in transferring purchasing power from buyers to sellers and from creditors to borrowers. Through a variety of specialized instruments, they also provide credit to importers of goods and services. Finally, they also reduce the risk associated with exchange rate movements through the facilities of the forward market and other hedging techniques.

The foreign exchange market includes a network of commercial banks and a small number of nonbank dealers or brokers. These firms buy and sell foreign exchange, generally in the form of demand deposits in foreign banks (bank deposits denominated in another currency). Banks usually trade in foreign currencies for their own account. Brokers serve an intermediary role between buyers and sellers of currencies. About two-thirds of the foreign exchange transactions in the U.S. market are handled by banks; the remainder involves broker transactions between banks. The major users of the exchange market are exporters, importers, investors, persons traveling to foreign countries, and others who transact business in world markets and are prepared to either buy or sell foreign currencies. During the 1950s and 1960s, a large share of transactions in foreign currencies were associated with merchandise trade. With the shift from pegged exchange rates and the advent of OPEC in the early 1970s, the volume of currency trading greatly expanded and became more closely related to capital movements.

The exchange market is worldwide, and because centers are located in the different time zones, activity occurs somewhere 24 hours of the day. According to a 1987 estimate, the daily foreign currency trading volume in the three major centers (London, Tokyo, and New York) amounted to about $250 billion. London, historically a major financial center and with the key location from a time perspective, accounts for about half of the trading volume. New York and Tokyo each handle about 25 percent of the total.[1]

Although a wide range of currencies is bought and sold, a small number predominate because they serve as trade and/or reserve currencies. In the New York market, the most important foreign currency traded is the German mark which accounts for about one-third of the total volume. The Japanese yen accounts for about 25 percent of the total; the British pound, almost 20 percent. Other currencies traded in order of importance are the Swiss franc, the Canadian dollar and the French franc.[2] These are also the *convertible* currencies—they can be exchanged freely for other currencies. Currencies of some countries are *inconvertible* in which case residents of the issuing country or nonresidents may not be able to freely convert to, or exchange for, another currency.

---

[1]James Kraus, "The Best Kept Secret," *The American Banker* (July 30, 1987), pp. 34-35; and Foreign Exchange Committee, "Summary of Results of U.S. Foreign Exchange Market Turnover Survey Conducted in March 1986 by the Federal Reserve Bank of New York," *Annual Report 1986*, Federal Reserve Bank of New York, 1987, pp. 59-69.
[2]"International Banking," *The Economist* (March 21-27, 1987), p. 34.

SPOT AND FORWARD MARKETS

The U.S. foreign exchange market includes a market for spot and forward transactions and a futures market. The former market centers in New York City, with the bulk of the currencies traded by about 100 banks and almost two-thirds of the volume of transactions taking place in the spot market. The spot or current exchange rate applies to transactions for which the delivery of the currency occurs within two days.

Forward rates cover transactions applicable to a future date usually for multiples of 30 days, generally to a maximum of one year. Customers of banks—exporters, importers, and investors—enter the forward market primarily to hedge. That is, they seek to avoid the risk of an adverse movement in the exchange rate as they anticipate a need in their business transactions to either buy or sell a foreign currency at some specified future date. For example, a U.S. exporter may expect to come into possession of 100,000 British pounds in 60 days as a result of shipments to Britain. To avoid the risk of an adverse movement in the exchange rate (a decline in the dollar price of pounds), he would enter the forward market at the present time and contract to sell the pounds at the forward rate. Delivery of the pounds received by the exporter would be made to the bank in 60 days; in the meanwhile he would not be affected by changes in the spot rate.

Sometimes the forward rate is higher than the spot rate (i.e., sells at a premium); sometimes the forward rate is lower (or sells at a discount). But if free market conditions prevail, there is a relationship between and among currency prices. According to the interest rate parity theory, the difference between the spot and the forward rate is governed by interest rate differentials on securities of similar risk in the countries of the relevant currencies. At equilibrium

$$1 + r_d = s/f(1 + r_f)$$

with r_d = domestic interest rate, s = spot rate, f = forward rate, and r_f = foreign interest rate.

In the absence of equilibrium, funds will be transferred to the area of highest return when both the spot-forward differential and the interest rate differential are taken into account. This transfer, in turn, affects the exchange rates and interest rates in a predictable fashion. At equilibrium, the return on funds invested in two markets with freely convertible currencies should be identical if adjustments are made for transaction costs. Thus the theory provides a basis for relating national money markets to foreign exchange markets.

Although banks participate both as buyers and sellers of foreign currencies, they are able to avoid the risk of an exchange rate movement by maintaining a covered position—matching agreements to buy a currency with corresponding agreements to sell. Much of a bank's activities designed to achieve a covered position is accomplished through transactions with other banks; this in turn leads to an extensive interbank market. Part of a bank's foreign exchange transactions involves swaps— the simultaneous purchase and sale of foreign currency at two different maturity dates. Such transactions (as described more fully in the following section) are used either to achieve a covered position or to fully utilize funds that might otherwise remain idle. Almost one-third of bank activities in the foreign exchange market involves swaps.

Although banks have traditionally functioned in the foreign exchange market as a service for their customers and for profits, the activity has become increasingly important as a source of profits. Banks secure income from foreign exchange transactions either from uncovered positions or as a result of the difference between what they must pay for and what they receive in currency exchanges—the "bid-ask" spread. Some banks serve as "market makers" in that they stand ready to buy or sell foreign currencies on a continuing basis in anticipation of a favorable change in the value of the currency or of a trade for another currency at a favorable price. Losses also occur as banks deal in the currency markets; in 1974, Bankhaus I.D. Herstatt (West Germany) and Franklin National (United States) experienced losses in foreign exchange trading that contributed to their insolvency. The foreign exchange activities of U.S. banks are not regulated, although guidelines have been established and prudent practices are presumed to be followed by commercial banks.[3]

For the major international banks, foreign currency trading is generally not considered an activity separate from other functions. Rather, it is interrelated with other international financial services particularly with major corporate clients. The exchange market is highly competitive,

---

[3]The Federal Financial Institutions Examination Council (representing the Office of the Comptroller of the Currency, The Federal Deposit Insurance Corporation, the Federal Reserve Board, the National Credit Union Administration, and the Federal Home Loan Bank Board) adopted a set of uniform guidelines in 1980 regarding foreign exchange trading and positions. A major requirement is that senior management of each bank provide written memoranda specifying the goals and policies for foreign exchange trading activities. Policies are expected to be comprehensive and to cover all aspects of a bank's participation in the exchange markets. Reporting procedures are to be sufficiently detailed to permit detection of discrepancies between stated policies and actual practices. See Federal Financial Institutions Examination Council, "Uniform Guideline on Internal Control for Foreign Exchange in Commercial Banks," press release, May 22, 1980.

Other guidelines that reflect changes in the nature of exchange market activity are provided in Foreign Exchange Committee, "Guidelines for the Management of Foreign Exchange Trading Activities," *Annual Report* 1986, Federal Reserve Bank of New York, 1987, pp. 20-28.

with some of the competition provided by foreign banks that have established offices in the United States, especially in New York City. Yet the market has provided an important source of profits for banks located in the major financial centers. In addition to the three major financial centers, other centers of importance include Zurich, Paris, Singapore, Frankfurt, Brussels, Hong Kong, Amsterdam, Toronto, and Sydney.

FOREIGN EXCHANGE FUTURES

Traders and investors hedge not only through the forward market but also through the futures market to eliminate or reduce an exposed or uncovered position in a foreign currency. This occurs in the International Money Market, a division of the Chicago Mercantile Exchange. The futures market in foreign exchange is separate and distinct from the spot and forward markets. The forward market is essentially an extension of the spot market; it involves transactions in foreign monies and demand deposits between banks and their customers, usually in amounts that meet the customer's specific needs. In contrast, the futures market in foreign exchange occurs in the commodities exchange market along with agricultural products, metals, and petroleum. Another major difference is that maturity dates and sizes of futures contracts are more standardized than in the forward market.

The futures and forward markets are limited to several of the major currencies including the British pound, Canadian dollar, Japanese yen, Swiss franc, and West German mark, as well as Eurodollar transactions (noted in Chapter 4). In contrast, a large number of currencies are exchanged in the spot market, with about 50 regularly listed in the financial papers. Although prices are usually more favorable to buyers in futures than in forward trading, the limited number of currencies and maturities reduces the flexibility and usage of the futures market.

FOREIGN EXCHANGE RISK MANAGEMENT

Since about 1982, hedging in the foreign exchange market has also been accomplished through the use of foreign currency options. An option provides the holder with the right, although not the obligation, to buy (a call option) or to sell (a put option) a specified amount of a foreign currency at a specified price on or prior to a designated date. As a result, the holder of the option, by paying an amount of money or a "premium" for this right, is able to avoid the risk of an adverse shift in the price of the foreign currency that he expects to buy or sell. The option is exercised if the price of the foreign currency shifts to the extent that the direct purchase or sale of the currency becomes more costly. In addition to their use as insurance against adverse exchange rate movements, options may be bought or sold for speculative purposes.

Options are traded on both the organized exchanges (for the British pound, West German mark, Canadian dollar, Japanese yen, and the Swiss franc) and in the over-the-counter market (for a larger number of currencies). United States commercial banks participate in the options market to accommodate the hedging requirements of their customers. This activity provides a fee income for banks and has become an important type of off-balance-sheet activity for such institutions.[4] The futures and options markets provide additional hedging facilities to accommodate traders and to add depth to the market for currency exchanges.

Commercial banks assist traders and investors in reducing exchange rate risk primarily through the forward market. Banks are also involved in currency swaps to avoid risks and regulatory controls in international transactions.

Currency swaps take various forms, but basically they involve an exchange of two currencies and an agreement to reexchange the currencies at some specified future date at the exchange rate prevailing at the time of the original exchange. Banks may be directly involved as a party to a swap, or they may act as an intermediary in which case they receive a fee for their service. Swaps are used for hedging purposes and to secure a foreign currency at a favorable rate or if it would not otherwise be available. Contracts generally range from $10 million to $50 million, with maturities ranging from 5 to 10 years. Although they involve the same basic principle, several different types of currency swaps have been developed, and the value of such transactions has increased dramatically. The instruments have increased in usage since the early 1980s and by 1988 new swap activity was estimated at $450 billion annually.[5]

THE INTERNATIONAL LENDING FUNCTION

United States banks are actively involved in international lending both from their home offices and their overseas branches and affiliates.

---

[4]A good summary of foreign currency options is provided in Maurine R. Bartlett and Kathleen W. Ludman, "Over the Counter Foreign Currency Options," *Annual Report* 1986, Foreign Exchange Committee, Federal Reserve Bank of New York, 1987, pp. 32-50.

See also Robert A. Feldman, "Foreign Currency Options," *Finance and Development* (December 1985), pp. 38-41.

[5]Steven Plaut, "Swaps and Bank Exposure," *Weekly Letter*, Federal Reserve Bank of San Francisco (April 1, 1988), pp. 1-3. Swaps are also examined in General Accounting Office, *Banking: Off-Balance-Sheet Activities* (Washington: 1988).

Historically, U.S. bank lending in the international markets was confined largely to the traditional role of trade financing. By its very nature this type of credit was short term in duration, loans were self-liquidating, and the associated risks were limited. But in the 1960s and 1970s, multinational corporations grew, expanded their operations, and turned to commercial banks to help finance their overseas activities. During the same period of time, many of the developing countries increasingly sought funding for a variety of purposes from commercial banks. Since the mid-1970s, borrowing also occurred to cover the cost of petroleum imports.

As a result of different types of needs of borrowers, international banking developed into two distinct types of activity. In the first type, the lending takes place in terms of, or involves, the *domestic* currency; for example, a U.S.-based bank extends a dollar loan to a German firm. In the second type, the loan is denominated in and involves the currency of a *foreign* country; for example, a London bank extends a dollar loan to a German firm. A substantial share of the growth in lending activities in recent years is related to the foreign currency types of lending.

Lending in international markets is somewhat more varied or assumes more forms than that occurring domestically. In addition to the straight or traditional loan to persons, companies, or governments, a part of bank operations in international commerce includes trade financing, including bankers' acceptances. *Bankers' acceptances* are drafts drawn by a company or an individual on a bank ordering it to pay a named individual (or the bearer) a specified amount at a specified time accepted by the bank. In effect, the bank makes an unconditional promise or guarantee that payment will be made on the draft at maturity date. United States bankers' dollar acceptances are a predominant form of lending usually to finance shipment or storage of goods. They amounted to about $80 billion outstanding by the end of 1982 and provided financing for about 31 percent of U.S. exports and 25 percent of imports.[6] Since that time, the market for dollar acceptances has generally contracted to about $70 billion by the end of 1987. The decline has been attributed to lower interest rates and to the use of other forms of financing. In addition, U.S. foreign trade has grown more slowly since 1980 as compared with preceding years.[7]

---

[6]"U.S. Bankers' Dollar Acceptances," *International Letter*, Federal Reserve Bank of Chicago (February 25, 1983), p. 3.

Bankers' acceptances are high-quality instruments that may be discounted by banks at the Federal Reserve to meet reserve requirements. The Federal Reserve, in turn, provides extensive guidelines on the usage of acceptances. Some of these are specified in the Export Trading Company Act of 1982.

[7]Frederick Jensen and Patrick Parkinson, "Recent Developments in the Bankers Acceptance Market," *Federal Reserve Bulletin* (Washington: January 1986), pp. 1-12.

Another major form of lending is the *interbank deposit*—a deposit usually short term in nature, placed in other banks. In fact, the largest share of outstanding debt claims of banks is made up of interbank lending.[8] Interbank lending enables banks to maintain a liquid position and to facilitate maturity matching of claims and counterclaims. It enables a bank to maximize the use of its deposits in an income-earning capacity. Interbank deposits provide a basis for correspondent bank relationships. A large share of interbank lending occurs within individual banking organizations—among the head office, branches, and subsidiaries of the same organization. They are also an important type of transaction in the Eurocurrency market, accounting for over one-half the value of gross Eurocurrency deposits.

Many large banks have become increasingly involved through their trust departments in the management and international investment of institutional funds including pension funds and funds of charities, foundations, and various tax-exempt organizations. This investment in foreign countries has expanded especially since 1985, in part as a result of the decline in the value of the U.S. dollar.

Banks also lend through the purchase of corporate securities—commercial paper, promissory notes, and other corporate bonds and securities. The purchase of short-term securities, such as Treasury notes of other governments, also represents a form of international lending.

Syndicated credits, lines of credit extended by groups of banks, became increasingly important in the 1970s, declined somewhat following the debt crisis of the 1980s, but at least partially recovered in importance in 1987. Credits of this type reflect both the commitments to lend and the lending that has actually occurred. Under these arrangements, a number of banks participate jointly in the extension of large loans to single borrowers usually on common terms. This permits the risk, which might be too great for one bank to accept, to be shared by several institutions. It is one way many large- and medium-sized regional banks located away from the major financial centers have been able to participate in international lending. This approach also facilitates the granting of loans that might otherwise be too large for one firm because of capital limitations. Typically one large bank performs the lead or agent role in exploring market opportunities; it secures information for use in judging the credit-worthiness of the potential borrowers, and in creating the loan agreements. For its efforts, the lead bank receives from the borrower a one-time management fee usually in the range of ½ to 1 percent of the loan value. Other banks then participate primarily as sources of credit. In addition to an interest return, they may receive a one-time participa-

---

[8]See U.S. Department of Commerce, *Survey of Current Business* (March 1987), p. 54.

tion fee ranging from ⅛ of 1 percent to 1 percent depending upon the extent of their participation. Syndicated lending is a widely used approach in large Eurocurrency loans.[9]

The maturity date is an important consideration in commercial bank lending. In order to remain in a liquid position, banks prefer to extend short-term loans (less than one year) or medium-term loans (a one- to ten-year maturity date). By the end of 1987, about two-thirds of the foreign loans outstanding of major U.S. banks had a maturity of one year or less.

Loans extended by U.S. banks to foreign private enterprises are not a large share of total bank loans. By the end of 1987, only about 23 percent of the total was accounted for by private nonbank borrowers, the remainder by banks and by public borrowers.[10] Several reasons exist for the preference for nonprivate borrowers. Not only is it more difficult to get credit information from private firms overseas, but frequently financial standards and norms of firms in foreign countries are different from those of U.S. companies and accordingly difficult to interpret for purposes of credit evaluation.[11] The resolution of problem loans is generally also substantially different from U.S. procedures. The absence of bankruptcy laws and settlement procedures in many countries is one of the major difficulties encountered by U.S. creditors.

Commercial banks also participate in world capital markets by underwriting bond issues for large borrowers such as major firms or a government agency. Underwriting is accomplished by a group of banks or a syndicate which subscribes to the issue on its own account; the securities are then sold to clients of the participating banks and other interested buyers.

Banks sometimes participate as a third party in countertrade (or bartering) in which there is a direct exchange of goods or commodities without the use of a currency. According to some estimates, the linking of import transactions with export transactions may account for as much as 25 percent of the total volume of world trade. A large share of the countertrade involves East-West transactions, but an increasing number of developing countries have encouraged the practice in an effort to

[9]For a description of the nature and problems associated with syndications, see Morris Le Compte, "International Loan Syndications, the Securities Acts, and the Duties of a Lead Bank," *Virginia Law Review* (Fall 1978), p. 897.; Frances W. Quantius, "Problems with International Loan Syndications," *The Bankers Magazine* (March-April 1983), pp. 18-21; J. A. Donaldson and T. H. Donaldson, *The Medium Term Loan Market* (New York: St. Martin's Press, 1982), pp. 43-51; and David B. Tinnin, "The War Among Brazil's Bankers," *Fortune* (July 11, 1983), pp. 50-55.

[10]See Federal Financial Institutions Examination Council, "Country Exposure Lending Survey," statistical release, April 1988.

[11]See G. N. Naidu, "Differences in International Financial Practices: Implications for Foreign Lending," *The Journal of Commercial Bank Lending* (April 1983), pp. 47-52.

overcome a shortage of convertible currencies. Commercial banks, including some from the United States, have established countertrade departments to assist in financing the exchanges, and to provide guidance and information to customers.[12]

The extent to which major U.S. banks participate in the different types of foreign lending varies from firm to firm. Among several of the largest lenders, the portion of foreign loans to total loans ranges from about 45 to 55 percent. Although there are many exceptions, generally the larger the lending capacity of a bank, the higher is the portion of foreign loans to total loans.[13]

NET U.S. BANK CAPITAL FLOWS

United States-located commercial banks are both lenders and borrowers in international capital markets. The net capital positions of banks depends upon changes in their claims on foreign residents and changes in liabilities to foreign residents over time. United States *bank claims* are defined to include claims on private sector foreigners (loans, collections outstanding, acceptances, deposits abroad, claims on affiliated foreign banks, foreign government obligations, and foreign commercial and financial paper). United States *bank liabilities* include liabilities to private sector foreigners and international financial institutions (demand, time and savings deposits, certificates of deposit, liabilities to affiliated foreign banks), and other liabilities.[14] Both assets and liabilities are as reported by U.S. banks for their own account and for the accounts of their customers.

Bank capital flows are affected particularly by trade financing. For example, a merchandise or service export might be paid for by a draft drawn by a foreign importer on dollar balances held in the United States, thus resulting in a *decrease* in U.S. *liabilities* to foreigners. Or if the payment were made by a bill of exchange drawn by the American exporter on the importer, U.S. bank *claims* on foreigners would *rise*. Similarly, an import of merchandise or services could involve an acceptance drawn by the foreign exporter and accepted by the U.S. importer, which would *increase liabilities* to foreigners. Or the U.S. importer could

---

[12]An analysis of the commercial aspects of countertrade is provided in Thomas B. McVey, "Overview of the Commercial Practice of Countertrade," in *Barter in the World Economy*, eds. Bart Fisher and Kathleen Harte (New York: Praeger Publishers, 1985), pp. 9-36.

[13]A list of the major foreign lending banks is provided in L. Michael Cacace, "Citibank, Bank of America are Top Lenders," *American Banker* (June 22, 1983), pp. 1, 28.

[14]Federal Reserve Bank of St. Louis, *International Economic Conditions* (August 1987), p. 6.

pay for the transaction with a draft drawing down balances on branches of U.S. banks located overseas; this would involve a *reduction* in U.S. bank *claims* abroad.

In addition, changes in interest rates, and interest rate differentials between the United States and the rest of the world contribute to bank flows. For example, liabilities of U.S. banks increase when U.S.-located banks borrow from their foreign branches in order to accommodate a strong domestic demand for funds and in response to high U.S. interest rates. Claims of U.S. banks have been increased as a result of U.S. money market fund purchases of negotiable Eurodollar certificates of deposit, particularly from British banks.

Although the volume of both bank claims and liabilities changes over time, the most important factor is the net difference—the amount referred to by the U.S. Department of Commerce as "net bank-reported capital flows."[15] During some years, including most of the 1970s and early 1980s, United States-located banks were net lenders in the international capital markets. During the four-year period 1983-1986, U.S. banks were large net borrowers in international capital markets. The major shift occurring in 1982-1983 appears to be closely related to the nature of trade financing and the U.S. current account deficit. As noted in Chapter 8, the change in bank flows is related to the shift of the United States to a net debtor country at that time. (A description of the U.S. balance of payments with emphasis on the relationship to bank activities is contained in Appendix A2.1).

VOLUME OF INTERNATIONAL LENDING

The importance of international commercial banking is reflected in estimates of the volume of worldwide lending. One of the few sources of data of this type is the Bank for International Settlements (BIS) located in Basle, Switzerland. The BIS figures indicate that the net international (or cross-border) lending of commercial banks amounted to an estimated $1770 billion by the end of 1986 (Table 2.1). The estimated $1770 billion volume of international bank lending is a cumulative or total figure that represents the amount outstanding at a particular point in time, in this case at the end of 1986. The amount of new loans during the preceding 12 months was about $160 billion—an indication of the change over a period of time. The $1770 billion figure is also a net figure; it excludes interbank deposits to avoid double counting resulting from the redepositing of funds between the reporting banks.

[15]Christopher Bach, "U.S. International Transactions, Fourth Quarter and Year 1980," *Survey of Current Business* (March 1981), pp. 40-67.

TABLE 2.1   Net International Bank Credit (Stocks at end of 1986 in billions of U.S. dollars)

	Sources	Uses
Industrial Countries[1]	1248.4	1031.9
Other developed countries	41.6	113.8
Eastern Europe	29.4	73.1
OPEC countries	143.8	116.4
Latin America	70.8	221.8
Middle East (non-OPEC)	22.7	16.9
Africa	12.6	22.8
Asia	89.2	103.6
Unallocated[2]	111.5	69.7
	1770.0	1770.0

[1]Industrial countries include Australia, Belgium, Luxembourg, Denmark, Finland, France, Germany, Ireland, Italy, Netherlands, Norway, Spain, Sweden, Switzerland, United Kingdom, Canada, Japan, and the United States, as well as banks engaged in international business in the Bahamas, Cayman Islands, Hong Kong, Singapore and offshore banking units in Bahrain, Netherlands Antilles, and U.S. bank branches in Panama.

[2]Includes international institutions other than the Bank for International Settlements.

Source: Bank for International Settlements. *International Banking and Finance Market Developments* (Basle, Switzerland: April 1987), pp. 9-10.

Commercial banks located in industrialized countries dominate the field of international banking. As reflected in Table 2.1, banks from these countries had provided about 70 percent of the cumulative net cross-border lending by the end of 1986. But it is also apparent from Table 2.1 that by far the greatest share of loans (about 58 percent) is extended to other industrialized countries. The OPEC countries are also net lenders (they are more important sources of bank credit than users of bank credit) although their position has declined somewhat in recent years.

United States banks play an important role in this market, although their relative position has declined since the early 1980s. In 1983 and subsequent years, for example, U.S. banks were net borrowers from abroad, a factor contributing to the U.S. status as a net debtor country since mid-1985.

A much higher degree of competition has developed in international lending in recent years as a result of a more aggressive attitude on the part of Japanese financial institutions. Prior to 1978, Japanese banks were virtually prohibited by their government from medium- and long-term foreign currency lending. As a result of a relaxation of prohibitions, external claims of banks in Japan increased from the equivalent of about $34 billion at the end of 1978 to over $1110 billion at the end of 1986. Although the rapid growth in Japanese bank lending may have caused some concern that the terms offered by these institutions to compete in the market have not been consistent with prudent lending practices, the overall effect has been to increase the volume of world credit.

The remaining areas identified in Table 2.1 are more important as users than as suppliers of bank credit. The major debtor status of Latin America is particularly significant, in part, as reflected in the region's sources and uses of bank credit. Borrowing by this group of countries from private sources has become more important since 1973 and the action of the OPEC countries in raising oil prices.

In relative terms, the centrally planned economies represent a small but rapidly growing source of demand for commercial bank funds. The Soviet Union is the most important borrower and is sometimes assumed to be an implicit guarantor of loans secured by other Eastern European countries. The recent decline in the growth of new loans to these countries appears to be the result of debt servicing problems experienced by Poland and Romania.[16]

Banks, of course, are but one source of funds. By their very nature as profit-oriented institutions, they perform a limited role in the allocation of world credit. Capital is also provided through private direct investment, and by national governments and international organizations, especially where assistance must be provided on concessional terms. However, commercial banks became a growing source of international capital during the late 1970s. International bank lending increased to the extent that by 1980 it was estimated to represent more than 50 percent of all international capital flows and more than 50 percent of the long-term external debt of the developing countries.[17] During 1982, 1983, and 1984, with the increased seriousness of debt servicing problems, commercial bank lending became a relatively less important source of international capital, although some recovery occurred beginning in 1985.

SECURITIZATION

Part of the relative decline in international bank lending is the result of "securitization" in the financial markets. Securitization is a process in

---

[16]Richard Williams and Peter Keller, "Eastern Europe and the International Banks," *Finance and Development* (December 1982), pp. 39-41.

[17]Paul Mentri, *The Fund, Commercial Banks, and Member Countries* (Washington: International Monetary Fund, 1984).

A source of an extensive amount of data on international activity of commercial banks by country since January 1984 is provided in International Monetary Fund, *International Financial Statistics* (Washington: monthly issues). Included are tables showing by country: foreign assets and liabilities of depository banks, cross-border interbank accounts, international bank credit to nonbanks, and international bank deposits of nonbanks.

which financial intermediaries extend loans (mortgages, car loans, and the like) which are then pooled and packaged in larger amounts and sold to investors. In effect, the intermediary converts illiquid assets (the loans) into a marketable security (the packaged debt instrument).

Securitization in a broader sense refers to a practice in which major commercial and government borrowers secure funds by selling securities directly to the public rather than by borrowing from banks. The process involves direct financing; savers are linked directly to the ultimate investors rather than through banks by way of the intermediation process. But while securitization in the broad sense may result in a reduction in the demand for bank loans, there may be an increase in the demand for backup services or credit enhancement facilities which banks and other financial institutions are able to provide.

What is the basis for the securitization approach being a substitute for the traditional intermediation process? With intermediation, funds are transferred from savers to investors through the financial intermediaries—banks, thrift institutions, and insurance companies. The intermediaries serve several functions—provision of liquidity for savers, evaluation of credit risk of borrowers, collection of funds, and so on. Securitization is sometimes described as a process that "unbundles" or divides the intermediary functions and permits the participants, including banks, to concentrate on functions in which they have a strong advantage. In some instances, for example, banks may be able to evaluate credit risks efficiently or, because their names are widely recognized, to participate in credit enhancement. Further, the banks may not always be the best source of funds because of limited capital or deposits.[18] Accordingly, to the extent that the functions of the participants in the financial markets have changed, the process whereby funds are transferred from savers to investors has also changed.

Securitization includes *commitments* in which a bank commits itself to provide credit to a customer at a future date, and *guarantees* in which a bank guarantees the obligation of a customer to a third party. One important form of guarantee is the *standby letter of credit* (SLC). With the SLC, a bank guarantees a contractual obligation of a customer to a third party; the bank substitutes its credit standing for that of a customer. If the customer defaults, the bank is obligated to pay the third party; the result is to enhance the credit rating of the borrower. Standby letters of credit are used primarily to back a customer's repayment on debt issues or to support a customer's obligation to provide goods and services to a third party. The risk associated with obtaining payment from a foreign

---

[18]An analysis of securitization is provided by M. K. Lewis and K. T. Davis, *Domestic and International Banking* (Cambridge, Mass.: The MIT Press), pp. 111-127.

importer or borrower may also be covered through the use of the letter of credit. Letters of credit take various forms. Under one arrangement, a bank obligates itself to a third party to cover maturing obligations upon default by a borrower or as a result of restrictions imposed by foreign governments for balance of payments purposes. As a result, the exporter or lender is assured of being paid in a timely fashion. The SLC is a good illustration of an off-balance-sheet activity in that the bank receives a fee income without affecting its balance sheet assets and liabilities.

Banks are also involved in the securitization process as a result of commitments, one of the more important being the *loan commitment*. This arrangement may take various forms, but basically a bank agrees to extend to its customer a specified amount of credit, for a specified period of time, at a specified rate of interest. For this agreement, the bank charges a fee based on the size of the total commitment; in some instances, the bank may also benefit by requiring the customer to hold a compensating balance (a deposit with the bank). Thus the loan commitment facilitates the securitization process; it is also an off-balance-sheet activity that provides a fee income with no direct impact on the bank's balance sheet.

One important commitment is the *note issuance facility* (NIF); short-term notes issued by commercial or government borrowers are under-written by banks, which distribute them to investors and savers, and guarantee to purchase unsold notes. Typically, a facility is established for a period of several years during which time the borrower issues short-term notes on a revolving basis. For their contribution of providing a back-up facility, banks receive a fee income. Because of a conflict with Glass-Steagall restrictions on securities underwriting, commercial banks within the United States have been restricted in the provision of NIFs and other underwriting activities.[19]

The securitization process is one of the more important developments occurring in international capital markets. Direct financing by borrowers has resulted in a relative decline in bank lending and interest income. But banks have accommodated the process through innovative techniques and procedures that frequently involve off-balance-sheet activities. One result (described in Chapter 14) is that traditional methods of supervising banks which focus on capital ratios have become less

---

[19]Under Glass-Steagall, U.S. banks are able to underwrite and deal in Treasury securities and securities issued and backed by federal agencies. They can underwrite general obligation municipal bonds but not most kinds of revenue bonds. They cannot underwrite corporate debt and equities. They are also able to underwrite and deal in corporate securities overseas. A few states (Arkansas, Rhode Island and New Jersey) permit state banks or their subsidiaries to be more extensively involved in underwriting activities. For a discussion, see Federal Deposit Insurance Corporation, "Glass-Steagall Act," *Mandate for Change* (Washington: 1987), pp. 35-45.

relevant. In addition, fee income has become increasingly important for commercial banks.

Some evidence exists that the shift away from intermediation that characterized the first part of the 1980s may have diminished. The BIS suggests that securitization in domestic markets has continued to expand. However, at the international level there has been renewed growth in commercial bank lending since 1985 and 1986, but a contraction in net new bond financing and Euronote facilities since 1987.[20] This may suggest that securization at the international level is in a transition period. This is a part of the change that is transforming international finance and commercial banking.

BASIS FOR INTERNATIONAL BANKING

Commercial banks undertake international activities in response to economic stimuli in much the same way as any enterprise responds to profit opportunities. But the basis for making profits in external financial markets may not always be readily apparent. For example, a bank investing in a foreign market is at a disadvantage because of its alien status and because it lacks familiarity with the political and socioeconomic conditions that an indigenous firm would possess. What is the basis for cross-lending activity—the simultaneous flow of funds in two directions? How is it possible that while U.S. commercial banks are a major force in lending abroad, banks of foreign countries are also active creditors within the U.S. market?

One basis for an explanation relates to the theory of international direct investment and the ownership of productive capacity abroad. According to this approach, an analysis of direct investment belongs more to the theory of industrial organization than to a theory of comparative advantage and capital movements. A firm, if it is to invest abroad, must overcome an inherent disadvantage that actual or potential local firms would have in terms of nearness to, and knowledge of, the market. Since direct investment would be ruled out in a perfectly competitive world, the investing firm must possess a monopolistic advantage based on product differentiation, patents or restricted technology, economies of scale, or government limitations on output or entry.[21]

A related effort to explain international banking attempts to identify the source of comparative advantage that an outside bank might

---

[20]Bank for International Settlements, *Fifty-Eighth Annual Report* (Basle, Switzerland: 1988), pp. 101-110.

[21]An analysis of the monopolistic advantage is provided in Charles P. Kindleberger, *American Business Abroad* (New Haven: Yale University Press, 1969).

have when faced with the competition of local banks having a familiarity with the local situation. Bank activity is separated into three functions— retail, service, and wholesale. A comparative advantage may exist in retail banking when the bank applies managerial know-how and technology developed for the home market to external uses at a low marginal cost. However, retail banking profits may not endure as local entrepreneurs gain sufficient knowledge and experience and, already possessing a knowledge of local conditions, are able to compete against outsiders.[22]

The second type of activity is a bank service function related to direct foreign investment. In this case, the banking institution extends to a foreign country a relationship with a subsidiary that already exists with the parent company in the home country. The availability of information and a personal contact are the major sources of advantage maintained by the foreign bank through its offices in the host country. Further, the foreign bank can provide services to local firms in the form of information in their native country.

Wholesale banking is usually identified with interbank transactions—the lending and borrowing undertaken by banks among themselves. Reasons for a favorable interest rate spread—the basis of an explanation for the international transactions—include certain intrinsic service values (for example, the traditional use of the dollar in international trade), governmental regulation (for example, the imposition of reserve requirements), and product differentiation (for example, dealing primarily with large customers).

Another explanation for international banking centers on efforts to reduce risk through foreign diversification of investments. Because economic conditions do not change in one country in the same way, at the same time, or to the same degree as in other countries, multicountry diversification may reduce the variability of the overall profit rate.[23]

Another study hypothesizes that banking is a mobile activity and that an increase in competition among banks may also give rise to competition among bank regulatory agencies themselves. The conclusion is drawn that while bank regulators seek to reduce the degree of risk in banking they also attempt to attract banking business to their countries by imposing a less restrictive degree of regulation. Although the focus of this hypothesis is on regulatory agencies, it complements or supports various theories of bank location. It is consistent particularly with an

---

[22]See Herbert G. Grubel, "A Theory of Multinational Banking," *Banca Nazionale del Lavoro Quarterly Review* (December 1977), pp. 349-363; and R. Z. Aliber, "International Banking: A Survey," *Journal of Money, Credit and Banking* (November 1984), Pt. 2, pp. 661-678.

[23]See, for example, Norman S. Fieleke, "The Growth of U.S. Banking Abroad: An Analytical Survey," *Key Issues in International Banking*, Federal Reserve Bank of Boston (October 1977), pp. 9-40.

industrial organization approach. Banks locate and do business on the basis of a noncompetitive advantage; this advantage is provided not by virtue of size or some other monopoly power, but rather as a result of an advantage granted by law or by the regulatory agency.[24]

Thus the ability of nonindigenous banks to operate in an alien economy in which they lack the familiarity with local customs and institutions may vary from country to country. However, the advantage that some larger institutions possess, the desire for diversification, and the type and degree of regulation imposed by the various countries are probably the most pervasive and important factors. For whatever reason, large banks find overseas activities profitable and are likely to continue to consider them an important source of earnings.

Some writers argue that the behavior of banks is affected to a great extent by political developments and that international banking and international politics are inextricably entangled. Despite their increasing interdependence, bankers and policymakers may have different motives and goals.[25] Furthermore, banks may not respond to economic considerations directly, but rather may also conduct activities on the basis of the way in which a government either has taken or will take action that ultimately affects economic considerations. For example, U.S. banks may be more willing to risk larger loans to Mexico than to an African country; Mexico is geographically closer and a large trading partner of the United States. As a result, the U.S. government is more likely to come to her aid for balance of payments purposes should the need arise.

SUMMARY AND CONCLUSIONS

International commercial banking includes a variety of services of a financial nature—accepting and creating deposits, buying and selling foreign exchange, extending credit of varying maturity dates to a wide range of borrowers, involvement in loan commitments and guarantees, and advising clients on foreign trade and investment opportunities. According to one survey, international bankers considered their most significant activities to include transactions in the foreign exchange market and servicing the overseas needs of domestic customers. Next

---

[24]Deborah Allen and Ian H. Giddy, "Towards a Theory of Interdependence in Global Banking Regulations," *Eastern Economic Journal* (December 1979), pp. 445-452.

[25]For a summary of political considerations, see Philip A. Wellons, "International Debt: The Behavior of Banks in a Politicized Environment," *International Organization* (Summer 1985), pp. 441-469. For a more comprehensive analysis, see Benjamin Cohen, *In Whose Interest? International Banking and American Foreign Policy* (New Haven, Conn.: Yale University Press, 1986).

in importance was direct lending to multinational corporations and the participation in syndicated Eurocurrency loans. Other activities included investment banking and local currency lending in overseas markets.[26] These functions are performed through domestic offices or through one of several types of offices that may be established in a foreign country. The nature of international capital markets has also changed particularly since the early 1980s. International bank lending declined at least through about 1985, but bank loan commitments and guarantees gained in importance.

Although a bank enterprise participating in a foreign market is at a disadvantage because it lacks familiarity with the legal and socioeconomic conditions that an indigenous firm would possess, it is apparent that outside banks can provide effective competition. This capability may be based on legal and regulatory constraints or the possession of some types of monopolistic advantage.

[26]Group of Thirty, *How Bankers See the World Financial Market* (New York: 1982), pp. 24-25.

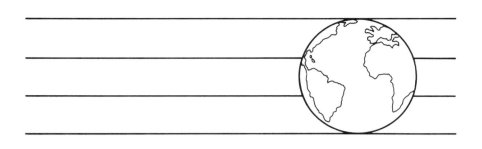

APPENDIX A2.1
THE U. S. BALANCE OF
PAYMENTS

The U. S. balance of payments can be described as a summary tabulation which, in principle, covers all trade, aid, and investment transactions between residents of the United States (business firms, government, and private individuals) and the rest of the world. The data it contains are estimated on an annual basis, although quarterly information is proved by the U. S. Department of Commerce.

The balance of payments statement can be presented in several different ways; Table A2.1 is a simplified version that identifies only the major categories of items. The official Department of Commerce statement lists as many as 70 different items.

As presented in Table A2.1, items in the left column are identified as credits, items that generate receipts, or items that give rise to foreign exchange available to U. S. residents. The right column of Table A2.1 shows debits, items that generate payments, or items that are ways in which U. S. residents use foreign exchange.

The first major group of items on the balance of payments includes merchandise and service exports and imports and net unilateral transfers (U. S. grants and gifts to foreigners less foreign gifts to the United States), and is generally referred to as the *current account*. Preliminary figures for

TABLE A2.1 U. S. Balance Of Payments, 1986

CREDITS (RECEIPTS)		DEBITS (PAYMENTS)	
Merchandise exports	$231	Merchandise imports	$381
Service exports	139	Service imports	115
		Unilateral transfers	15
Current Account	370		511
Capital inflows including:		Capital outflows including:	
Foreign official	33	U. S. government	2
Direct investment	26	Direct investment	32
Bank liabilities	77	Bank claims	57
Treasury securities	9	Other private claims	5
U. S. securities other than	71		
Treasury securities			
Capital Inflows	213	Capital Outflows	100
Statistical Discrepancy	27		

Source: Derived from U. S. Department of Commerce, *Survey of Current Business* (Washington: March 1987), p. 44.

1986 indicate that receipts on current account amounted to $370 billion; payments amounted to $511 billion. Accordingly, the United States experienced a current account deficit of $140 billion; United States imports of goods and services, plus gifts and grants to foreigner, exceeded the exports of goods and services by $140 billion.

The second major category is referred to as the *capital account.* Capital inflows (left column) are credits and indicate U. S. borrowing from foreigners during the year. The 1986 inflow took the form of an increase in foreign official holding of U. S. assets ($33 billion), an increase in foreign direct investment in the United States ($26 billion), an increase in foreign claims against U. S. banks ($77 billion), increased foreign holding of Treasury securities ($9 billion), and increased foreign holdings of other U. S. securities ($71 billion).

The debit side of the capital account (right column)indicates U. S. lending abroad—in 1986, in the amount of $100 billion. This included a growth in U. S. government claims against foreigners ($2 billion), additional U. S. direct investment abroad ($32 billion), increased claims of U. S. banks on foreigners ($57 billion), and increases in other private claims ($5 billion). A large statistical discrepancy ($27 billion) indicates the problem associated with deriving highly accurate estimates for the balance of payment components.

The excess of receipts over payments in the capital account (including the statistical discrepancy) indicates a surplus in the capital account, or that the United States borrowed more from abroad ($140 billion) than it lent to foreigners during 1986. The amount borrowed during the year equals the current account deficit; it indicates how U. S. residents paid for the surplus of imports.

Aggregate credits in the balance of payments must equal aggregate payments, since each recorded transaction involves a receipt and a payment. As a simplified example, a U. S. merchandise export (a credit) might be financed by a transfer of a demand deposit from the foreign importer to the U. S. exporter (a debit)—either an increase in U. S. deposits in foreign banks or a decrease in foreign deposits in U. S. banks (a short-term capital outflow). Similarly, a U. S. import of merchandise (a payment) would be financed by a short-term capital inflow (a credit)—either a decrease in U. S. deposits in foreign backs or an increase in foreign deposits in U. S. banks.

Commercial bank involvement in the balance of payments is largely the result of accommodation of international financial transactions. For example, a U. S. bank sells foreign exchange (a deposit in a foreign bank) to a U. S. importer; when the U. S. importer pays for the imports, the deposits are transferred to the overseas exporter, U. S. deposits in a foreign bank decreased, and a short-term capital inflow has occurred. Generally, most international economic transactions—goods, services, and investment flows—are accommodated by transfers of bank deposits which appear in the balance of payments as short-term capital movements.

Developments in the 1986 U. S. balance of payments situation also indicate changes in the U. S. investment position in the world economy. The current account deficit in 1986 was offset by a capital account surplus—the United States residents bought more goods and services from abroad than foreigners bought from the United States, and foreigners expanded their net holding of claims against the United States. The current account deficit and capital account surplus have characterized the U. S. balance of payments position for the last several years, with the result that the U. S. is now the major debtor country. For many years prior to the 1980s, the United States experienced a surplus on current account transactions and a deficit on capital account transactions; the United States was a net lending country.

3

FRAMEWORK FOR INTERNATIONAL FINANCIAL ACTIVITY

Within any given country, banking and other commercial activity are governed by a legal framework of facilitating laws, enforceable contracts, and other national institutional arrangements. International transactions are conducted within a framework of conventions and rules agreed upon by the governments of the individual nations and administered by international organizations. The most important of these has been the International Monetary Fund (IMF).[1]

THE IMF

The IMF was established in 1945 as part of the Bretton Woods Agreement with a membership of 45 countries. As a result of the creation of new countries and the potential benefits of membership, participation has expanded to include over 150 countries. Although the role of the

[1]Material in this chapter is based in part on Charles W. Hultman, "G-5 Market Intervention and Commercial Policy," *Journal of World Trade Law* (May-June 1986), pp. 287-293.

Fund has changed over the years, efforts toward promoting economic and financial cooperation among member countries remain central to its activities. At the time the IMF initiated operations near the end of World War II, international trade and payments occurred largely in accordance with wartime requirements. Commodity and service flows were based to a great extent on emergency needs, with the United States the major supplier of a large share of export items. Most countries employed exchange controls to conserve their limited foreign exchange for essential imports. The currencies of nearly all countries, with the exception of the U.S. dollar, the Canadian dollar, and those of a few Central American countries, were inconvertible or could not be freely exchanged for other currencies because of governmental regulation. The economies of many countries had experienced severe wartime damages which contributed to large import requirements and a serious dollar shortage. Exchange controls were accepted by IMF members as an expedient to cope with foreign currency shortages and balance of payments deficits. Such quantitative restrictions on international payments were to be removed as soon as governments believed their economies could adjust to the free market forces of supply and demand for foreign currencies. In addition, international cooperation in financial matters was emphasized in order to preclude a resurgence of competitive exchange devaluation and the restrictive commercial policies that characterized the 1930s. The IMF's approach was to encourage policies leading to currency convertibility and the pegging of exchange rates to gold or a major currency unit through the use of stabilization funds. These funds consisted of official holdings of gold, foreign exchange (holdings of short-term claims denominated in terms of convertible foreign currencies), reserve position with the IMF, and, since 1969, Special Drawing Rights (SDRs), a new reserve created by the IMF. The U.S. dollar was the major reserve currency, and the U.S. government stood ready to permit foreign official institutions to exchange their dollar holdings for gold.

By the early to mid-1950s, recovery from the war devastation in Europe and Japan was approaching completion. The IMF continued to make financial resources available to member countries experiencing short-term balance of payments problems, but the availability of assistance came to be directed more toward eventual removal of exchange controls and achievement of currency convertibility. In addition, attention shifted somewhat toward the resource needs of the low-income countries.

By the early 1960s, many countries were able to remove most exchange controls and thus to restore currency convertibility. In accordance with IMF principles, most of the member countries pegged their exchange rates and maintained official par values for their currencies. Exchange rate stability was achieved by the intervention of monetary and treasury authorities in the foreign exchange markets. Stability was largely accomplished by appropriate foreign exchange purchases and sales on the part of the authorities to keep the market rate within one percent above and below the established par value. A country experiencing a balance of payments problem and unable to maintain the declared par value because of a shortage of its own exchange reserves could borrow a predetermined amount from the IMF to carry out the intervention. If the country experienced a fundamental disequilibrium, then under the direction and guidance of the IMF the exchange rate could be adjusted through devaluation to a more realistic level. With the strong support of the IMF and participating countries, the pegged exchange rate system (frequently called the Bretton Woods System) remained in effect until the early 1970s.

THE COLLAPSE OF THE PEGGED EXCHANGE RATE SYSTEM

The pegged exchange rate was the key component of the international financial system during the early post-World War II period. Although freely floating or flexible exchange rate systems had been proposed in which prices of foreign currencies could change daily in response to free market forces, such a system had never been adopted on an extensive basis, and there were some fears that it would lead to unstable currency prices and a decline in world trade and investment. It was not until the 1970s, following a serious decline in the U.S. trade position, that the system of officially established and maintained international currency values could no longer be readily sustained and the need for change became apparent. Even then, the move to floating rates occurred more by default than as a planned effort on the part of major trading countries.

Conditions in the exchange market approached crisis proportions in 1971 as central banks attempted to support the value of the dollar by purchasing unprecedented sums with their currencies. As a result, convertibility of the dollar into gold was suspended by the United States in August 1971; in December 1971, the U.S. government announced a devaluation or change in the official price of the dollar by 10 percent. But the problems persisted, and further devaluation of the dollar and revaluation of several major currencies were undertaken in early 1973. Finally, in March of 1973, currency values were "set afloat" to be determined by free market conditions. Efforts to reestablish a global pegged exchange rate system were abandoned. Following intensive discussions among member countries, the nature of the new international exchange market gradually commenced to take form. Canada and the United Kingdom decided to continue to permit their currencies to float; Italy and Japan decided they would initiate similar action. The majority of the remaining countries eventually tied their currencies to one of the more widely used currencies or some other monetary asset.

SURVEILLANCE PROCEDURES

The action of the various countries was eventually formalized by the IMF. Provisions of the IMF (Second Amendment) permit countries the choice among several alternatives: to allow their currencies to float; to maintain the value of their currency in terms of another currency, Special Drawing Rights, or some currency composite; or to establish a link with other currencies on some variable basis. However, member countries are obligated to provide a framework for order and stability in the exchange markets. Under the surveillance principles adopted in April of 1977, countries are to strive for the orderly underlying conditions essential for financial stability, to intervene to counter disorderly conditions in the exchange market, and yet to avoid manipulation of exchange rates in order to gain an unfair advantage in world commerce. Essentially, the governments of member countries are expected to maintain internal balance (price stability and full employment) and to even out short-term fluctuations in exchange rates. However, they are expected to refrain from influencing long-term trends in the exchange markets, particularly with the objective of maintaining a depreciated currency simply to promote a favorable trade balance.

NATURE OF POST-BRETTON WOODS
EXCHANGE RATE SYSTEM

An indication of the structure of the system that evolved is provided in Table 3.1. The currencies of a large number of countries are pegged, although not to gold. This occurs when a country maintains a fixed relationship between the price of its currency and some other price, such as that of the currency of another country. About 40 countries relate their currencies to the U.S. dollar and about 15 to the French franc. The constant value relationship with the dollar, franc, or other currency is maintained either through exchange controls or by market intervention

TABLE 3.1 Exchange Rate Arrangements as of March 31, 1988

Pegged					Flexibility Limited vis-a-vis a Single Currency or Group of Currencies		More Flexible		
Single currency			Currency composite						
U.S. dollar	French franc	Other	SDR	Other	Single currency	Cooperative arrangements	Adjusted according to a set of indicators	Other managed floating	Independently floating
Afghanistan Antigua and Barbuda The Bahamas Barbados Belize Djibouti Dominica Ecuador El Salvador Ethiopia Grenada Guatemala Guyana Haiti Honduras Iraq Lao People's Democratic Republic Uganda Venezuela Liberia Mozambique Nicaragua Oman Panama Paraguay Peru St. Kitts and Nevis St. Lucia St. Vincent Sierra Leone Somalia Sudan Suriname Syrian Arab Republic Trinidad and Tobago	Benin Burkina Faso Cameroon Central African Republic Chad Comoros Congo Cote d'Ivoire Equatorial Guinea Gabon Mali Niger Senegal Togo	Bhutan (Indian rupee) Kiribati (Australian dollar) Lesotho (South African rand) Swaziland (South African rand) Tonga (Australian dollar)	Burma Burundi Iran, Islamic Republic of Jordan Libya Rwanda Seychelles	Algeria Austria Bangladesh Botswana Cape Verde Cyprus Fiji Finland Hungary Israel Kenya Kuwait Malawi Malaysia Malta Mauritis Nepal Norway Papua New Guinea	Bahrain Qatar Saudi Arabia United Arab Emirates	Belgium Denmark France Germany, Federal Republic of Ireland Italy Luxembourg Netherlands	Brazil Chile Colombia Madagascar Portugal	Argentina China Costa Rica Dominican Republic Egypt Greece Guinea-Bissau Iceland India Indonesia Jamaica Korea Mauritania Mexico Morocco Pakistan Singapore Sri Lanka	Australia Bolivia Canada The Gambia Ghana Guinea Japan Lebanon Maldives New Zealand Nigeria Philippines South Africa Spain United Kingdom United States Uruguay Zaire

TABLE 3.1 (cont.)

Pegged					Flexibility Limited vis-a-vis a Single Currency or Group of Currencies		More Flexible		
Single currency			Currency composite						
U.S. dollar	French franc	Other	SDR	Other	Single currency	Cooperative arrangements	Adjusted according to a set of indicators	Other managed floating	Independently floating
Viet Nam				Poland				Tunisia	
Yemen Arab Republic				Romania				Turkey	
Yemen, People's Democratic Republic of				São Tomé and Principe				Yugoslavia	
Zambia				Solomon Islands					
				Sweden					
				Tanzania					
				Thailand					
				Vanuatu					
				Western Samoa					
				Zimbabwe					

Source: International Monetary Fund, *Annual Report 1988* (Washinton: 1988), p. 87.

in the form of the purchase or sale of the appropriate currency.[2] Typically, a country ties to a currency that is stable and important in world trade, or to the currency of a country with which it conducts a substantial amount of trade or with which a colonial relationship might have prevailed.

Pegging to the SDR or some other currency composite generally provides even greater stability than a link with a single currency. As noted in Table 3.1, almost 40 countries have currencies pegged to either the SDR or some other currency composite. The currencies of Hungary, Poland, and Romania are pegged to currency composites. The Soviet Union is not a member of the IMF; accordingly, the exchange rate system applicable to the ruble is not included in Table 3.1.

Another small group of countries achieves limited flexibility by maintaining the value of their currency within about 2 ¼ percent of that of some other currency, usually the U.S. dollar. The eight countries participating in the cooperative exchange arrangements include members of the European Monetary System and the European Economic Community. Each country maintains its currency within a narrow margin of the currencies of remaining members.

The exchange rates of about 45 countries are in the "more flexible" category. They are either adjusted according to a set of indicators, are part of a managed float system, or else are allowed to float independently. About 20 countries are in the floating category which includes the United States, Canada, Japan, and the United Kingdom.

Thus the policy regarding exchange rates and markets varies from country to country. Furthermore, these arrangements are not necessarily permanent. Some revisions have occurred over time in the types of systems maintained by individual countries. For example, the number of currencies linked to the U.S. dollar and the pound sterling has declined. In turn, an increased number of governments permit the exchange rates to float—to respond either fully, or at least partially, to free market forces of supply and demand.

How can the present exchange rate system be described or identified? To characterize it as a freely floating regime can be misleading. Although the system is frequently termed a "managed float," this too may be misleading in that the great majority of countries are categorized as having pegged rates—rates pegged to a single currency, SDRs, or a currency composite. More accurately, perhaps, it might be characterized as a system which permits floating rates that are to be modified by

[2]A description of the various ways by which the central banks of the industrialized countries intervene in the foreign exchange market and an analysis of the success of such efforts is provided in Dean Taylor, "The Mismanaged Float: Official Intervention by the Industrialized Countries," *The International Monetary System: Choices for the Future*, ed. Michael B. Connolly (New York: Praeger Publishers, 1982), pp. 49-84.

occasional central bank intervention in accordance with International Monetary Fund principles. The system is so complex and varies so widely among the various groups of countries that a single descriptive phrase is inadequate.

INITIAL EXPERIENCE WITH THE FLOATING RATE

The U.S. dollar, the British pound, the German mark, the Japanese yen, and other major currencies have floated since the early 1970s. Is the floating exchange rate a viable part of the international financial system, given the developments of the 1970s and expectations for the remainder of the 1980s and for the l990s? Or must a new system be developed to cope with the stresses and strains of severe inflation, uneven rates of growth among countries, and a possible tendency toward restrictive commercial policies? After 15 years of use it is possible to offer at least a limited evaluation of the experience with the floating exchange rate. Basically, an assessment of the system involves two issues. First, is the exchange rate sufficiently stable in the short run to readily accommodate the flow of trade and financial flows across international boundaries? Second, does the exchange rate shift appropriately in connection with payments imbalances and thus accommodate the long-term adjustment process?

One of the more important statements on the managed float regime is that developed by the Consultative Group on International Economic and Monetary Affairs (the Group of 30) as a result of a 1979 survey of commercial banks and multinational corporations. Results of the survey were generally optimistic. However, some disadvantages of the floating exchange rate system were identified. Generally, it was observed that exchange rates and markets exhibited a greater degree of instability under the floating system. In addition, business firms were required to devote more time and resources to the observation and analysis of the impact of foreign exchange market developments. Yet the study concluded that both the foreign exchange markets and international business adapted well to the exigencies of the floating system. In fact, it suggested a number of benefits that have developed: the market has become more competitive with the entry of new banks and the growth of new financial centers; a global, 24-hour foreign exchange market has developed; nonbank customers have benefited from reduced margins; and an increase has occurred in the number of options available to accomplish an exchange transaction.

The Group's survey of major corporations indicates that there has been an acceptance of floating rates and that they have neither led to extensive disruption of their international transactions nor adversely affected future investment opportunities. Although floating increased the costs marginally for the major users, the Group of 30 concluded that there was a preference by industrial corporations for floating rates.[3]

Essentially, banks and businesses have found it both necessary and possible to adapt to the floating system. Indeed, institutional arrangements have been modified and new ones developed to accommodate trade and investment in a system in which exchange rates rise and fall in response to market conditions and government intervention.

A second concern with the floating exchange rate related to the long-term balance of payments adjustment process, the extent to which trade and capital flows are altered or shift under such a system to correspond with structural changes in the world economy. The nature of the impact of floating exchanges on the level and pattern of trade flows was examined in an empirical study undertaken under the auspices of the General Agreement on Tariffs and Trade (GATT) in 1980. GATT itself has been concerned over the years primarily with the liberalization of barriers to trade across national boundaries. Yet it implicitly recognizes that trade flows depend not only upon the removal of tariffs, quotas and similar devices, but also on the existence of a system that fosters a high degree of certainty in payments for commercial transactions.

The GATT study was basically supportive of floating rates. The authors contended that the additional costs associated with uncertainties in the exchange market have not caused a decline in the rate of growth in world trade. They also concluded that the system has not contributed significantly to shifts in the trade balances of individual countries during the period under study. Finally, a comparison was made of the impact on trade of floating rates with the lowering of trade barriers. While the liberalization of trade barriers has an impact primarily only on the affected industries and products, exchange rates movements affect the real price of all exports and imports and accordingly the competitiveness of all industries.[4]

RECENT EXPERIENCE WITH THE FLOAT

Recent evidence suggests that short-term exchange rate variability increased beginning in the early 1980s. In addition, the greater variability

[3]"Group of 30 Study Finds Banks and Business Adapt to Floating Rate System," *IMF Survey* (April 7, 1980), pp. 108-109.
[4]"Effects of Floating Rates on World Trade Are Analyzed in Study Published by GATT," *IMF Survey* (November 1981), p. 372.

has increased the difference between forward exchange rates and future spot rates (the actual spot rate at the future date). This difference is a reflection of the degree of risk associated with exchange transactions. As a result of the increase in risk associated with transactions, there has been a growth in both the volume and the cost of hedging.[5]

An IMF study notes that although floating exchange rates have been in operation for several years, experience with the system does not appear to have lessened the variability of exchange rate fluctuations. Yet there is no evidence that the volume of world trade and investment have been adversely affected by the exchange rate system.[6]

A related concern is that on occasion there is a tendency for the exchange rate to "over-adjust"; if the rate starts to move in a particular direction, cumulative forces in the exchange market lead to excessive movements and, accordingly, a more volatile system. The foreign exchange market may exhibit excess short-term volatility as compared with conditions expected to prevail when determined by long-term factors.

A follow-up survey of exchange market participants by the Group of 30 in 1985 suggested continued support for the existing system. Exchange rate volatility and currency realignments were believed to be the result of different economic conditions and contrasting economic policies. Accordingly, corrective action should be directed toward those basic conditions and policies rather than toward the foreign exchange rate system.[7]

The Bank for International Settlements noted in 1988 that long-term exchange rate fluctuations have adversely affected resource allocation, encouraged protectionist tendencies, and increased the risks associated with international investment decisions. The Bank concluded that there is a need for increased international coordination of economic policies and a stronger determination to maintain exchange rates that are both stable and predictable.[8]

Generally there has not been widespread support for a major alteration of the exchange rate system, but the defects are apparent. The managed float has been in existence for well over a decade, and its

[5]International Monetary Fund, *Annual Report 1982* (Washington: 1982), pp. 42-45.

[6]International Monetary Fund, *Exchange Rate Volatility and World Trade* (Washington: July 1984), pp. 35-37.

[7]Group of Thirty, *The Foreign Exchange Market in the 1980s* (New York: 1985), pp. 1-2.

A 1986 study of the impact of exchange rate uncertainty during the period 1974-1984 concluded that the reductions in total U.S. trade were modest but probably had the greatest impact on agricultural products, manufactured goods classified by material, and crude materials. See Keith Maskus, "Exchange Rate Risk and U.S. Trade: A Sectoral Analysis," *Economic Review*, Federal Reserve Bank of Kansas City (March 1986), pp. 16-28.

[8]Bank for International Settlements, *Fifty-Eighth Annual Report* (Basle, Switzerland: 1988), pp. 175-179.

continuation is likely but by no means a certainty. Opposition to the arrangement is reflected, for example, by the French government, which has insisted on a revamping of the international monetary system in order to eliminate its instability. Supporters of the present system, in turn, argue that existing defects could be alleviated by closer cooperation and coordination of economic policies among major trading countries. Others have argued for a more managed system based on target zones and the use of economic indicators to guide policy actions related to the exchange rates of the major industrialized countries.[9]

The deficit on the U.S. current account is a central consideration in the policies adopted regarding the exchange rate. The ability of the United States to eliminate or at least reduce its current account deficit will have an important bearing on the form of any exchange rate regime that develops in the future.

The desirability of a flexible exchange rate regime has been debated for many years and will probably continue to be an issue among economists, bankers and those involved in international commerce. The shift to a new system of exchange rates in the early 1970s did affect the activities of commercial banks. Yet banks and other participants in international commerce have adjusted to the short-term fluctuations in currency prices. The variability of exchange rates is probably less than expected although more than desired; this variability appears to have had no significant impact on the total volume of world trade and investment, although it has affected the balance of payments position of individual countries in recent years.

UNITED STATES EXCHANGE RATE POLICY

Provisions of the IMF allow countries to choose among several alternative exchange rate regimes, but they are obligated to maintain a framework for order in the exchange markets. Of central importance are the system and policies adopted by the United States, the major trading and investing nation. What is an appropriate exchange rate policy for the United States, given that the dollar is a key currency in international commerce?

The U.S. policy on official intervention in the foreign exchange market has varied over time since the collapse of the pegged exchange rate system in 1971. Initially, U.S. monetary authorities intervened in the

[9]For an analysis of economic indicators in exchange rate policy, see International Monetary Fund, "The Use of Indicators," *Annual Report 1987* (Washington: 1987), pp. 31-33.

exchange market in mid-1972 in an effort to stabilize an unsettled market. This approach continued through 1976. Under the Carter administration, a nonintervention policy was initially attempted but was soon abandoned when the dollar began to show erratic movements.

The policy established and pursued under the Reagan administration beginning in April of 1981 called for abstaining from intervention in the foreign exchange market except in emergency situations. In other words, the administration maintained a relatively "clean" float; the authorities generally refrained from currency purchases or sales to influence the value of the dollar.[10] The exception to this rule occurred in instances in which a dramatic event or a major development appeared likely to create unsettled conditions and lead to unusual instability in the foreign currency markets. For example, concerns arose in March of 1981 (the time of the attempted assassination of President Reagan) and in June of 1982 (following a major currency realignment of the European Monetary System).[11]

The Reagan administration's initial nonintervention posture was criticized by several European governments. The administration's position was consistent with its general policy of limiting the role of the federal government in economic affairs of the country. At least until mid-1983, of the major industrial countries, the United States intervened least frequently and then only to offset abnormal trading conditions.[12] The degree of exchange market intervention varies from country to country. In some instances, it is limited to the short-term objective of countering a noneconomic shock that might otherwise lead to unsettled conditions in the exchange markets. In other instances, it may take the form of action to offset an undesired seasonal or even a long-term trend toward currency appreciation or depreciation. Usually the level of exchange rates desired by the authorities is not specified.

---

[10]The nonintervention policy of the United States is summarized in "A New U.S. Official Foreign Exchange Market Intervention Policy," *International Letter*, Federal Reserve Bank of Chicago (May 8, 1981), pp. 1-2.

[11]Michael Hutchinson, "U.S. Intervention Policy," *Weekly Letter*, Federal Reserve Bank of San Francisco (June 10, 1983), pp. 1-3.

A description of stabilization activities of the Federal Reserve Board and the Treasury's Exchange Stabilization Fund is provided on a regular basis in the monthly *Federal Reserve Bulletin*. See, for example, Sam Y. Cross, "Treasury and Federal Reserve Foreign Exchange Operations," *Federal Reserve Bulletin* (Washington: July 1988), pp. 430-434.

[12]"Studies of Foreign Exchange Market Intervention," *IMF Survey* (May 9, 1983), pp. 137-138.

See also, "The Effectiveness of Foreign Market Intervention," *International Letter*, Federal Reserve Bank of Chicago (June 17, 1983), pp. 1-3; and "U.S. Government Intervention in the Foreign Exchange Markets," *International Letter*, Federal Reserve Bank of Chicago (August 12, 1983), pp. 1-3.

UNITED STATES CURRENT ACCOUNT DEFICIT AND NET DEBTOR STATUS

Concern over a major appreciation and then depreciation in the value of the dollar since 1979, the U.S. current account deficits since 1982, and the shift of the United States to a net debtor status in 1985 has caused the United States to pursue a more active exchange market policy. The three related developments were the result of several factors or conditions in the U.S. economy and the world economy. Inflation and high interest rates in the United States during the late 1979s and early 1980s in conjunction with a growing federal deficit provided a strong incentive for foreign countries to invest in the United States. The purchase of U.S. dollars by foreigners to accommodate the investment contributed to the appreciation of the dollar through early 1985. The appreciated dollar, in turn, contributed to a relative decline in the value of exports and a relative increase in imports eventually leading to a current account deficit. The deficit, in turn, was offset by the U.S. capital account surplus—the United States became a major borrowing country.

The U.S. current account deficit (with the value of imports of goods and services exceeding the value of exports of goods and services) was also expanded as a result of relative economic stagnation in many European countries. As a consequence, their demand for U.S. goods and services fell short of the amounts that would have been imported under conditions of full employment and prosperity.[13] A related development was the decline in U.S. private direct investment overseas following 1981.

The change in the U.S. balance of payments and investment position was a reversal of its growing importance as a major creditor nation during the 1970s. The peak creditor status had been achieved in 1981, with net claims of all types against foreigners, including net bank claims, amounting to $140 billion. But this country's investment status altered dramatically, leading to a net debtor position; by the end of 1987, this amounted to $368 billion.

The U.S. debt is perceived by some as a potential problem in that it involves foreign ownership of United States-located property and financial assets, and that it leads to a net outflow of debt service payments. However, the U.S. concern is not simply the large debt to foreigners but also the large current account deficits that are an integral part of foreign lending to the United States and to the growth of the debt. The current account deficit is considered by some as a major factor contributing to

---

[13]See Ralph C. Bryant and Gerald Holtham, "The External Deficit: Why? Where Next? What Remedy?" *The Brookings Review* (Spring 1987), pp. 28-36.

unemployment in this country, which has also led to strong protectionist tendencies within Congress.

G-5 EFFORTS

Because of the sharp and continued appreciation of the dollar beginning in late 1979 and the subsequent current account deficits, U.S. monetary authorities came to intervene in the exchange markets on a regular basis. In addition, the U.S. government secured the cooperation of other G-5 (Group of Five) countries (Great Britain, France, West Germany, and Japan) in 1985 in undertaking official coordinated intervention in the exchange market to achieve a depreciation of the dollar. Two additional countries—Canada and Italy—decided to participate, with a resulting G-7 (Group of Seven) arrangement. The G-7 effort, although based on informal and voluntary action, appears to represent a new aspect of commercial policy in the postwar period. Actions require the coordinated efforts of several governments; further, coordination efforts apply not only to the exchange markets but also to internal economic policies. Coordinated G-7 action continued although on a somewhat erratic basis as the dollar depreciated in the exchange markets from early 1985 though 1987. At that time, concerns arose that the value of the dollar may have dropped too far, and a reverse action was initiated by some of the participants to prevent their own currencies from continued appreciation. The establishment of international currency values that are acceptable to all participating countries is an important problem in such arrangements.

Traditionally, the presumption has been made that in the long run the international value of currencies or exchange rates would move toward a purchasing power parity equilibrium. At equilibrium, the exchange rate would equal the ratio of the foreign and domestic price levels.[14] Stated in terms of the "law of one price," goods would sell for the same price worldwide when adjusted by the exchange rate. In the "absolute" version of purchasing power parity, the exchange rate reflects the ratio of the price indexes of two countries. In the "relative" version,

---

[14]For example, if a given bundle of goods and services cost 100 British pounds in the United Kingdom and the same bundle cost $250 in the United States, then the equilibrium exchange rate would be $2.50 = 1 pound.

An analysis of purchasing power parity is provided in Jacques R. Artus, "Methods of Assessing the Longer-Run Equilibrium Value of an Exchange Rate," *Finance and Development* (June 1978), pp. 26-28; Michael Melvin, "Purchasing Power Parity," *International Money and Finance* (New York: Harper & Row, Publishers, Inc., 1985), pp. 74-87; and Jacques R. Artus and Malcolm Knight, *Issues in the Assessment of the Exchange Rates of Industrial Countries* (Washington: International Monetary Fund, July 1984).

a *change* in the exchange rate would correspond to a *change* in the price indexes of the two countries.

Application of the purchasing power parity concept poses both conceptual and empirical problems relating to the measurement of price levels, the types of items to be included in the indexes, impediments to trade, and choice of a base period. Nevertheless, the theory is helpful in understanding the complex relationship between price levels and exchange rates.

At the February 1987 Paris meeting of G-7 countries, it was agreed (the Louvre Accord) that the governments would foster stability of exchange rates around the current level.[15] Subsequently, the participants agreed to the use of a set of economic indicators as a guideline for stabilizing the market. In practice, the governments have attempted to maintain exchange rates within an undisclosed range. By the time of the annual meeting of the IMF and World Bank in September of 1987, the G-7 countries were prepared to reaffirm the decision to cooperate closely to promote exchange rate stability around the existing level.

The G-5 (or G-7) approach is advantageous in that the likelihood of unilateral action is reduced because coordination is emphasized—essentially the cooperation of several governments to achieve specified objectives. Yet there are problems associated with such arrangements. To what extent can the governments, treasuries, and central banks of several different countries agree upon objectives? To what extent are they willing to pursue policies that may come to be perceived as incompatible with the domestic goals of each of the respective economies? This is a particularly important consideration, given that exchange market intervention has far-reaching consequences for participating countries. Intervention has two impacts: (1) altering the relative exchange market values of the currencies being bought and sold and (2) altering the monetary base of the intervening countries. There were indications that some of the G-7 participants, especially Japan and West Germany, were unwilling on occasion to appreciate their currencies to the extent desired by the United States. And where central banks are relatively independent (as is the Federal Reserve Board), the precise policy desired by the legislative or executive branches may not be accepted and fully adopted by these institutions.

Even if intervention to alter the exchange market values of currencies is accomplished, there may be a resistance to the secondary impact—permitting the monetary base of the affected countries to be altered. To the extent that a central bank "sterilizes" the monetary impact of ex-

---

[15]For an analysis of the extent of these implications, see Joseph Kvasnicka, "Central Banks Move to Halt the Dollar's Rise," *International Letter*, Federal Reserve Bank of Chicago (March 8, 1985), pp. 1-3.

change market intervention, it may eliminate or reduce any impact on underlying conditions that caused the imbalance in the first place. Generally, the Federal Reserve has routinely sterilized the monetary impact of exchange market intervention. Although the action is consistent with stated U.S. monetary targets, it significantly weakens the impact of the intervention efforts.[16]

A fundamental risk with exchange market intervention is that it may become a substitute for the type of internal corrective action prescribed by the IMF's Articles of Agreement. Article IV specifies that each member shall:

    i. endeavor to direct its economic and financial policies toward the objective of fostering orderly economic growth with reasonable price stability, with due regard to its circumstances;

    ii. seek to promote stability by fostering orderly underlying economic and financial conditions and a monetary system that does not tend to produce erratic disruptions;

    iii. avoid manipulating exchange rates or the international monetary system in order to prevent effective balance of payments adjustments or to gain an unfair competitive advantage over other members.

The G-7 countries have engaged in extensive discussions regarding initiation of policies to correct underlying conditions, yet action to correct basic conditions through monetary or fiscal policy has been limited.

GOLD AND OTHER OFFICIAL RESERVES

The exchange reserves that were required under the Bretton Woods pegged exchange rate system remain central to the floating system to the extent that governments find it desirable to intervene in the exchange markets. An important concern of some of the international financial institutions as well as the central banks of most countries pertains to the level and distribution of international reserves. The four types of reserves that are maintained by central banks and treasuries are gold, historically the most important international asset; Special Drawing Rights, first created by the IMF in 1969; reserve positions of IMF members in the Fund; and official holdings of foreign exchange. Official international reserves are held by countries for various related purposes—to maintain the exchange value of the domestic currency rela-

---

[16]For an analysis of problems associated with coordination, see C. Fred Bergsten, Etienne Davignon, and Isamu Miyazaki, *Conditions for Partnership in International Economic Management* (New York: The Trilateral Commission, 1986).

tive to all other currencies, and as a reserve to continue essential imports or to service external obligations during periods when current export earnings fall below a desired level. In some countries, such reserves, especially gold, serve as a backing for the domestic supply of money and credit. Although officially held exchange reserves are not part of the asset structure of private commercial banks, the use of such reserves by central banks and treasuries for stabilization measures does affect the domestic monetary base and position of commercial banks.

The historical importance of gold is probably best manifested in the international gold standard in the 1800s and first part of the 1900s. Gold and the U.S. dollar were the major international reserves in the early post-World War II period, but decisions were made in the 1960s and 1970s to *demonetize* gold—to lessen its importance as a monetary asset. These efforts were reflected in several different actions taken with regard to the use of gold. Since 1965, the Federal Reserve System is no longer required by law to maintain the basic domestic monetary reserves in the form of gold. In 1969, member countries of the IMF agreed to authorize the creation of SDRs, a transferable reserve claim sometimes called "paper gold." In mid-1971, the U.S. government suspended the convertibility of officially held dollars into gold. The dollar was devalued in 1971 and in 1973, and since then the value of the dollar is no longer tied to gold.

Another action which served to *demonetize* gold occurred in 1974, when the value of the SDR came to be determined not by the value of gold but by a composite or basket of currencies. In addition, following a decision made in 1975, the IMF sold part of its gold stock at auction; through mid-1980 it has disposed of about 25 million ounces in this fashion. Finally, since 1978, member countries of the IMF are no longer authorized to define their respective currencies in terms of gold.

What is the appropriate role of gold in the world economy today? Is it realistic to assume that some type of international gold standard could or should be reestablished? In general, gold has fewer official functions, yet it continues to be one form of international monetary reserve. Gold is also traded more widely in private markets including the United States for speculative purposes and as a store of value. In some countries gold is held in private hoards as protection against hyperinflation and political disturbances. The Bank for International Settlements estimates world production of gold had gradually increased to about 1375 metric tons by 1987. Official gold stocks decreased slightly, with the result that about 1765 metric tons were absorbed for nonmonetary purposes— industrial uses, jewelry, and private hoards.[17] Although gold does not

---

[17]Bank for International Settlements, *Fifty-Eighth Annual Report* (Basle, Switzerland: June 1988), p. 184.

provide an interest return to the holder, its price has increased in several recent years as a result of inflation and frequently, at least in the short run, in connection with a decline in the value of the U.S. dollar. Although the world market price of gold rose sharply for a time during the early 1970s, its value has vacillated in more recent years. For example, it reached a high of $750 per ounce in 1980, but by early 1984, sold at a price of about $375 per ounce and by early 1988, $430 per ounce.

The shift away from official uses of gold by the United States and various other countries, in part, may be based on the fact that the major beneficiaries are the Soviet Union and South Africa, the two major producers. Yet demonetization does not rule out completely the consideration of gold in some official capacity in the future. However, the actual nature of a gold standard that might be adopted can be perceived in different ways. As a minimum, it entails an arrangement requiring the Federal Reserve System (and other central banks) to maintain gold reserves against bank deposit reserves and currency in circulation as it did prior to 1965. In the most comprehensive form it implies defining monetary units in terms of gold and instituting an international gold standard similar to that prevailing prior to the 1930s. Interest in some type of gold standard seems greatest when inflationary pressures are most severe because of a belief that monetary stability would be restored under a system of this type.

At the time that the U.S. Congress authorized an increase in the U.S. quota in the International Monetary Fund in 1980, a Gold Commission was created to serve as a study group under the Secretary of the Treasury. It was hoped that questions regarding the future role of gold could be resolved. The Commission was requested to "assess and make arrangements with regard to the policy of the U.S. government concerning the role of gold in the domestic and international monetary systems..." The first meetings of the Gold Commission were conducted in mid-1981. Initially, there was some sentiment in favor of a limited form of the gold standard by at least a few of the seventeen Commission members and by a part of the U.S. public particularly because of an inflation rate in excess of 10 percent at that time. However, it appears that the use of other alternatives to achieve monetary stability is a more predominant view in the United States and that sympathy for a return to a form of the gold standard was, in fact, reflected by but a few members of the Commission. The final recommendation of the Commission was that there be no change in the role of gold.[18]

---

[18]See A. J. Schwartz, "Reflections on the Gold Commission Report," *Journal of Money, Credit, and Banking* (November 1982), pp. 538-551.

SPECIAL DRAWING RIGHTS

In an effort to supplement gold as a form of international reserve, the IMF created Special Drawing Rights in 1969, essentially as book entries of credit in its ledgers. The SDRs were initially denominated in terms of the gold equivalent of one U.S. dollar. Subsequently a weighted average of 16 currencies was used in their valuation, but since January 1, 1981, only the five major currencies (U.S. dollar, West German mark, Japanese yen, French franc, and the British pound) are included in the weighted average. At the time of the initial issue, SDR 6 billion were created. By March of 1988, SDR 20.5 billion were held as official reserves, the equivalent of about $28 billion. Also, by this time, SDR 1 = $0.452 + 0.527 DM + 1.02 franc + 33.4 yen + 0.0893 pound sterling.

Special Drawing Rights are a unique form of reserve; they are used as a medium of exchange only in transactions involving the IMF, central banks, or treasuries of member governments and certain other prescribed holders. For example, the government of one country might transfer its holdings of SDRs to another country in exchange for currency of the second country that is needed for balance of payments purposes. Holders are also permitted to buy and sell SDRs forward, and to use them in swaps and other financial exchanges. In addition to the IMF and member governments, SDR holders include the Bank for International Settlements, the World Bank, the International Development Association, and several multinational development banks. Special Drawing Rights are not used as a medium of exchange by private traders or for commercial transactions.

The SDR is also employed outside the Fund by governments and by the private sector as a valuation technique or an international unit of account.[19] The price of an item is stated in terms of SDRs; actual payment is made with a national currency at the existing price of that currency in terms of SDRs or with the five constituent currencies of the SDR. Items traded internationally especially have been priced in terms of SDRs rather than in terms of dollars, pounds, marks, or francs. When the Suez Canal was reopened for service, shipping rates were denominated in terms of SDRs rather than Egyptian pounds. OPEC has on occasion considered basing world oil prices on the SDR rather than on the U.S. dollar.

The major advantage of SDR pricing is that the variability of the price of the item being traded is reduced. In some instances, the value of

---

[19]D. M. Sobol, "The SDR in Private International Finance," *Quarterly Review*, Federal Reserve Bank of New York (Winter 1981-1982), pp. 29-41.

the SDR may be better known than that of the currencies, particularly when the latter are not widely traded in commerce. Over a dozen international and regional organizations use the SDR to express monetary magnitudes; these include the Asian Development Bank, the European Conference of Postal and Telecommunications Administration, the International Centre for Settlement of Investment Disputes, and the International Development Association.

By the early 1980s, a large number of commercial banks were offering time deposits denominated in SDRs, and at least a few European banks have established SDR-denominated current account deposits. In these cases, the SDR is used only for valuation purposes or as a unit of account; it is not actually used to accomplish this payment. Eurobonds have also been issued denominated in terms of SDRs.

Related to the unit of account function, the SDR is also used as a currency peg. About ten of the smaller countries fix the value of their currency in terms of the SDR (see Table 3.1). Changes of this type are expected to enhance the use of the SDR for this purpose in private transactions outside the IMF.

Although gold is the oldest and SDRs are the newest of the international reserves, by far the greatest share of reserves are the official holdings of foreign exchange (Table 3.2). The largest growth has also occurred in this type of reserve. Essentially, these are the holdings by treasuries and central banks of short-term government securities and bank deposits denominated in terms of a readily convertible currency such as the dollar, pound, mark, or yen.

During the period 1980 through March of 1988, the aggregate value of the three basic types of reserves increased from about SDR 321 billion to about SDR 517 billion. What is the value of the reserves in terms of

TABLE 3.2   OFFICIAL RESERVES OF IMF COUNTRIES 1980 and 1988* (in billions of SDRs)

	1980	1988
Special Drawing Rights	11.8	20.5
Reserve positions in IMF	16.8	30.7
Foreign exchange holdings	292.8	465.6
Total reserves less gold	321.4	516.7
Total reserves including gold	761.9	828.3

*Gold is valued at London market price. Figures for l988 are for March of that year.

Source: International Monetary Fund, Annual Report 1986 (Washington: 1986), p. 58; and Annual Report 1988, (Washington: 1988), page 66.

dollar equivalents? With an SDR worth about $1.38 in March of 1988, the SDR 517 billion was worth about $713 billion.[20]

THE EUROPEAN MONETARY SYSTEM

Another institutional arrangement noted previously that plays a central role in European (and accordingly international) financial affairs is the European Monetary System (EMS). The EMS came into existence in 1979, subsequent to the abandonment of the pegged exchange rate system, primarily to establish exchange rate stability and certainty among participating countries. As a result, the price of currencies of West Germany, France, Italy, Netherlands, Belgium, Luxembourg, Denmark, and Ireland are tied or permitted to deviate only within a narrow range of central exchange rates (plus or minus 2.25 percent with the exception of the Italian lira, which can deviate by 6 percent) as part of the Exchange Rate Mechanism (ERM). The central exchange rates have been altered on several occasions to reflect changes in balance of payments positions of participating countries. In some respects, the EMS is similar to the IMF's pegged exchange rate system that prevailed from the mid-1940s through the early 1970s. However, EMS exchange rates are permitted to float freely vis-a-vis all other currencies.

The EMS has also established the European Currency Unit (ECU) to serve as a unit of account, a means of settling payments imbalances, and a reserve asset for participating countries. The ECU is a composite currency containing specified amounts of currencies of ten European countries (the eight EMS countries plus the United Kingdom and Greece which are expected to eventually participate in the EMS). As a composite, its value is generally subject to less variation than that of any of the individual currencies.

The ECU is used extensively in financial markets. Many European banks accept deposits and make loans denominated in ECU terms. The ECU is becoming a widely used unit in the international bond market. ECU travelers checks are now available. The growth in the use of the ECU in recent years has led to suggestions that it take the place of the U.S. dollar as a major reserve asset.[21] It could conceivably become a common currency and take the place of national currencies should the European Community continue to integrate economically and politically.

---

[20]For an extensive treatment of the various forms of international reserves and their legal status, see Joseph Gold, *SDRs, Currencies, and Gold: Seventh Survey of New Legal Developments* (Washington: International Monetary Fund, 1987).

[21]Robert Triffin, "The International Monetary System and the European Monetary System," *EFTA Bulletin* (March 1987), pp. 10-13.

Although the EMS has forced member countries to coordinate economic policies, balance of payments strains remain a recurring problem. Yet it has contributed to a greater degree of stability in the group's trade and investment relationships with the rest of the world than would have been likely for individual member countries. A British decision to participate in the ERM would further enhance the system's role in the world economy.

In addition, closer economic integration would result if the European Economic Community were to adopt a set of proposals contained in the Second Council Directive. One of the key provisions of the Directive removes the remaining restrictions on commercial banks licensed by any member state of the Community to establish branches or supply services in any other member country beginning in 1993.[22]

OTHER INTERNATIONAL FINANCIAL INSTITUTIONS

Although the IMF plays a central role in the international finance system, several other institutions, especially the Bank for International Settlements (BIS), are also an important part of the world monetary structure. The BIS, established in 1930, is principally a European institution with headquarters in Basle, Switzerland. The BIS is managed by a board of directors with representatives of central banks from Belgium, France, Germany, Italy, the United Kingdom, and several other participating countries. The U.S. Federal Reserve failed to subscribe to stock in the BIS at its inception, although U.S. commercial banks did purchase shares in the institution. In addition, the United States plays a major role in the activities and policies developed by the BIS.

The BIS performs a number of functions, one of the most important being that of facilitating cooperation and consultation among central banks.[23] The BIS engages in transactions generally with central banks; it also serves as an agent or trustee for several regional and international institutions. The BIS remains an important organization for promoting monetary cooperation among the industrialized countries, performing its most essential role during periods of financial stress and instability. For example, the multilateral agreement to assist the Mexican government in overcoming its external debt problems in 1982 was accomplished under the aegis of the BIS. The BIS has been involved in numerous debt

---

[22]Commission of the European Communities, *Proposal for a Second Council Directive* (Brussels: February 16, 1988).

[23]An excellent source of information on international financial matters is provided in Bank for International Settlements, *Annual Reports* (Basle, Switzerland: various issues).

reschedulings since that time. And, finally, the BIS played a central role in establishing the Basle Concordat as well as, at the instigation of the United States, encouraging the establishment of bank capital adequacy guidelines among industrialized countries (described in Chapter 14).

Another institution of major importance in world capital markets is the International Bank for Reconstruction and Development (IBRD or World Bank). The IBRD commenced operations in 1946 with an emphasis on provision of long-term loans for reconstruction and development purposes. This institution is a lender of last resort and provides long-term capital on a concessionary basis. As discussed in Chapter 13, its efforts are of particular value to the developing, borrowing countries, especially in terms of the impact on external debt obligations.

SUMMARY AND CONCLUSIONS

The institutions and arrangements that provide the framework within which international commercial banking occurs have evolved over many decades, but some of the most important changes have taken place since the end of World War II. For example, a central feature of the international gold standard, a key institution of the late 1800s and early 1900s, was fixed exchange rates, and gold was the major international reserve asset. When the IMF came into existence in the late 1940s, fixed exchange rates were maintained through exchange controls or stabilization funds, but even this arrangement gave way to a floating exchange rate system in the early 1970s. And gold, along with the Special Drawing Rights, is only one of several reserve assets held by central banks and treasuries. The IMF remains a central international institution, continuing to provide guidelines and assistance to insure stability and efficiency in the exchange market.

Exchange rates have become somewhat more volatile than was hoped would be the case. The appreciation of the U.S. dollar during the years 1980 through early 1985 also created balance of trade problems for the United States. This, in turn, led to the G-5 and G-7 efforts designed to shift relative currency values to more acceptable levels.

International banking is obviously affected by the framework within which it operates. The institutional arrangements that evolve influence the volume of world trade and investment, which in turn have an impact on the nature and volume of bank activity. The type of exchange rate system affects the way in which banks establish procedures and instruments to meet the requirements of commerce. In addition, banks are affected by the policies established by international agencies to cope with Third World debt problems, restrictions on international trade and investment, and the settlement of disputes in international commerce.

Developments in exchange rates and the exchange market are but one part of the total change occurring in international finance. As noted in the following chapters, which examine both the U.S. and foreign money and capital markets, new attitudes and policies, and revised legislation and regulations are profoundly affecting the world of finance and credit. Financial institutions are both introducing innovation and being forced to adjust to new conditions at a pace never before experienced.

The Eurocurrency market, which encompasses a system composed of claims amounting to a value in excess of $4500 billion, was largely unheard of prior to the mid-1960s. This market, along with the Asian currency market and other financial innovations, is examined in the following chapter.

4

INNOVATION IN WORLD FINANCIAL MARKETS

The framework of international financial activity described previously considered governmental and intergovernmental institutions created to accommodate world trade and financial activities. The volume of activity in world financial markets has increased since the end of World War II, not only as a direct result of the growth in world trade but also because of a variety of innovations that have been introduced. The innovations, in turn, are a result of such factors as improvements in technology (especially in communications), efforts on the part of banks to avoid burdensome regulations, and the desire on the part of financial institutions to meet the demands of international and multinational corporations.

The present chapter focuses on a major nongovernmental phenomenon that has been central to international commercial banking since the early 1960s—the Eurocurrency market. The Asian dollar market, a more recent development, is also examined. And, finally, off-balance-sheet activities, innovative efforts that have been either initiated or developed by banks primarily since the early 1970s, are considered.

EUROCURRENCY MARKET

One of the most unusual developments in post-World War II international commerce, but one having a pervasive impact on international banking, is the *Eurocurrency market*. The Eurocurrency market is essentially a short-term capital market of money deposited in banks outside the country that issued the money. *Eurodollars*, which make up the largest part of the market, are defined as deposits denominated and payable in U.S. dollars in banks located, for the most part, outside the United States. The deposits are in large amounts ($100,000 or more) and take the form of time deposits or certificates of deposit; essentially the market functions at the wholesale level and involves short-term claims. The participating depository banks can be either foreign or overseas offices of a U.S. bank.

Eurodollars are created when an American or foreign owner of a dollar deposit in a bank in the United States transfers the funds or deposits them with an offshore bank—any bank located outside the United States. Usually the owner makes the transfer to obtain a higher rate of return abroad. Foreign banks are willing to accept the deposits because they can make dollar loans and secure a favorable return—these loans are termed *Eurocurrency bank credits*.

The basis for Eurodollars arises initially, for example, when a foreigner comes into possession of a demand deposit in a New York bank as a result of the export of products to the United States. The exporter's alternative uses of the dollar deposit include the purchase of U.S. securities or the sale of the deposit for a European currency and the subsequent purchase of European securities. But the exporter might find that the highest rate of return could be secured by making a deposit denominated in dollars in a European bank, for example, a London bank. Eurodollars are created when there is a transfer of ownership of a dollar deposit by the foreigner to the London or other European bank. The volume of deposits in the New York bank does not change, although, of course, the deposits are held by a different party—in this case, the London bank.

The London bank, now a holder of a deposit asset and an interest-bearing liability, must lend the dollars at a higher rate of return if it is to make a profit. A positive margin may exist for the London bank intermediary for any one of several different reasons—if different-sized loans can be made, if loan maturity dates are different from the initial deposit, if the London bank has a better knowledge of market opportunities, or if it is able to assume a larger risk. Generally, however, Eurobanking is profitable because it is less regulated in terms of reserve requirements and deposit insurance premiums. As a result, the participating bank can offer higher interest rates on deposits and extend loans at lower interest rates (i.e., a narrower spread) than can a United States-located bank.

Equally important is that if the London bank makes a loan to another financial institution such as a bank, rather than holding the deposits for its own liquidity needs, another dollar deposit is created. In fact, as noted later, interbank deposits represent about 80 percent of gross Eurocurrency liabilities.[1] They are central to the market as a means whereby major banks with large currency deposits not needed directly are provided to other banks and ultimately to final borrowers. The interbank depositing does not affect the volume of deposit liabilities of the New York bank; such deposits may eventually be drawn down if they come to be held by a nonbank borrower that desires to import from the United States or to discharge an obligation.

Many of the participating banks are located in London, which is the center of the market. Those that accept the deposits and make loans are sometimes called Eurobanks, although they have no unusual features or characteristics. Further, Eurobanking is only part of the overall activities of such banks, which also accept demand deposits and make loans in the domestic currency. Countries in which Eurobanks are located regulate banking activities in the domestic currency, but Eurocurrency transactions are basically unregulated.

The interest paid to banks on Eurodollar loans exceed deposit rates by a relatively narrow margin. Loan interest rates are generally specified in terms of some percent above LIBOR (the London interbank offered rate, the rate charged by the six major London banks for loans to each other.)

In addition to the dollar deposits, a market exists for deposits of other currencies not denominated in the currencies of the banks accepting the deposits. The major remaining currencies that are lent and borrowed include sterling, Deutsche marks, French and Swiss francs, and the yen. Along with the U.S. dollar, they make up the more inclusive Eurocurrency market. As convertible currencies, they are widely used in international trade and accordingly are particularly appropriate for this type of market.

Are Eurodollars a component of the U.S. money supply? Those held by *foreigners* are not. Some deposits held by nonbank *U.S. residents* may be included as part of certain monetary aggregates. For example, Eurodollars held by U.S. residents are not included in M1, the most narrowly defined monetary aggregate that corresponds with the function of money as a medium of exchange. However, overnight Eurodollars is-

---

[1]A detailed analysis of the Eurocurrency market is provided in John Hewson, *Liquidity Creation and Distribution in the Eurocurrency Markets* (Lexington, Mass.: D.C. Heath and Company, 1975).

sued to U.S. residents by foreign branches of U.S. banks are included in the more broadly defined M2 and M3. M3 also includes term Eurodollars held by U.S. residents at all foreign branches of U.S. banks and at all banking offices in the United Kingdom and Canada.[2] The rationale is that Eurodollar deposits are close substitutes for domestic deposits.

An important development in the Eurodollar market was the U.S. authorization of International Banking Facilities (IBFs) in late 1981. IBFs (described more fully in Chapter 10) are arrangements which permit deposits to be held by *foreigners* in United States-located banks. These deposits are denominated primarily in terms of dollars but also in terms of other currencies; they are exempted from reserve requirements and deposit insurance coverage. This enables U.S. banks to participate directly in the Eurocurrency market rather than having to go through an overseas office. Both the dollar and nondollar deposits are considered part of the Eurocurrency market even though the dollars are in United States-located banks because they are not subject to all United States banking regulations. By early 1988, nondollar currency deposits in U.S.-located banks amounted to about $40 billion; dollar deposits, about $231 billion.[3] In a late 1988 ruling, the Federal Reserve Board authorized U.S. banks to accept foreign currency deposits from U.S. residents effective at the end of 1989. The major purpose was to give small businesses and investors greater flexibility in the exchange markets.

The Eurocurrency markets are distinctive in that the transactions are "offshore"—currencies are deposited in banks and loans are obtained from banks located outside the country of the currency in question (or at least not subject to the regulations of the host country, as in the case of IBFs). Such transactions occur in a nonregulated environment which permits the payment of a higher rate of interest on deposits; it also enables the extension of a greater volume of loans insofar as legally

---

[2]For an analysis of conceptual problems in the composition of U.S. monetary aggregates, see Daniel J. Larkins, "The Monetary Aggregates: An Introduction to Definitional Issues," *Survey of Current Business* (January 1983), pp. 34-46. The current status of Eurodollars as part of M2 and M3 is provided by Federal Reserve Board, *Federal Reserve Bulletin* (monthly).
By mid-1988, U.S. residents held about $15 billion in overnight Eurodollars (included in M2 and M3) and about $86 billion in term Eurodollars (included in M3). See "Other Components of M2 and M3," *Monetary Trends*, Federal Reserve Bank of St. Louis (April 1988), p. 6.

[3]Federal Reserve Board, "Monthly Report of Assets and Liabilities of International Banking Facilities," *Statistical Release* (various issues). A good statement of the nature of IBFs as part of the Eurocurrency market is provided by Marvin Goodfriend, "Eurodollars," *Current Readings on Money, Banking, and Financial Markets*, ed. James A. Wilcox (Boston: Little, Brown and Company, 1987), pp. 330-341; and Henry S. Terrell and Rodney H. Mills, "International Banking Facilities and the Eurodollar Market," *Staff Studies* (Washington: Federal Reserve Board, August 1983).

required reserves do not exist.[4] Yet the nonregulated nature of the market does not necessarily imply a high risk for participants. The safety of the system depends largely upon the prudence of depository institutions—a degree of caution must be exercised regardless of the extent of government regulation.

SIZE AND OTHER FEATURES OF THE EUROCURRENCY MARKET

Although the origin of Eurodollars is subject to debate, some of the earliest Eurodollar deposits developed in the 1950s when the Soviet Union chose to hold dollar claims in European banks that it believed might otherwise be frozen or confiscated by the United States. Subsequently other holders of dollars discovered the interest rate advantage associated with depositing in European banks. A major incentive to the growth of Eurodollar activity arose in the mid-1960s as a consequence of efforts of the U.S. government to control capital outflows and to place a ceiling on interest payments by banks on short-term deposits. In addition, most foreign banks are subject to a lower noninterest-bearing asset requirement against deposit liabilities than are U.S. banks. Accordingly, there is an incentive in the form of a higher rate of return for banks to participate in this market.

For a time, it was believed that the Eurocurrency market was temporary in nature, one that would disappear with a decline in regulations on capital movements and in rigidities in interest rate patterns. In fact, the Eurocurrency market has become institutionalized and has grown dramatically in size—from an estimated $485 billion to $4561 billion in gross terms over the period 1975 through March of 1988. Because of its nature, a highly accurate picture of the size of this market is not readily available. Figures on the Eurocurrency market in Table 4.1 are based on data from the Federal Reserve Board and Morgan Guaranty Trust Company.

As indicated, the estimated value of the Eurocurrency market by early 1988 was $839 billion in terms of liabilities to nonbanks. The difference between this figure and the gross figure of $4561 billion (i.e., $3722 billion) to a great extent represents interbank lending and borrowing.

---

[4]Since November of 1980, Eurocurrency liabilities of all types held by United States-located banks are subject to a 3 percent reserve requirement. However, the Depository Institutions Act of 1982 provided that $2 million of reservable liabilities (including Eurocurrency liabilities) of each depository institution be subject to a zero percent reserve requirement.

TABLE 4.1   Eurocurrency Market
A. Eurocurrency Market Size[1]
(billions of dollars at end of period)

	1980	1982	1984	1986	1988
Gross liabilities to:					
Nonbanks	$278	$432	$497	$699	$839
Central banks	128	91	96	105	144
Other banks	1172	1645	1793	2879	3577
Total	1578	2168	2386	3683	4561
Eurodollars as % of total gross liabilities of all Eurocurrencies	76%	80%	82%	71%	67%

B. Eurodollar Deposit Rates (percent)[2]

	1980	1982	1984	1986	1988
Overnight	21.11	8.75	7.81	14.48	6.49
7-day	19.88	9.60	8.52	9.00	6.66
One month	19.33	9.26	8.34	6.92	6.69
Three month	17.79	9.36	8.61	6.35	6.78
Six month	16.69	9.64	9.11	6.19	6.99
Twelve month	14.98	9.76	9.86	6.17	7.43

[1]Based on foreign liabilities of banks in major European countries, the Bahamas, Bahrain, Cayman Islands, Panama, Canada, Japan, Hong Kong, and Singapore. Year-end data except for I988, which shows data for the end of March.

[2]Bid rates in London at or near end of year except for I988, which shows the rate for March.

Source: Federal Reserve Board and Morgan Guaranty Trust Company. Derived from data published in *International Economic Conditions,* Federal Reserve Bank of St. Louis (various issues).

Interbank lending, a major form of international lending, is an important characteristic of the market; if the demand for loans from a particular bank does not match the supply of deposits, the excess (or deficit) may be loaned to (borrowed from) other banks.

The significance of the Eurodollar component of the Eurocurrency market is also indicated in Table 4.1. Generally this has ranged in the neighborhood of 65 to 80 percent, much higher than the U.S. share in world trade and investment. The relatively large share reflects the extensive use of the dollar for the invoicing of world trade and the use of the dollar as a reserve currency. The dollar also plays a key role as a vehicle currency, or medium of exchange, to accommodate exchanges of other currencies. In the foreign exchange market, the dollar is particularly beneficial in an intermediary role when it involves a currency that is not heavily traded.[5] The extensive use of the dollar is also the result of high reserve requirements and deposit insurance applicable to United States-located banks that encourage the development of offshore deposits.

Eurodollar deposit rates for different maturity dates are also indicated for several recent years. Generally, these have declined since the early 1980s as part of a general trend toward lower rates. Both the level and the changes in three-month Eurodollar deposit rates (annual average) have been very similar to those of U.S. six-month certificate of deposit rates. Since 1966, the three-month Eurodollar rate (annual average) has ranged from a low of about 5.5 percent (1967 and 1972) to a high of about 17 percent (1981).

The narrow interest rate differentials between the United States and European countries is a reflection of the international scope of the Euro-currency market. Interest rate differentials remain relatively constant between markets, although the rates rise or fall over time. If, for example, rates rise in the United States, there is greater incentive for an investor to switch from a Eurodollar deposit to domestic U.S. bank deposits, short-term government securities, or other financial claims. Such arbitrage activity introduces upward pressure on Eurodollar rates until the original equilibrium differential is established.

Foreign branches of U.S. banks are major participants in the Euro-dollar market. Borrowing by U.S. branches has tended to exceed their Eurodollar lending, with the excess maintained as current accounts at head offices in the United States for use in an effort to meet rising credit demand at home. United States monetary authorities imposed a reserve requirement on borrowing in the Eurodollar market above a specified base in October of 1979 in part as an effort to curb credit expansion of banks in the United States. In July of 1980, the requirement was removed on the grounds that credit conditions had improved in the United States and that the restriction was no longer needed.

The Euromarket provides a useful alternative for U.S. firms attempting to either place or raise funds. Empirical evidence suggests that the Euromarket has been more important as an outlet for deposits (or place to invest funds) for U.S. residents than as a source of loans. For example, as a result of lending, U.S. residents held over $90 billion in

---

[5]For example, rather than a direct currency A-currency B transaction, currency A is traded for dollars, and dollars in turn for currency B. The dollar as a vehicle currency is analyzed in Paul Krugman, "Vehicle Currencies and the Structure of International Exchange," *Journal of Money, Credit, and Banking* (August 1980), pp. 513-526. See also M. K. Lewis and K. T. Davis, *Domestic and International Banking* (Cambridge, Mass.: The MIT Press, 1987), pp. 224-232.

Euromarket deposits in U.S. branch offices overseas at the end of 1985. Borrowing from these banks amounted to slightly less than $20 billion.[6]

EURODOLLAR FUTURES MARKET

Although only a relatively small volume of deposits denominated in terms of a foreign currency is held in United States-located banks, the U.S. financial community is sensitive to this market in a number of ways. Since late 1981, futures trading in Eurodollars has been authorized on the International Money Market, a part of the Chicago Mercantile Exchange. Trading involves 90-day Eurodollar time deposits in $1 million denominations. The Eurodollar futures market is designed specifically for the international market with much of the activity from sources external to the United States; participants are provided with an opportunity to hedge against movements in interest rates on Eurodollars. This market is used primarily by large banks and multinational corporations desiring to avoid the risk associated with interest rate movements in international financial transactions.[7]

The demand for a market of this type has been greater in recent years, given the severe inflation that has characterized many countries along with wider movements in interest rates and exchange rates under the managed float system. In fact, on the basis of the number of contracts outstanding, it has grown since 1981 to become the largest U.S. futures market, surpassing even the Treasury bond futures market. Comparable growth in Eurodollar futures characterizes markets in other centers, including Singapore and London. The market is expected to continue to expand along with the growth of the Eurodollar market and with continued uncertainty of the value of the U.S. dollar in the exchange markets.

EUROCURRENCY CREDITS

The initial deposits that are made in the Eurocurrency transactions are usually liquid and short term. Subsequent action of banks to secure

[6]Ramon Moreno, "Euromarkets and Monetary Policy," *Weekly Letter*, Federal Reserve Bank of San Francisco (January 23, 1987), pp. 1–3.

[7]"Future Trading in Eurodollars," *International Letter*, Federal Reserve Bank of Chicago (December 18, 1981), pp.1–2; Sharon Reier, "Th Disappointing Debut of Eurodollar Futures," *Institutional Investor* (May 1982), pp. 201–6; and Steven Plaut, "The Eurobond Market—Its Use and Misuse," *Weekly Letter*, Federal Reserve Bank of San Francisco (June 10, 1988), pp. 1–3.

higher returns results in longer maturities and the generation of Euro-currency credits or Euroloans. Specifically, *Eurocurrency credits* are loans with a maturity of more than one year extended by banks as a result of the Eurocurrency funds deposited with them or borrowed by them in the Eurocurrency market. Thus the loans are not made in the currency of the country in which the lending is located; in fact, about three-fourths of the volume represents Eurodollar transactions.

Syndicated credits generally involve large loans in which several financial institutions offer funds on common terms to a single borrower. Syndicates are headed by a lead bank, with other banks participating as sources of funds. Such arrangements not only facilitate the extension of large loans but also permit lenders to diversify risk more easily. Syndicated credits formed an important part of the "recycling" of currency deposits of the oil-producing countries to the less developed importing countries.

ASIAN DOLLAR MARKET

The term Eurocurrency is used because most loans and deposits are made in Western Europe with London the major center of the market. The prefix "Euro" serves to focus on the offshore or external nature of the market; any deposits or loans in a currency outside its country of origin can be termed a Eurocurrency transaction. A component of this market has come to be known as the Asian dollar market.

The Asian dollar market consists of dollar deposits in banks in Asia, but principally in Singapore and Hong Kong. The Asian currency market is simply a broader concept, reflecting the deposit of several currencies along with the dollar in banks in countries other than those in which they originate.

Asian currency transactions originated in the late 1960s in part as a result of Singapore's decision to promote the local financial services sector. This was accomplished by the provision of tax concessions and relaxation of regulations pertaining to bank deposits and loan activity. As might be expected, the major incentive for these offshore operations are the minimal restrictions that permit banks to operate with a narrower spread.

One factor contributing to the development of the market is the time zone difference of the area from that of Western Europe. Most banks in the Far East could not transact business in one day with London banks, which were closed during most of the Far East working day; one advantage of Singapore is that there is an overlap of a few hours with London in the normal working day.[8]

In most respects the Asian currency market is similar to the Eurocurrency market, the major difference being geographical in nature. The dollar also predominates in this market, but it also includes the Dutch guilder, Swiss franc, German mark, and Japanese yen.

Some uncertainty exists in this market regarding the role of Hong Kong as a result of the Sino-British Accord. After a transition period, Hong Kong will come under Chinese rule in 1997. As a result, the role of Hong Kong as a major financial center under Beijing and a Communist regime remains open to question. Although the ultimate role depends upon a complex set of political and economic considerations, it is possible that the area will become relatively less important as a banking center as the transition is completed.

MONETARY CONTROL AND THE OFFSHORE MARKET

The Eurocurrency market was initially perceived as a relatively unregulated market with funds flowing freely across national boundaries, deposit liabilities subject to low or no reserve requirements, and the possibility of extensive deposit creation. Accordingly, the conclusion was sometimes drawn that the market would lead to uncontrolled monetary expansion, increased liquidity, and greater inflation, since the action of monetary authorities to alter bank reserves and reserve requirements would no longer be effective. It has also been suggested that, because of the international character of the market, individual banks may be under less pressure to maintain prudent policies regarding liquidity and quality of credit.

Concern over the Eurocurrency market continues. Some of the issues remain controversial, but at least the worst fears appear to have been allayed. While it is true that the market is largely unregulated, the potential monetary and liquidity expansion is not as great as was initially thought to be the case. For one thing, as time deposits, Eurocurrency accounts are not as liquid as demand deposits. Empirical studies and other analyses, while recognizing the complexity of computing the money multiplier in the Eurocurrency market, suggest that the expan-

---

[8]For an analysis of the Asian dollar market, see Kenneth Bernauer, "The Asian Dollar Market," *Economic Review*, Federal Reserve Bank of San Francisco (Winter 1983), pp. 47-62.

sion potential was initially overstated.[9] In addition, even in the absence of a legal reserve requirement, depository banks hold reserves as a prudent measure and must in their own interests exert caution in their lending activities. And while the market is essentially unregulated, it is carefully monitored by central banks and could be subjected to their control if necessary to maintain the integrity of national monetary systems. There are also benefits associated with an unregulated market. As noted, for example, by the Bank for International Settlements, the benefits of banking deregulation "... have been in terms of cheaper loans to borrowers and higher returns to savers via a compression of margins."[10]

Finally, it is generally accepted that the Eurocurrency market is central to international commercial banking. The system contributes to an integrated world money and capital market as funds respond to interest rate differentials across national boundaries. Borrowers and lenders are more inclined to secure and provide funds on a worldwide basis and thus contribute to economic efficiency in the markets.

Some regulation of the Eurocurrency market may occur as a result of Great Britain's Financial Services Bill, which went into effect in January of 1987. The bill authorizes the British Secretary of Trade and Industry to establish a regulatory framework for both sterling and nonsterling markets in the United Kingdom. This action may have a significant impact on the Eurocurrency market, since it is centered in London.

IMPACT OF OPEC

Both the Eurocurrency market and in part the Asian currency market are central components of international banking, and yet both are post-World War II developments. Another major development, one that has contributed to the growth of the Eurocurrency market and also has affected the international banking community during the last decade, was the agreement reached by OPEC (Organization of Petroleum Exporting Countries) to restrict the supply and raise the price of petroleum. The OPEC policy dramatically affected the balance of payments position of most petroleum exporting and importing countries, and, in turn, the international sources of supply and demand for capital. OPEC

---

[9]For a thorough survey and summary of the literature concerning the relationship between inflation and the Eurocurrency market, see R. M. Pecchioli, "International Bank Activities and Inflation: A Survey," *The Internationalization of Banking* (Paris: Organization for Economic Cooperation and Development, 1983), pp. 195-203.

[10]Bank for International Settlements, *Fifty-Seventh Annual Report* (Basle, Switzerland: 1987), p. 85.

action introduced balance of payments strains that were unusually severe in 1974, 1979, and 1980 following relatively sharp increases in petroleum prices. Since 1973 and the initial action by OPEC, the role of commercial banks as intermediaries in international lending has become even more crucial.

During much of the period 1974-1983, the oil exporting countries experienced a cash surplus largely as a result of current account surpluses from oil sales. These surpluses led to deposits of the oil exporting countries with international banks. Part of OPEC's cash surplus has also been invested in U.S. government securities and in the stocks and bonds of companies located in the United States and other countries. In more recent years, an increased share of new bank deposits of OPEC countries has been placed in the United Kingdom, to a great extent in the form of Eurocurrency deposits.[11] According to IMF statistics, during the period 1974-1983, OPEC's cash surplus amounted to the equivalent of about $458 billion. Of this amount, $81 billion (18 percent) was used for loans and grants to nonoil-developing countries; $232 billion (51 percent) was used for the purchase of government and corporate securities, prepayments for imports, and real estate and direct investment, and the like; $20 billion (4 percent), in transactions with the IMF and World Bank; $93 billion (20 percent), for Eurocurrency deposits; and $32 billion (7 percent), bank deposits in industrial countries.[12]

A large share of the cash surplus generated by OPEC accrued to a relatively small number of countries (generally those with small populations) within the group. Several of the OPEC participants remained borrowers, and a few greatly expanded their external obligations during the 1974-1983 period. International commercial banks played a key role as intermediaries during this period; they transferred purchasing power from OPEC to the payments deficit oil consuming countries. This "recycling" activity of banks has caused the holdings of private financial institutions of the guaranteed long-term debt of the oil consuming countries to increase from $58 billion in 1978 to $223 billion in 1987. In relative terms the share of government-guaranteed debt held by private financial institutions has grown from 21 percent of the total in 1978 to 34 percent in 1987.[13] Although action by the commercial banks alleviated the initial

---

[11] A description of balance of payment's current account positions of the oil-exporting countries, the industrial countries, and the non oil-developing countries is provided in International Monetary Fund, *Annual Report 1982* (Washington: 1982), pp. 17-40. See also "The OPEC Cash Surplus," *International Letter*, Federal Reserve Bank of Chicago (August 13, 1982), pp. 2-3.

[12] International Monetary Fund, *World Economic Outlook 1983* (Washington: 1983), p. 195.

[13] International Monetary Fund, *World Economic Outlook 1986* (Washington: 1986), pp. 246-247.

balance of payments strain experienced by many oil-importing countries, the subsequent debt servicing requirement has in many instances intensified the risk for the lending institutions.

For the fuel-exporting countries as a group, the net cash surplus derived from current account transactions dropped sharply from the equivalent of over $100 billion in 1980 to annual deficits averaging from $10 billion to $15 billion since 1982.[14] The decline in petroleum prices caused by a reduction in world demand, the inability of OPEC to maintain production controls, and an increase in energy production in other parts of the world has had a serious impact on the current account position of some of the countries in this group. Further, OPEC countries are now generally not sources of new loanable funds, as they were in the 1970s.

INTERNATIONAL BOND MARKET

Commercial banks participate in the international money and capital markets not only as a source of funds, but also as underwriters of bond issues bought and sold by other parties. As underwriters, the banks provide a ready market for bonds primarily for their clients and other institutions, but also in part for their own portfolios.

Bonds represent instruments containing a promise to pay a specified sum by a certain date and to pay interest to the holder. Usually they are issued in standard denominations and are negotiable. Bonds are classified in different ways, depending upon where they are sold and how they are sold (Table 4.2). *International bonds*, unlike domestic loans, are those issued by a borrower of a nationality different from the country of the market in which the bonds are issued. International bonds may be either Eurobonds or *foreign bonds*. Foreign bonds are those issued in a market of a single country and are usually underwritten by a bank syndicate from one other country. The bonds are issued in accordance with security laws and are denominated in terms of the currency of the market country.

Eurobonds, which came to be used in the early 1960s, are underwritten and sold in more than one national market simultaneously. Typically this is accomplished through an international syndicate of banks, a cooperative effort on the part of major banks from several industrial countries.[15] Eurobonds are not subject to the security laws of any one

---

[14]International Monetary Fund, *World Economic Outlook 1985* (Washington: April 1985), pp. 236-237.

[15]For a description of the types of bonds and their importance in world markets, see World Bank, *Borrowing in International Capital Markets* (Washington: May 1980).

TABLE 4.2   Types of Bonds

International bond (sold outside country of borrower)

a. Foreign bond. Underwritten by syndicate of banks all from the same foreign country, usually in the currency of that country.
b. Eurobonds. Underwritten by international syndicate of bands; sold in countries other than the country of currency in which the issue is denominated.

Domestic bond (sold in country of borrower)

country, although the market is monitored by regulatory authorities; they are long-term securities and may be denominated in terms of any major currency or even in terms of such international units as Special Drawing Rights or European Currency Units.

Since about 1975, a growing proportion of Eurobond issues were in the form of floating rate notes (FRNs). Floating rate notes carry an interest rate that varies over the life of the loan. The rate is adjusted every three to six months at some specified margin or spread over either the U.S. prime rate or the London interbank offered rate (LIBOR). (The U.S. prime rate is presumably the rate set by major banks for loans to their best customers. As noted previously, LIBOR is essentially an average of the rate that six major London institutions charge for Eurocurrency loans.) The FRNs accounted for about one-half of the Eurobond market, but usage declined sharply in 1987, apparently as a result of uncertainties in exchange rate and interest rate movements.

Investors in the Eurobond market are largely of an institutional type, especially insurance companies and pension funds. Borrowers, or issuers of Eurobonds, include sovereign governments as well as major private companies that are well known. Almost 90 percent of the borrowers are residents of industrialized countries. Commercial banks serve as managers or co-managers to underwrite Eurobond issues. United States commercial banks located in the United States have not participated in underwriting activities, but some overseas subsidiaries and affiliates of U.S. banks are involved in efforts of this type.

United States corporations, especially manufacturing establishments and utilities, have increasingly turned to European markets as borrowers in recent years by selling dollar-denominated foreign bonds. Eurobonds have generally been tax-exempt and frequently not subject to registration and disclosure requirements. United States companies frequently have found relatively large sums available at a favorable interest rate as compared with domestic loans. Most of the Eurobonds sold by U.S. firms have been issued through subsidiaries in the Netherlands

Antilles to take advantage of a U.S. government tax treaty with the Netherlands Antilles.[16]

The volume of Eurobond financing has grown rapidly since the 1960s, primarily because interest rates have been more favorable to borrowers than other alternatives. According to one estimate, total international bond placements amounted to about $166 billion in 1985. Eurobonds accounted for about $135 billion; foreign bonds, about $31 billion. Although dollar bonds continue to predominate, a growing share of the total is denominated in terms of the yen, mark, and Eurocurrency unit.[17]

One result of the dramatic and unregulated growth is that some problems have arisen regarding price quotations and investor protection, in part because of the exemption from registration and disclosure requirements. Given the growth of the market and the absence of the centralization of information and activity, there is the likelihood that the market will be subject to a degree of regulation.[18] There is also evidence that the growth of the Eurobond market has diminished somewhat.

A related source of funds for nonbank institutions—the *Eurocommercial paper* market—has also expanded in importance. This market consists of unsecured promissory notes with a fixed maturity date (ranging from 7 to 365 days) issued by commercial borrowers outside the country of the currency in which the securities are denominated. Frequently, however, it involves some form of backup or support facility provided by banks.

In general, international lending, including both the issuance of bonds and bank lending, has grown in recent years. However, a significant share of the growth through 1985 was in bond financing rather than bank lending. Bank lending has recovered somewhat since that time. In part, the bond financing has been facilitated by innovative financing instruments. These instruments and procedures are sometimes defined as part of the "securitization" process. In the broadest sense, securitization includes certain off-balance-sheet activities used by commercial banks to function more effectively in the rapidly changing financial markets.[19]

[16]See Richard Karp, "Catching the Eurobond Habit," *Institutional Investor* (August 1982), pp. 208-212.
The tax advantage associated with the use of the Netherlands Antilles for financial transactions is summarized in "Netherlands Antilles Finance Affiliates," *Survey of Current Business* (June 1982), p. 41.

[17]Maxwell Watson, et al., *International Capital Markets* (Washington: International Monetary Fund, December 1986), pp. 26-30.

[18]See, for example, John J. Duffy, "The Eurobond Market Faces Regulation," *American Banker* (January 29, 1987), pp. 1, 10.

[19]A useful analysis of securitization is provided by Christine Cumming, "The Economics of Securitization," *Quarterly Review*, Federal Reserve Bank of New York (Autumn 1987), pp. 11-23.

INNOVATION IN FINANCIAL INSTRUMENTS

The Eurocurrency and Asian currency markets were among the first major institutional innovations in the financial markets since the end of World War II. Another group of innovations is a broad category of bank activities that generally has taken the form of off-balance-sheet (OBS) commitments. Off-balance-sheet activities involve a variety of financial techniques or instruments including loan commitments, acceptances, note issuance facilities, swaps, foreign currency options, standby letters of credit (described in Chapter 2), and several other bank transactions that are not included as assets or liabilities on a bank balance sheet but which subject a bank to some degree of risk. The bank transaction is typically fee-based, but does not involve holding an asset or taking a deposit. Off-balance-sheet items applicable to international commerce include commercial letters of credit (used in the financing of international trade), foreign currency options, currency swaps, and various contingent liabilities and commitments relating to foreign banks and governments.

Many of the innovations are of recent origin. They have been prompted by such factors as the growth in borrowing by large manufacturers through the use of commercial paper and the subsequent reduction in bank lending, the expansion of international banking, internationally integrated financial and capital markets, and the shift to floating exchange rates. In the Eurodollar market, note issuance facilities and other guarantees have been used to facilitate corporate borrowing. From a bank perspective, the innovations have been prompted by government regulations and supervision that concentrate on balance sheet conditions to foster safety and prudent policies in bank operations. From a borrower's perspective, the instruments permit substitute approaches to securing funds.

The basic reason for the growth and development of new OBS activities is the opportunity for profits in an increasingly competitive industry. The instruments and techniques associated with OBS transactions involve a service to customers designed to improve a bank's return on assets without lowering capital ratios. For some of the larger U.S. banks, OBS exposure amounts to two to three times the value of their assets. Some of the major U.S. banks that have been active in OBS activities include Citicorp, J.P. Morgan & Company, Chase Manhatten Corporation, Bank of America Corporation, and Manufacturers Hanover Corporation.

The gains from OBS activities cannot be readily determined. According to one estimate, "other noninterest income" of all FDIC-insured banks (which includes income from OBS activities) increased from about

1.03 percent of bank net assets in 1983 to 1.55 percent of bank net assets in 1987.[20]

Off-balance-sheet activities are considered beneficial because they promote efficiency in resource allocation in the financial markets. The regulatory concern is based on the fact that a bank commits itself to a service or activity that is not risk-free. To the extent that regulators evaluate liquidity and solvency solely on the basis of capital/asset and other standard balance sheet ratios, an important type of risk is not included. For example, with the traditional loan commitment, a bank receives a fee income; until the loans are requested, they do not appear on the balance sheet, although the bank has a legally binding obligation that it may be called upon to honor.

Since 1983, large U.S. banks have disclosed off-balance-sheet activities on Schedule RC-L of their quarterly Report of Condition (call reports). By mid-1987, reporting banks indicated OBS activities in the amount of $3.1 trillion, in excess of an estimated $2.9 trillion bank industry assets at that time. By far the greatest share (45 percent) was represented by foreign exchange commitments (commitments or contracts to buy foreign or U.S. currencies). Two other major activities were loan commitments and interest rate swaps, each representing about 17 percent of total activities.

By far the greatest share of OBS efforts in the United States are conducted by major banks—those with assets of at least $10 billion. According to one estimate, this group of 34 banks accounted for over 85 percent of the $3.1 trillion in OBS activities.[21]

The concern with OBS activities is not that banks have shifted to an unusually high risk venture and are necessarily following imprudent practices. Rather, it relates more to the rapid growth in an element of banking that has not been closely monitored in the past and which has not been included in the standard ratios used for guidelines. In addition, in some instances it is difficult to determine the degree of risk associated

---

[20]Mary McLaughlin and Martin Wolfson, "The Profitability of Insured Commercial Banks in 1987," *The Federal Reserve Bulletin* (July 1988), pp. 403-418.

[21]General Accounting Office, *Off-Balance-Sheet Activities* (Washington: March 1988), pp. 9-13. Of growing importance since the early 1980s is the interest rate swap in which two parties exchange each others' interest payments. The interest payment streams are of a different character, with each party (which may include a bank) preferring the payment it secures in the exchange. Frequently a variable rate obligation is exchanged for a fixed rate obligation. Maturities range from 1 to 12 years. The amount of interest paid is based on some specified principal amount which is termed the "notional" principal because it is not exchanged in the transaction. In addition, only a *net* interest amount is transferred to cover payment obligations. An extensive survey of the nature and use of interest rate swaps is provided in Larry D. Wall and John T. Pringle, "Interest Rate Swaps," *Economic Review,* Federal Reserve Bank of Atlanta (November/December 1988), pp. 22-40.

with such activities.[22] One difficulty encountered by regulatory agencies is that of differences in risk associated with various forms of off-balance-sheet activities. The risk may vary depending upon the type of commitment or instrument, the maturity date, and the nature of the obligor. For example, OBS activities involving international transactions may reflect a higher degree of risk than domestic transactions because of the currency risk—the possibility that the obligation cannot be serviced because of currency inconvertibility. Another difference relates to the type of commitment. For example, short-term self-liquidating trade-related contingent liabilities related to merchandise shipments are believed to involve less risk than standby letters of credit serving as financial guarantees for loans and securities.[23]

Because of the acceleration in OBS activity, new regulatory guidelines have been established requiring that capital be set aside against such commitments. As described in Chapter 14, the regulatory agencies have established guidelines that would tie capital requirements to both on- and off-balance-sheet risk. The Financial Accounting Standards Board (FASB) is also considering guidelines that would increase the disclosure of OBS information. Some banks have already started to include such obligations in notational form in their annual reports.[24]

SUMMARY AND CONCLUSIONS

One of the more important innovations in international finance since the end of World War II is the development and growth of the Eurodol-

[22]Potential benefits and risks of one form of OBS activity, the standby letter of credit, are analyzed in Chris James, "Off-Balance-Sheet Banking," *Weekly Letter*, Federal Reserve Bank of San Francisco (September 18, 1987), pp. 1-3.

[23]Committee on Banking Regulations and Supervisory Practices, "Proposals for International Convergence of Capital Measurement and Capital Standards" (Basle, Switzerland: Bank for International Settlements, December 1987, mimeo).

[24]For a detailed analysis of off-balance-sheet activities and bank disclosure requirements under Schedule RC-L of the regulators' Report of Condition, see David C. Cates and Henry A. Davis, *Off-Balance—Sheet Banking and the Changing Nature of Financial Risk* (Philadelphia: Robert Morris Associates, 1987). Analyses of off-balance-sheet activities are also provided in David Cates and Henry Davis, "Revealing the Invisible Ink: The Disclosure of Off-Balance-Sheet Activity," *The Journal of Commercial Bank Lending* (February 1987), pp. 9-18. See also Bank for International Settlements, *Recent Innovations in International Banking* (Basle, Switzerland: April 1986); and Nicholas Lash, *Banking Laws and Regulations* (Englewood Cliffs, N.J.: Prentice-Hall, Inc., 1987), pp. 142-160. Among the items included in RC-L are commitments to make or purchase loans or external credit in the form of lease financing arrangements, futures and forward contracts, standby contracts and other option arrangements, commitments to purchase foreign currencies and U.S. dollar exchange, standby letters of credit, commercial and similar letters of credit, and participations in acceptances. See Federal Financial Institutions Examination Council, *Call Number 162, FDIC-OCC Sample* (Washington: December 31, 1987).

lar and the broader Eurocurrency markets. The Eurocurrency market has contributed to an integrated world money market by promoting the movement of capital among the major money centers. It has reduced global interest rate differentials and has given borrowers access to a larger number of capital sources.

Although the market is largely unregulated, many of the early concerns that it would lead to uncontrolled inflation and ineffective monetary policies have diminished. An Asian currency market has also been created in a more planned fashion to service financial markets of southeast Asia and to integrate global transactions more fully.

The process of borrowing has also changed. Large corporations that used the Euromarkets for bank loans have turned to securitized financing. In an effort to improve profit positions, major banks have increased their off-balance-sheet activities. These activities are not readily controlled by traditional regulatory methods, but are coming under increased scrutiny. As described in Chapter 14, OBS transactions have provided the impetus for uniform bank capital adequacy guidelines among the major industrial countries.

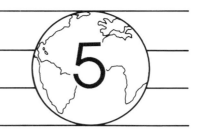

NATURE OF THE U.S. MARKET—A NATIONAL PERSPECTIVE

International commercial banking involves the provision of financial services across national boundaries as well as the establishment by banks of offices in external markets to accommodate customers. United States banks have played a major role in world financial activity from both domestic and foreign locations. But the importance of this role is related to the fact that the United States is also a choice area of location for foreign banks performing various intermediary functions.

ATTRACTIONS OF THE U.S. MARKET

The rapid growth in foreign commercial banking in the United States is to a great extent the result of the size of the U.S. market, its diversified money and capital markets, and a desire on the part of foreign banks to expand financial services to subsidiaries located in the U.S. As foreign manufacturing and service corporations established an increasing number of plants in the United States, offices of foreign banks found it advantageous to be conveniently located to provide loans, foreign exchange facilities, and export-import trade accommodations. Frequently, the service relationship in the United States stemmed from a parent company and parent bank relationship abroad.[1]

The importance of the dollar as a reserve currency and as a currency in which much of the world's trade occurs is also an important consideration. Historically, the value of the dollar has remained reasonably stable over time, and a large share (about two-thirds) of the official foreign exchange reserves held by foreign governments are in the form of short-term U.S. government securities. The United States also remains the world's most important exporter and importer of goods and services. If banks of a particular country are to assume a role of any significance in world trade, they must be in a convenient position to buy and sell dollars.

Although its investment status changed in 1985, the United States has long been a major creditor nation. United States-located banks, along with their foreign affiliates, have served an intermediary capacity in the flow of long-term funds especially to Western Europe, Canada, and Latin America.

The regulatory environment and political climate of the United States have also been relatively favorable to foreign institutions of both a financial and nonfinancial nature. Foreign banks are subject to chartering conditions, reserve requirements, supervision, and regulation; yet they are able to establish offices and operate in many states in much the same way as a domestic bank.

GENERAL NATURE OF FOREIGN PRESENCE

Foreign banks have been extensively involved in a variety of types of financial activities in the United States for many years. Comparatively little was known for a long time about the functions and services performed by foreign firms in the American economy. However, these services came to be accelerated in the late 1960s; by the end of 1987, over 800 foreign-owned or affiliated banking institutions were operating in this country with U.S. office assets of $452 billion (exclusive of International Banking Facility assets of about $176 billion held by branches and

[1]Some of the differences in practices and operating strategies of U.S. and foreign banks in the U.S. market are described in Stephen W. Miller and Seung H. Kim, "Marketing International Banking Services in the U.S.," *The Bankers Magazine* (March-April 1984), pp. 62-69. See also H. L. Brewer, "An Analysis of Foreign Bank Entry Into the U.S.," *The Mid-Atlantic Journal of Business* (Winter 1983/1984), pp. 21-30.

Material in this chapter is based on Charles W. Hultman, "Foreign Banking in the U.S.; A Review of Recent Developments," *Rivista Internazionale di Scienze Economiche e Commerciali* (October-November 1983), pp. 1022-1038.

agencies).[2] As indicated in Table 5.1, subsidiaries and branches predominate both in terms of number and value of domestic assets. In conjunction with the expansion in foreign banking activity in the United States, there has been a trend toward branches and subsidiaries, which, unlike agencies, can generally provide a full range of banking services. During the 1970s, the shift was toward branches, although entrance into the market through subsidiaries has also gained in importance. The extent to which these institutions represent foreign ownership varies depending upon the type of office. Three types of offices of foreign banks—branches, agencies, and New York State Chartered Investment Companies—are by their very nature part of the parent company and owned totally by foreign interests. This is not the case, however, with the 228 U.S. chartered commercial banks and 32 Edge Act and Agreement Corporations of foreign banks for which partial ownership sometimes prevails. As indicated in Table 5.2, about three-fourths of the Edge Act and Agreement Corporations held by foreigners are totally owned by the foreign interests. About 60 percent of the U.S.-chartered commercial banks with foreign ownership are truly subsidiaries in that they are either totally or at least 50 percent owned by foreign interests. However, almost one-fourth of the banks with at least some foreign ownership (many of which are located in Colorado, Florida, and Texas) involve less than 10 percent foreign ownership. This group of 50 banks could probably best be described as having a limited affiliation with foreign interests rather than being foreign-owned.

TABLE 5.1   Foreign Bank Offices In The United States (December 31, 1987)

	Number	Domestic assets (billions)
U.S. chartered insured commercial banks with some foreign ownership	228	$198.6
U.S. branches of foreign banks	360	195.1
U.S. agencies of foreign banks	205	53.1
Edge Act and Agreement Corporations of foreign banks	32	1.6
New York Chartered Investment Companies	11	3.9
	836	$452.3

Source: Federal Reserve Board, *Foreign Investment in U.S. Banking Institutions* (Washington: 1988), computer printout.

[2]Federal Reserve Board, "Monthly Report of Assets and Liabilities of Large International Banking Facilities as of December 31, 1987." Washington: January 20, 1988.

TABLE 5.2   United States-chartered Banks, Edge Act And Agreement Corporations
With Foreign Ownership
(December 31, 1987)

Percent of Foreign Ownership	U.S. Chartered Banks	Edge Act and Agreement Corporations
Less than 10 percent	50	2
10 to 24.9 percent	26	1
25 to 49.9 percent	12	1
50 to 99.9 percent	84	3
100 percent	56	25
TOTAL	228	32

Source: Federal Reserve Board, *Foreign Investment in U.S. Banking Institutions* (Washington: 1988) computer printout.

INITIAL LEGAL FRAMEWORK FOR FOREIGN BANKS

The International Banking Act of 1978 is the single most important law specifying the legal environment for foreign banks operating in the U.S. market, but earlier legislation influenced the financial activity of external institutions both directly and indirectly. Although several pieces of legislation are particularly important, the overall framework was established by the Federal Reserve Act of 1913.

The Federal Reserve Act provided the foundation for the banking system in this country and also permitted U.S. banks to set up branches in foreign countries. Under the Edge Act of 1919, special corporations known as Edge Act corporations (EACs or Edges) could be established as subsidiaries of U.S. banks to assist in commercial activities with foreign companies. Edge Act Corporations were severely restricted in their domestic activity, but they were relatively free to engage in international transactions including foreign equity investments. The Glass-Steagall Act of 1933 prohibited U.S. commercial banks from investment banking and securities transactions.

The McFadden Act of 1927 and the Banking Act of 1933 essentially set a geographic limit on branching activities of U.S. domestic banks. Banking institutions cannot establish full service branches outside their home state, although they can and do participate in some other forms of interstate activities and can set up branches in a foreign countries. (State laws, of course, are frequently more restrictive on branching practices of domestic banks within the state.) However, offices of foreign banks that were of minor importance at the time were generally state chartered and not subject to the McFadden Act; accordingly, they were not prevented from establishing branches in more than one state.

The U.S. banking system is sometimes referred to as a dual banking system with some institutions chartered and regulated at the state level, and others chartered at the national level and under the direction of or regulation by one or more federal agencies. It is a complex structure consisting of over 14,500 commercial banks. In addition, a wide range of nonbank financial institutions, such as savings and loan institutions, insurance companies, credit unions, and finance companies perform a variety of functions in the money and capital markets similar to those offered by commercial banks.

CONCERN WITH FOREIGN BANKS

The depression of the 1930s had a disastrous impact on international banking; world trade dropped sharply, and failure to make repayment on international debts was widespread. During World War II, free trade in goods and services was limited, and a large share of international finance was undertaken on a government-to-government basis. Significant growth in post-World War II international banking commenced in the 1960s along with activity in the Euromarkets.

The competitive presence of foreign banks in the United States was not felt until the 1960s and early 1970s. During these years, the United States and many other countries pursued a policy of reciprocity—not allowing foreign banks to operate within their borders unless the home country of those banks offered reciprocal treatment. One of the factors that kept U.S. doors to foreign offices open was the desire on the part of U.S. banks to set up offices abroad. Foreign bank activities were regulated by the individual states; except for subsidiaries and affiliates, no applicable federal regulation existed, and thus foreign banks enjoyed certain competitive advantages not shared by U.S. firms. For example, unlike U.S. banks, foreign banks could secure charters to conduct full service banking activities in more than one state. Some of the world's largest foreign banks maintained multistate offices (usually in New York, California, and Illinois), including Banque Nationale de Paris, National Westminster Bank, Sumitomo Bank, Swiss Bank Corporation, and Barclay's Group. State-chartered offices also had an advantage with respect to the level and holding of required reserves. Another factor was that unlike domestic banks, agencies and branches of foreign banks were not subject to the restraints of the Glass-Steagall Act, which separated commercial bank activity from investment banking and underwriting of securities.

In addition, foreign banking activities were not subject to the degree of regulatory control believed necessary to develop and implement an effective monetary policy; more than three-fourth of the assets of foreign offices were held by agencies and branches that were not subject to federal control or supervision. By 1977, offices of foreign banks located in the United States had expanded to the point where they held about 10 percent of all business loans. In 1978, the International Banking Act (IBA) was passed.[3]

PROVISIONS OF THE INTERNATIONAL BANKING ACT

A major objective of the IBA was to create a regulatory structure at the federal level that would embody a policy of national treatment or competitive equality among United States-located banks whether they were domestic or foreign-owned. Some of the key features of the IBA are as follows:

1. Provision is made for the *federal* licensing of branches and agencies of foreign banks.
2. The Federal Reserve Board imposes reserve requirements on branches and agencies of foreign banks having worldwide consolidated assets in *excess* of $1 billion.[4]
3. Federal insurance on deposit liabilities is available to branches of foreign banks.
4. Foreign banks in the United States have access to various Federal Reserve services such as discounting and check clearing.
5. Foreign banks are restricted in their ability to establish branches in more than one state.
6. Edge Act Corporations may be owned by foreign firms.
7. Foreign banks are subject to the same restrictions on nonbanking activities as domestic bank holding companies.

---

[3]A detailed description of the laws affecting foreign banking operations is provided in Lucian Weeramantry, et al., *Banking Law* (New York: Matthew Bender, 1983), Vol. 9, Chapters 191 through 198.

Federal Reserve regulations implementing the IBA of 1978 are included in Federal Reserve Regulation K. A description of provisions pertaining to Edge Act Corporations, powers of foreign branches of U.S. banks, and international banking operations generally is contained in *Federal Register*, Vol. 44, No. 120 (June 20, 1979), pp. 36005-36012.

[4]As noted in a subsequent section, the Monetary Control Act of 1980 imposed uniform reserve requirements on all depository institutions.

THE IBA, NATIONAL TREATMENT, AND RECIPROCITY

The basic philosophy embodied in the IBA is that of equality of competitive opportunity based on a national treatment policy. With the national treatment approach, U.S. regulators are expected to implement provisions of the IBA and other laws in a way that avoids preferential treatment for either foreign or domestic institutions. A framework was to be developed that would be nondiscriminatory in its effects on banks regardless of the country of origin.

The use of a reciprocity principal—according foreign banks the same treatment U.S. banks receive abroad—was presumed to pose certain problems in terms of implementation and of ultimate impact and was rejected by Congress. Implementation of such a provision would require complete and continuing knowledge of banking laws and regulations of every foreign country with banks interested in entering the U.S. market. However, the major disadvantage of reciprocity is that, by its very nature, the ultimate results are likely to be restrictive. Each country, for example, could be as restrictive on bank entry as the country from which that firm originated. This could precipitate a negative approach to foreign bank entry as regulators reacted to restrictive foreign measures.

The national treatment approach is consistent with the open policy the United States takes toward most types of foreign investment in domestic markets. It is a positive approach that presumably encourages foreign governments to offer treatment that is at least as nonrestrictive as that found in the United States.[5]

The task of developing an appropriate philosophy, laws, and regulations pertaining to operations of external banks is complex. Differences in banking systems make it difficult to construct a regulatory framework that is in the best interests of the United States in its role in the world economy. In addition, although the U.S. Congress espoused the principle of national treatment for foreign banks through the IBA, the idea does not necessarily extend to all of the states. As noted in the following chapter, individual states have the ultimate authority to determine the level and type of foreign bank activity within their respective borders even if the banks have a national charter. Furthermore, not all U.S. legislators have been supportive of the national treatment approach. As late as September of 1984, a bill was considered that would authorize the Comptroller of the Currency to consider reciprocity among the

---

[5]The implications of reciprocity and national treatment are examined in U.S. Department of the Treasury, *Report to Congress on Foreign Government Treatment of U.S. Commercial Banking Organizations* (Washington: September 1979), pp. 1-5.

factors in acting on an application by a foreign bank to establish a federal branch or agency.[6]

RESULTS OF THE IBA

The overall impact of the International Banking Act cannot be clearly assessed as a result of two major factors. Although enacted in 1978, guidelines and regulations to implement the act were generally not put into effect until late 1980.[7] In addition, a number of comprehensive regulatory changes were being made in the domestic financial structure, particularly as a result of the Depository Institutions Deregulation and Monetary Control Act of 1980. These changes affect not only commercial banks but also the thrift institutions. The most important of these changes relates to the authority given to thrift institutions to offer checkable deposits. Uniform reserve requirements were established on all depository institutions. Limits placed on interest rates paid by financial institutions have also been removed.

Foreign banks have also found the use of another new arrangement—International Banking Facilities (IBFs)—to be most advantageous. International Banking Facilities (described more fully in Chapter 10) were first authorized in 1981. Essentially, they are deposits held by banking institutions that are not subject to reserve requirements and Federal Deposit Insurance Corporation (FDIC) insurance. About 70 percent of IBF assets are held by agencies and branches of foreign banks located in the United States.

Provisions of the IBA of 1978 were both significant and comprehensive, although the most direct and immediate impact was on foreign branches and agencies. The most important changes pertain to foreign ownership of Edge Act Corporations, federal licensing of branches and agencies, restrictions on interstate banking, and the availability of FDIC coverage. Other important developments relate to the increasing use of bank holding companies and Edge Act Corporations.

What has been the overall impact of these changes on subsidiaries, agencies, and branches—the three basic types of foreign offices? The basic forms of foreign offices in the United States have continued to expand, although at a decreasing rate, since the 1960s (Table 5.3). In terms

---

[6]"National Treatment of Banks," *Hearings Before the Committee on Banking, Housing, and Urban Affairs*, U.S. Senate, 98th Congress, (Washington: September 26, 1984).

[7]Analyses of the results of the International Banking Act of 1978 are provided in James C. Baker, "Is the International Banking Act of 1978 Working?" *The Bankers Magazine* (May-June 1982), pp. 15-19; and Neil J. Pinsky, "Implications of the International Banking Act for Competition in Banking," *Issues in Bank Regulation* (Autumn 1979), pp. 16-24.

TABLE 5.3   Number And Asset Value Of Foreign-owned Agencies, Branches, And Subsidiaries In The U.S., 1976-1987

	1976	1978	1980	1982	1987
Agencies: Number	91	140	177	191	205
Asset value	$30.1	$39.8	$58.1	$54.1	$53.1
Branches: Number	67	110	169	250	360
Asset value	$26.9	$62.5	$89.7	$153.6	$195.1
Subsidiaries: Number	33	39	121	245	228
Asset value	$15.5	$22.8	$88.2	$160.5	$198.6
Total number of offices	191	289	467	686	793
Total asset value	$72.5	$125.1	$236.0	$368.2	$446.8

Source: Federal Reserve Board, *Foreign Investment in U.S. Banking Institutions* (Washington: various issues), and other Federal Reserve publications. Figures for 1976 and 1978 are not strictly comparable with those for the following years. Values for assets of International Banking Facilities included. Figures are year-end values except for l987 which are mid-year.

of numbers and value of assets, branches have increased most rapidly. The number of agencies and subsidiaries has also grown since that time, although there has been a decrease in the number of subsidiaries since the early 1980s. As a result, the relatively uniform growth that characterized each of the three forms of organization through the early eighties no longer applies since that time. Much of the shift relates to developments in several states that either are, or may become, centers of financial activity—New York, Illinois, California, Florida and Texas—states that are hosts to over 90 percent of foreign offices.

SUBSIDIARIES

The decrease in the number of subsidiaries since 1982 (Table 5.3) is somewhat surprising and whether or not the trend will continue is difficult to predict. One contributing factor may be the appreciation of the U.S. dollar during the period 1980-1984 and the associated increase in costs of takeovers of U.S. banks by foreign banks. An earlier study notes, for example, that growth in foreign banking in the 1970s showed a strong statistical association with the *declining* value of the dollar.[8]

However, a comparison of figures for 1982 and 1987 may be misleading because of a sharp decline of about 60 in the number of subsidi-

[8]Lawrence G. Goldberg and Anthony Saunders, "The Determinants of Foreign Banking Activity in the United States," *Journal of Banking and Finance*, Vol. 5 (1981), pp. 17-32.

aries in one state (Florida) during that period.[9] In several other important host states, (New York, California, Texas) the number of foreign subsidiaries has remained about constant or has increased slightly. Finally, subsidiaries are being established for the first time in still other states (Wisconsin, Arkansas). Accordingly, a nationwide trend since 1982 is not readily discernible. Variations among individual states include an increase in the number of subsidiaries in some states that have not been considered major financial centers in the past. This development may simply reflect the nature of some subsidiaries that emphasize retail activities and concentrate their efforts on penetration of new markets of this type.

Several of the major United States-chartered insured commercial banks with majority foreign ownership are indicated in Table 5.4. Marine Midland is by far the largest of this group for which foreign ownership exceeds 50 percent of the total. It also represents a relatively recent (1980)

TABLE 5.4   **Major United States-chartered Insured Commercial Banks With Majority Foreign Ownership (December 31, 1987)**

Bank	Country	State	U.S. Assets (billions of dollars)
Marine Midland Bank	Hong Kong	New York	$17.6
Republic National Bank of N.Y.	Netherlands	New York	10.1
National Westminster Bank USA	United Kingdom	New York	10.1
Union Bank	United Kingdom	California	8.9
Harris Trust & Savings Bank	Canada	Illinois	7.6
European-American Bank		New York	5.7
California First Bank	Japan	California	5.6
Sanwa Bank California	Japan	California	4.9
Bank of Tokyo TC	Japan	California	4.4
Bank of California	Japan	California	3.7

Source: Federal Reserve Board, *Foreign Investment in U.S. Banking Institutions* (Washington: 1988), computer printout.

[9]The number of foreign-owned subsidiaries in Florida declined from about 80 to slightly more than 20 during the two-year period. This was the result of liberalized state banking laws, extensive consolidation on the part of many banks, and the purchase of a major foreign multibank holding company by domestic interests. See Federal Reserve Board, *Foreign Investment in U.S. Banking Institutions* (Washington: various issues); and Larry A. Frieder, "Florida's Interstate Banking Debate," *Economic Review*, Federal Reserve Bank of Atlanta (May 1985), pp. 20-33.

acquisition by foreigners. Marine Midland is the lead bank for the parent company, Hongkong and Shanghai Banking Co., which has an extensive interstate presence, with several branches in New York, Wilmington, Miami, Chicago, Houston, Los Angeles, San Francisco, Portland, and Seattle. Some perspective on the size of this institution is provided by a comparison with other United States-owned banks. In terms of volume of assets, Marine Midland is significantly smaller than Citibank of North America, the largest U.S. bank, with assets of over $100 billion.[10]

Many of the United States-chartered subsidiaries of foreign banks have one or more U.S. branches which afford a geographical extension of their activity. Marine Midland for example, has about 330 branches; National Westminster has almost 150 branches. These are not to be confused with the 360 United States-located branches of *foreign-chartered* banks.

AGENCIES

The leveling off in the number of agencies and the slight decline in the value of their assets since 1980 is related to state laws as well as the IBA. Federal agencies (and branches) can be established only in states where their operation is expressly permitted; they are not expressly permitted in a number of states, including some of the more important financial centers. Only in Florida has the number of agencies continued to increase to a significant extent. By the end of 1987, agencies (whether state or federally licensed) existed in only eight states.

Part of the decline in the use of agencies is also the result of changes in foreign banking laws. New York, for example, under a reciprocity provision, would not authorize Canadian banks to establish branches in New York, although Canadian agencies were allowed. Subsequently, Canada changed its banking law. As a result, in order to conduct full service operations, Canadians increased the number of branches and decreased the number of agencies in New York. In some instances, agencies were converted directly into branches.

The major U.S. agencies of foreign banks are presented in Table 5.5. As noted, most are located in California, and most of the parent banks of this group are Japanese. Mitsubishi Bank Ltd. is the largest and is located in California.

---

[10] "The Top 25 Banks Deposits and Assets," *American Banker* (June 1987).

TABLE 5.5   Major U.S. Agencies Of Foreign Banks
             (December 31, 1987)

Bank	Country	State	U.S. Assets (billions of dollars)
Mitsubishi Bank Ltd. Agency	Japan	California	3.8
Bank of Nova Scotia Agency	Canada	Georgia	3.1
Fuji Bank Ltd. Agency	Japan	California	2.7
Da-Ichi Kangyo Bank Agency	Japan	California	2.5
Bank of Nova Scotia Agency	Canada	California	2.2
Tokai Bank Ltd. Agency	Japan	California	2.2
Intern. Comm. Bank of China Agency	Taiwan	New York	2.1

Source: Federal Reserve System, *Foreign Investment in U.S. Banking Institutions* (Washington: 1988), computer printout.

BRANCHES

The IBA prohibits foreign banks from establishing full service branches in more than one state—the selected home state.[11] Limited service or restricted branches may be set up in other states but only if expressly permitted by the state and approved by its bank regulatory agencies. Activities of restricted branches are limited in much the same way as those of Edge Act Corporations in that they are not authorized to accept domestic demand deposits. As a result, only about 15 percent of branches are of a limited service type. In addition, all United States-located branches are required to maintain reserves against deposit liabilities as a result of the IBA and the Monetary Control Act of 1980.

Dramatic growth has occurred since 1978 despite IBA restrictions on branch establishment. Much of the expansion has occurred in New York and California. The growth in New York reflects the state's continued dominance as a financial center as well as changes pertaining to subsidiaries and agencies noted previously. The growth in California is largely the result of availablility of FDIC coverage required by California law.

[11]Full service branches and subsidiary banks of foreigners in the United States were expected to designate a home state by March 31, 1981. Of the 112 full service branches and subsidiaries operating in the United States and representing 33 foreign countries on that date, 79 designated New York as the home state; 27, California; two, Florida; two, Illinois; one, Massachusetts; and one, the District of Columbia. Once the foreign bank selects a home state, it faces the same regulations as domestic banks. Thus the basic rules governing acquisitions are now identical for all banks operating in U.S. markets, whether foreign or domestic. See Board of Governors, Federal Reserve System, press release, Washington (June 5, 1981).

TABLE 5.6 Major U.S. Branches Of Foreign Banks
(December 31, 1987)

Bank	Country	State	U.S. Assets (billions of dollars)
Dai-Ichi Kangyo Bank Ltd.	Japan	New York	$9.7
Swiss Bank Corporation	Switzerland	New York	9.4
Bank of Tokyo Ltd. Agency	Japan	New York	8.6
Mitsubishi Bank Ltd.	Japan	New York	6.3
Fuji Bank Ltd.	Japan	New York	5.8
Sanwa Bank Ltd.	Japan	New York	5.7
Sumitomo Bank Ltd.	Japan	New York	5.4

Source: Federal Reserve Board, *Foreign Investment in U.S. Banking Institutions* (Washington: 1988), computer printout.

The largest branches of foreign banks are located in New York, the major U.S. financial center (Table 5.6). Home countries of the parent banks of the largest branches are Switzerland and Japan.

EDGE ACT CORPORATIONS

Although the IBA was restrictive toward agencies and branches of foreign banks, a partially offsetting and important change provided by the act was that for the first time EACs could be owned by foreigners. The IBA also authorizes EACs to branch freely in other states, an important consideration, since the formation of a branch from an existing EAC is less costly than setting up a new EAC. In addition, EACs are no longer subject to a 10 percent requirement on U.S. deposits, although they may be subject to the same reserve requirements as U.S. banks. Second, EACs are now permitted to finance export *production*, as well as export *transactions*.[12]

What has been the result of changes introduced by the IBA of 1978? Edges are attractive to foreign banks located in the United States, since they are already involved in international transactions; in addition, they open up out-of-state banking possibilities that were otherwise restricted by other provisions of the IBA. As indicated in Table 5.7, by the end of 1987, foreigners had established 32 Edge and Agreement Corporations with U.S. assets of about $1588 million. This represented about 20 percent

[12]For a detailed description of Edge Act Corporations, see James Houpt, "Edge Corporations," *International Banking: U.S. Laws and Regulations* (Washington: American Bankers Association, 1984), pp. 10-1 to 10-55.

TABLE 5.7   Foreign-owned Edge And Agreement Corporations

	1980	1987
Number of offices	16	32
Number of U.S. branches	1	15
Assets at U.S. offices	$431m	$1588

Source: Federal Reserve System, *Foreign Investment in U.S. Banking Institutions* (Washington: various issues), computer printout.

of all Edge and Agreement Corporations (including both main offices and branches). Several of the Corporations have also established branches in other states or the Cayman Islands in order to expand the geographic scope of their operations.

REPRESENTATIVE OFFICES

Section 10(a), Representative Offices, of the IBA specifies that any foreign bank that maintains an office other than a branch or agency shall register with the Secretary of the Treasury. However, establishment is not authorized in contravention of state law. Representative offices are used by many foreign banks in U.S. markets for a variety of purposes. Although they are severely limited in terms of permissible activities, such offices generally play an important liason role in the solicitation of new business for the parent bank. Representative offices can be set up relatively easily and in some instances are a first step in promoting customer relations for the subsequent establishment of full service operations. In some states, these offices serve as loan production offices performing certain specified functions in the loan extension process; usually they are prohibited from approving loans and disbursing funds. By late 1986, there were about 410 representative offices of foreign banks located in U.S. markets.[13]

SAVINGS AND LOANS ASSOCIATIONS

Foreign interests, especially Canadian, have also entered the U.S. thrift industry, although on a limited scale. By the end of 1987, part or full ownership of 18 savings and loan associations (S & Ls) was held by

[13]Department of the Treasury, *National Treatment Study: 1986 Update* (Washington: 1986), p. 20.

residents of foreign countries. The associations were located in about ten different states and held assets of approximately $19 billion.[14]

Foreign interest in U.S. savings and loan institutions has been limited, in part because the associations are largely domestically and retail-oriented. As with other depository institutions, foreign-owned S & Ls must hold reserves against deposit liabilities. However, this interest may increase as a result of the authority granted to S & Ls to hold checkable deposits (Negotiable Order of Withdrawal or NOW accounts) and to make some commercial loans.

SOURCE OF CHARTER/LICENSE

The IBA gave agencies and branches of foreign banks the option of being licensed by the federal government (the Comptroller of the Currency). With a federal license, an office could be established in any state in which no agency or branch of that foreign bank existed and where state law permits the office to be established. An initial advantage was that the offices were given the right to utilize a wide range of services available to Federal Reserve banks, including borrowing from the Federal Reserve and check collection services. Since 1980, all U.S. depository institutions have had access to such services.

Federal licensing may also permit a foreign country to establish a branch in some states where entry is otherwise restricted. For example, some states have reciprocity requirements under which a foreign bank can establish an office only if its country of origin permits U.S. banks to establish offices there. However, the Comptroller of the Currency has power to override reciprocity requirements in licensing federal branches under the IBA.[15]

How have foreign offices responded to the new licensing option? Since 1978, somewhat more than half of the newly established U.S. branches of foreign banks have selected a federal rather than a state license. The greatest share of those securing a national license have located in New York, with a relatively smaller portion in Illinois, California, and other states.

Agencies of foreign banks, in contrast, have been far less inclined to opt for a federal license. Because agencies generally have limited functions, they are less likely to benefit from federal services. Only about

[14]Federal Reserve Board. *Foreign Investment in U.S. Banking Institutions* (Washington: 1988), computer printout.

[15]For an analysis of the advantages and disadvantages of federal licenses and FDIC coverage, see Steven M. Lucas and Scott A. Anenberg, "Regulation of Foreign Banks in the United States," *International Banking: U.S. Laws and Regulations* (Washington: American Bankers Association, 1984), pp. 11-1 to 11-46.

five percent of all agencies have selected the federal license; most of these have located in Florida.

Agencies and branches of foreign banks established prior to the IBA of 1978 are also permitted to shift from a state to federal license. Actually very few of the institutions have made such a shift.

Subsidiaries of foreign banks located in the United States had the choice of either state or federal charters even prior to 1978 and the IBA. Of those established before 1978, about one-third were national banks. Since 1978, a somewhat greater share of newly established foreign subsidiaries have become national banks which is consistent with a broader trend. Since the beginning of 1982, well over half of all newly established U.S. banks (both domestic and foreign-owned) chose national charters; in contrast, during the preceding years, one-third or less selected national charters. Thus foreign-owned subsidiaries have followed the trend of all United States-chartered banks in the choice of a charter.

One consideration in making a charter decision is that in recent years some states have taken the lead in the authorization of new powers for commercial banks, especially in the areas of insurance, real estate, and securities activities.[16] One advantage previously available stemming from lower reserve requirements was eliminated by Congressional action in 1980 (the Monetary Control Act) to place a virtually uniform reserve requirement on all depository institutions. As a result, the advantage generally associated with lower reserve requirements for institutions that chose to be state banks was no longer available. In addition, all banks subject to Federal Reserve requirements can borrow from the Fed to improve their reserve positions.

DEPOSIT INSURANCE

The IBA requires that branches of foreign banks located in the United States accepting deposits of less than $100,000 obtain deposit insurance from the Federal Deposit Insurance Corporation. Coverage is optional for other offices. The insurance requirement for bank offices taking "small" deposits was designed to require coverage for retail banks.[17]

---

[16]See Victor L. Saulsbury, "State Banking Powers: Where Are We Now,?" *Regulatory Review,* Federal Deposit Insurance Corporation (Washington: April/March 1987), pp. 1-16. Of course, Congress or the federal regulatory authorities are able to limit state action regarding availability of new powers for state banks.

[17]This requirement provides protection for bank customers in retail banking. Retail deposits are usually defined as those of less than $100,000 each; wholesale deposits are those of $100,000 or more each. See General Accounting Office, *Despite Positive Effects, Further Foreign Acquisitions of U.S. Banks Should be Limited Until Policy Conflicts are Fully Addressed* (Washington: August 1980), glossary.

Insurance coverage is advantageous to a foreign bank seeking to attract retail deposits on the same basis as any other United States-chartered bank. Yet, in addition to its cost (1/12 of 1 percent of covered liabilities), FDIC coverage subjects an office to a number of regulatory burdens and consumer-oriented laws that may not otherwise apply. For example, the FDIC requires a foreign bank with an insured branch to pledge assets equal to 5 percent of the branch's liabilities. Assets are pledged to the FDIC (or its designee) to be used if needed to protect the deposit insurance fund. The insured branch must also maintain a "capital equivalency" ledger account (a liability account) equivalent to at least six percent of the value of its liabilities.[18] Accordingly, by the end of 1986, only about 16 percent of foreign branches had secured FDIC coverage indicating primarily that most branches engage in wholesale banking— dealing mostly with governments, large corporations and other banks for which deposits exceed $100,000.

In contrast, subsidiaries of foreign banks, regardless of the date of establishment, maintain FDIC coverage, which is generally mandatory under state and federal law. Among other things, subsidiaries tend to be more retail-oriented than branches, catering to a major extent to the small depositor. Although offices of foreign banks generally tend to be wholesale- oriented, a number of Japanese subsidiaries have been successful in the California market, and the British National Westminster has conducted extensive retail activities in the New York area.

RELATIVE IMPORTANCE OF FOREIGN OFFICES

Another way to assess the impact of the IBA on foreign offices in U.S. markets is to examine trends in the relative importance of deposit and lending activities. As reflected in Table 5.8, the share of total assets of all offices of foreign banks increased from almost four percent at the end of 1973 to 19 percent by the end of 1987. In general, about three-fourths of the total is accounted for by agencies and branches; the remainder, by subsidiaries.

Frequently, bank size and importance are measured in terms of total deposits. The share of total deposit liabilities in the United States held by all foreign banks increased from 1.7 percent in 1973 to 14.1 percent in 1987.

[18]See *12 Code of Federal Regulations*, Subpart C, 346.9-347.6 (Washington: January 1, 1987), pp. 310-319. See also William Ryback, "Federal Supervision of Branches and Agencies of Foreign Banks," *International Banking: U.S. Laws and Regulations* (Washington: American Bankers Association, 1984), p. 12-11.

TABLE 5.8 Relative Importance Of Offices Of Foreign Banks In U.S. Markets 1973-1987

Year	All Offices (percent)				Subsidiaries (percent)				Agencies and Branches (percent)			
	Total Assets	Total Loans	Business Loans	Total Deposits	Total Assets	Total Loans	Business Loans	Total Deposits	Total Assets	Total Loans	Business Loans	Total Deposits
1973	3.8	3.7	7.6	1.7	0.6	0.6	1.1	0.7	2.9	2.9	6.0	0.8
1974	4.9	5.1	9.5	2.3	1.0	1.0	1.4	1.1	3.6	3.9	7.5	1.0
1975	5.3	5.7	10.4	2.9	1.2	1.3	1.7	1.2	3.9	4.2	8.1	1.4
1976	5.8	6.4	10.2	3.1	1.3	1.4	1.9	1.3	4.3	4.9	8.0	1.6
1977	6.4	6.6	10.3	3.6	1.3	1.3	1.8	1.4	5.0	5.1	8.2	2.1
1978	8.0	8.8	13.1	4.5	1.5	1.5	2.0	1.6	6.4	7.2	10.8	2.7
1979	9.9	10.9	16.3	5.6	2.2	2.3	3.0	2.3	7.5	8.4	13.0	3.2
1980	11.9	13.4	18.2	6.6	3.0	3.1	3.9	3.1	8.8	10.0	13.9	3.4
1981	13.5	15.4	19.2	7.7	4.1	4.6	5.1	4.0	9.2	10.6	13.8	3.7
1982	14.4	16.3	18.8	10.4	4.3	4.9	5.5	4.2	10.0	11.1	13.0	6.1
1983	14.6	15.6	18.3	11.1	4.3	5.0	5.8	4.2	10.1	10.3	12.2	6.8
1984	15.9	15.1	21.6	12.9	4.8	5.4	7.1	4.7	11.0	9.6	14.2	8.1
1985	16.1	15.4	22.5	12.1	4.6	5.1	7.1	4.6	11.4	10.2	15.1	7.4
1986	17.3	15.6	23.3	12.8	4.1	4.6	6.4	4.0	13.1	10.9	16.6	8.7
1987	19.0	16.6	26.4	14.1	4.1	4.7	6.7	4.1	14.8	11.7	19.4	10.0

Source: "Share tables" of Federal Reserve Board. Data from Federal Financial Institution Examination Council's Reports 002, 031, 032, 033, and 034, and Federal Reserve Reports 886a and 105. Includes data on books of International Banking Facilities.

The relative growth in total loans and business loans as a share of U.S. loans is also reflected in Table 5.8. As indicated, business loans have become relatively more important to foreign offices than have total loans; by the end of 1987, slightly more than one-fourth of the volume of business loans made by United States-located banks were made by offices of foreign banks.

Offices of foreign banks have become competitive in U.S. financial markets within a relatively short period of time. Although the IBA was designed to eliminate an advantage that foreign agencies and branches held primarily in establishing interstate networks, the act has not lessened the growth in the overall operations of foreign banks.

FOREIGN REPRESENTATION

Almost all countries have banking offices in this country. Generally the growth in foreign participation was greatest just prior to 1978 as the anticipated passage of the International Banking Act provided incentive to establish operations before a more restrictive legal environment could come into existence. An indication of the source of foreign ownership is provided in Table 5.9. By far the largest number of financial institutions have parent companies in Japan, Canada, and several European countries. Canadian firms, as far back as the late 1800s, were among the first to show a sizable interest in U.S. commercial banking markets. By the end of 1987, about 90 Canadian banking offices were conducting business in the United States. Canadian institutions are located in several

TABLE 5.9 Foreign Ownership Of U.S. Banks
(December 31, 1987)

	Number of Subsidiaries[1]	Number of Branches[2]	Number of Agencies
Japan	27	49	32
United Kingdom	8	25	23
Canada	59	18	13
Germany (West)	0	16	6
France	1	18	14
Switzerland	3	12	6
Hong Kong	4	23	4

[1]Includes all banks with some foreign ownership.

[2]Several branches are identified as agencies with power to accept deposits from U.S. residents.

Source: Derived from Federal Reserve Board, *Foreign Investment in U.S. Banking Institutions* (Washington: 1988) computer printout.

TABLE 5.10 United States Banking Assets Of Major Foreign Countries, 1986 (In billions of dollars)

Country	Amount	Percent
Japan	$245.4	8.7%
Canada	42.4	1.5
United Kingdom	40.6	1.5
Italy	36.4	1.4
Switzerland	24.5	0.9
France	22.4	0.8
West Germany	11.0	0.4
All other Countries	103.9	3.8
Total for foreign countries	526.6	19
Total for domestic industries	2285.9	81
Total for all	2812.5	100.0

Source: E. Gerald Corrigan, "A Prespective on the Globalization of Financial Markets and Institutions," *Quarterly Review*, Federal Reserve Bank of New York, (Spring 1987).

northern cities, but a large share is situated in the state of Colorado through the use of a bank holding company arrangement.

If the importance of foreign ownership in U.S. markets is measured in terms of total deposits or total assets rather than number of offices, the results are altered somewhat. Yet banks from Japan, the United Kingdom, and Canada predominate regardless of the measure used. Other countries of importance in terms of assets of U.S. offices of their banks include West Germany, France, Italy, and Switzerland (Table 5.10).

JAPANESE BANKS

If Canadian and British banking activities in the United States are of interest because of the early origin, then Japanese banks are of equal interest because of the strength of their recent participation. During the 1970s and early 1980s, a number of changes were introduced by the Japanese government to liberalize the monetary structure of the economy in order to tie their money and capital markets more closely to the world financial system. One change occurred with the Japanese Banking Law of l982, which embodied the principle that foreign bank branches be accorded equal treatment with Japanese banks. As a result, Japanese banks attempting to establish branches in the United States were no longer restricted by state reciprocity provisions regarding branches. By late 1983, Japanese banks owned several of the largest foreign banking offices located in the United States. Also, by the end of l987, Japan had the largest number of branches (49) and agencies (32) as well as 27 subsidiaries in the United States and held almost half of the assets of all foreign banks in the United States. (Table 5.10). The rapid growth since the early 1980s suggests that the IBA has not had an adverse impact. Japan's participation has been relatively recent, but with over 100 offices in this country the strength of her interest is apparent.[19] Most of the branch banks are located in New York but most of the agencies are located in California. The location of Japanese banking offices has been limited largely to California, New York, and Illinois.

The Japanese presence has also been somewhat unique in that virtually all of the subsidiaries are either totally or majority owned by Japanese interests. For most other countries, ownership of many United States-located subsidiaries involves less than majority control. Another difference is that most Japanese banks chartered in the United States are owned by banking organizations rather than by individuals or families. Finally, virtually all of Japan's major banks (which include three long-term credit banks, seven trust banks, and 13 city banks) as well as several regional banks have established at least one but frequently several offices in the United States.[20]

NATURE OF INTERNAL CHANGES

Although foreign banking in the United States has been affected primarily by the IBA, several other changes have altered the financial environment. Traditionally, banks have carefully monitored assets in an effort to achieve a balance between liquidity (holding a sufficient amount of reserves and government bonds) and profitability (holding customer loans to secure a high rate of return). The position on liabilities was largely passive. But in the late 1960s and the 1970s, inflation and high interest rates resulted in disintermediation and subsequent efforts by banks to offer claims that would be more attractive to depositors, particularly NOW accounts and C.Ds.[21] In addition to the growing

[19]Summaries of Japanese bank activities in the United States are provided in Douglas Ostram, "Japanese Banks in the United States," *JEI Report* (January 22, 1988); and Bruce Stokes, "Banking on the Future," *National Journal* (January 30, 1988), pp. 246-250.

[20]The thirteen city banks are national in scope with branches throughout Japan with a focus on short-term and trade finance. The three long-term credit banks work closely with the Japanese government to provide long-term industrial loans. The seven trust banks also lend for long-term industrial expansion. The smaller regional banks participate in commercial financing. See Andreas Prindl, *Japanese Finance: A Guide to Banking in Japan* (New York: John Wiley & Sons, 1981), pp. 21-33; and Japan Economic Journal, *Japan Economic Almanac 1987* (Tokyo: 1987), pp. 304-305.

[21]A detailed analysis of asset and liability management for the United States and other Organization for Economic Cooperation and Development countries is provided in R. Harrington, *Asset and Liability Management by Banks* (Paris: Organization for Economic Cooperation and Development, 1987).

competition from the thrift industry and the need for liability management, banks found that revenues could be expanded through fee income on several types of assumed obligations, including letters of credit and note issuance facilities.

Even the official definition of monetary aggregates has changed in recent years to reflect new institutional prerogatives and social attitudes. Basic definitional changes in these aggregates were introduced in the United States in 1980 but the continuing innovations and regulatory developments since then suggest that even these definitions are no longer adequate. For example, in early 1987, the Federal Reserve Board decided to abandon the targeting of the basic money supply, M1, at least temporarily. Part of the difficulty related to an appropriate definition of the composition of M1. Another factor was that the growth rate of Ml had for some time greatly exceeded the targeted range.

The definition of commercial banks is also being reexamined. Traditionally, banks have been defined as institutions that accept deposits and extend commercial loans. In recent years, private nonbank companies have been able to enter the banking business on a limited basis by operating institutions that have come to be known as "consumer" banks or *nonbank banks*. These institutions either do not make commercial loans or else do not accept demand deposits and, accordingly, are not included in the legal definition of banks. As a result they escape many of the regulations applicable to banks, including the prohibitions on interstate banking. Major firms already participating in these activities include American Express, Merrill Lynch & Co., Prudential Insurance, and Sears, Roebuck and Company.[22]

A number of legislative proposals have been made to prevent financial institutions from escaping regulation. Finally, in 1987, Congress passed the Competitive Equality Banking Act of 1987, which placed a ban on the chartering of additional nonbank banks. In effect, the act closed the nonbank bank loophole, although a large number of institutions already in existence were exempted from the ban. It also expanded the definition of a bank to include all institutions insured by the Federal Deposit Insurance Corporation.[23] The future structure and regulation of the entire financial industry may be affected significantly by this and other changes in the legal definition of a commercial bank. Among other things, some of the major U.S. banks have considered the possibility of

---

[22] A list of nonbank banks along with their parent companies is provided in Victor L. Saulsbury, "Commercial Banks: An Endangered Species?" *Regulatory Review*, Federal Deposit Insurance Corporation (Washington: March 1986), pp. 1-24.

[23] The Competitive Equality Banking Act of 1987, P.L. 100.86. Although about 160 nonbank banks had already been chartered, only about one-third were affected by the 1987 act. The remaining institutions are industrial banks or trust companies and are not subject to its provisions.

dropping their bank charters in order to gain the regulatory freedom of the nonbanks.[24]

Another possible option available to banks is to shift from a national to a state charter. In addition, some state banks may choose to drop their membership in the Federal Reserve System. Decisions of this type, of course, reflect a drastic change for a bank but have a potential advantage in states that permit state banks to underwrite securities and perform other functions that have not been open to national banks. Many of the larger banks have sought legislation that would allow them to perform additional functions including securities underwriting and insurance activities. One change likely to occur is a modification of the Glass-Steagall Act in order to allow bank holding companies to underwrite securities.[25] As a result, bank organizations could diversify into other product lines, yet commercial banks would remain legally separate from operations perceived as involving greater risk.

The trend toward diversification is reflected in decisions by several major nonbank corporations to offer customers a wider variety of financial services. In some instances mergers or acquisitions have been undertaken in an effort to combine investment funds, individual retirement accounts, insurance, automobile and real estate financing, and cash management services. In addition to the blurring of differences of service activities of commercial banks and other related financial institutions, some forms of interstate banking that were severely restricted are now occurring particularly with multibank holding companies through out-of-state acquisitions.

The adoption of risk-based capital guidelines by the regulatory agencies in late 1988 (described in Chapter 14) will also affect the type and nature of foreign bank activity in the United States. As a result of the guidelines, banks are required to maintain a larger amount of capital and, accordingly, to incur a greater cost to support commercial loans than to support most other assets including mortgages. As a result, foreign banks may find a greater incentive to shift toward retail banking.

The dramatic increase in commercial banking activity has also led to the development of a more efficient system for the transfer of dollar holdings among banks of the world. Through electronic funds transfer services, it is possible to facilitate and expedite interbank transfers by

[24]See Andrew Albert and Robert M. Garrison, "Major Firms Mull Over Idea of Dropping Bank Charters," *American Banker* (October 29, 1986), pp. 1, 8.

[25]A change in the Glass-Steagall Act to permit bank holding companies to underwrite securities was proposed by Alan Greenspan, "Statements to Congress," *Federal Reserve Bulletin* (Washington: February 1988), pp. 91-103. Several European banks grandfathered under the IBA, including Swiss Banking Corporation, Union Bank of Switzerland, and Credit Lyonnais, have been able to continue to conduct securities and investment banking.

performing a clearing function and also by handling the basic accounting function for each transaction.

SUMMARY AND CONCLUSIONS

Foreign banks have been a part of the U.S. financial community for many years. However, the belief that they operated at a competitive advantage in U.S. markets coupled with a major increase in the activity of these institutions ultimately led to the passage of the International Banking Act in 1978 and even to a temporary moratorium on the foreign acquisition of U.S. banks. Other legislation has introduced comprehensive regulatory change in the domestic financial structure that affects both banking and nonbanking institutions.

Several important changes have occurred in foreign bank organization and activity during the past several years. The overall results can be best summarized as continued growth in participation in U.S. financial markets, increased consolidation or formation of operational networks, and to the extent feasible, a shift to less regulated types and areas of activity. The changes that are occurring also vary somewhat from state to state. This is the result of new economic opportunities arising in some states; in others, it is the result of the IBA of 1978 or changes in state laws.

Generally, it was presumed that the IBA would restrict agency and branch activity while subsidiary activity would remain unaffected. In fact, the number of subsidiaries has declined relatively as has the number of agencies, but the number of branches has continued to grow. In addition, a substantial amount of growth has occurred in Edges and bank holding company activities. And the predicted impact of the IBA may have been modified by economic conditions and changes in state laws in the major financial centers.

By the end of 1987, approximately 250 major banks maintained a banking office of some type within the United States. These banks represented almost 100 different countries, and included all major countries except some from the communist bloc and from Africa.

The nature of the developing structure of the U.S. financial sector is the result of changes in economic conditions and legislation in addition to those included in the International Banking Act. If there is evidence of an overall resulting trend in foreign banking in the United States, it is that new legislation and economic conditions have promoted the most growth in wholesale and international banking as opposed to the largely domestic retail type banking. Foreign banking activity can be expected to continue to increase in the United States in the foreseeable future. However, this growth is likely to be commensurate with that of domestic institutions so that the share of the market held by foreign institutions increases more slowly. This does not mean, of course, that the dynamic character of United States-located banking will in any way be diminished. The final effects of financial deregulation have not yet been completely felt. The trend toward interstate banking is not likely to be reversed, and the growing shift to a service dominated economy will have a continuing impact on the structure of banks and other financial institutions and the way they operate.

THE U.S. MARKET—A STATE
PERSPECTIVE

Although foreign banking assets as a share of total banking assets have expanded significantly since the end of 1973, over half of the 50 states retain laws or administrative regulations that effectively prohibit agencies and branches and, in some instances, subsidiaries of foreign banks.[1] Why do some states encourage and others discourage a banking presence? And what methods do the various states employ to accomplish their objectives?[2]

The purpose of this chapter is to examine from a state's perspective the potential advantages and disadvantages of a foreign banking presence in the form of agencies, branches, or subsidiaries. In addition,

---

[1]*National Treatment of Banks*, Hearings Before the Committee on Banking, Housing, and Urban Affairs, U.S. Senate, 98th Congress, Second Session (Washington: September 1984), p. 73; and Federal Reserve Board, *Selected Assets and Liabilities of U.S. Offices of Foreign Banks* (Washington: April 1987).

[2]"State Laws on Foreign Banks Categorized," *The Banking Expansion Reporter* (July 2, 1984), pp. 5-7.

An analysis of the importance of state governments in affecting U.S. international commercial policy using bank legislation as an example is provided by John M. Kline, "Foreign Banking Legislation," *State Government Influence in U.S. International Economic Policy* (Lexington, Mass.: D.C. Heath and Co., 1983), pp. 157-185.

provisions used by various states to shape the role of foreign activities within their jurisdiction are analyzed.[3]

GENERAL NATURE OF STATE LAWS

Although the federal government has granted foreign banks the same treatment accorded domestic banks since 1978, this type of approach is not generally employed by the states. The regulatory nature of the U.S. dual banking system generally permits states to exclude most types of offices of foreign banks.

A first group of states—well over half the total—has chosen to exclude the basic offices of foreigners. In some of these states, however, foreign-owned Edge Act Corporations, bank holding companies, loan production offices, and in several instances, subsidiaries, have the authority to initiate and conduct banking activities.[4]

A second group of states (about fifteen in number) permits entry by either agencies *or* branches, but not both.[5] States that permit agencies only in effect limit the foreign office to international commerce. Another small group of states is completely open to various offices of foreign banks.[6]

However, by far the greatest share of foreign banking activity occurs in states that have, or have had, some form of reciprocity provi-

[3]Material in this chapter is based on Charles W. Hultman. "The Foreign Banking Presence: Some Cost-Benefit Factors," used with permission from the *Banking Law Journal* (July-August 1987), pp. 339-349. Warren, Gorham & Lamont, Inc. 210 South Street, Boston, MA 02111. Copyright 1987.

[4]The position of some states is not always clear. For example, some states do not permit an agency or branch of a foreign bank to do business in the state. But frequently the laws list a variety of activities not considered doing business, including making and servicing loans, suing and being sued, and related activities. In some instances, state laws are silent on foreign banks. States that appear to exclude agencies and branches include Arizona, Arkansas, Colorado, Connecticut, Idaho, Indiana, Iowa, Kansas, Maine, Minnesota, Montana, New Hampshire, New Jersey, New Mexico, North Carolina, North Dakota, Ohio, Oklahoma, Rhode Island, Tennessee, Utah, Vermont, Virginia, West Virginia, Wisconsin, and Wyoming.

Louisiana law is unusual in that it expressly prohibits a foreign bank from establishing branches or agencies within the state. However, an exception is provided in that subject to the rules of the International Banking Act, a foreign bank may establish and operate a federally licensed agency in any parish in the state having a population of more than 500,000. See LA. REV. STAT. 6:550 A and B (West 1986).

Included in the states that exclude agencies and branches but in which a significant number of subsidiaries, Edge Act Corporations, or bank holding companies exist are Wisconsin, Arkansas, and Colorado.

[5]States or areas in this group include Alabama, District of Columbia, Delaware, Guam, Hawaii, Illinois, Massachusetts, Michigan, Maryland, Mississippi, Oregon, Pennsylvania, and Texas. Missouri's Rev. Stat. 362.420 appears to exclude foreign banking, but 362.423 permits foreign banking corporations to undertake various kinds of banking business.

[6]States in this category are Alaska, Nebraska, South Carolina, and South Dakota.

sion. States utilizing these provisions require that U.S. banks be allowed to establish and conduct comparable operations in the home country of the bank interested in establishing an office. This group includes California, Florida, Georgia, Illinois, Pennsylvania, Massachusetts, Texas, and Washington. New York, the single most important host state for foreign banks, deleted the reciprocity provision in 1984.[7] In some instances (Texas, Florida, and Georgia), states apply reciprocity but also limit the types of offices that are allowed.

ADVANTAGES AND DISADVANTAGES OF FOREIGN OFFICES

Interest on the part of states in the implications of international banking was particularly strong in the late 1970s and early 1980s following the enactment of the IBA. Determination of an appropriate state policy has become even more complex because of the increase in regional banking arrangements and interstate banking. Actually, in many respects the impact of regional and interstate banking is similar to that of international banking; developments in both cases affect money flows, interest rates, resource allocation, and the potential for local development. In fact, opposition of some states to outside banking applies not only to foreign banks but also to those from other states. The arguments used in favor of or against foreign banks are to a great extent analogous to those applied to out-of-state firms.

Why the significant variations in state laws? In general, a foreign banking presence in an area provides such additional financial services as deposit taking, lending, and other standard functions performed by intermediaries. The unique service likely to be offered by a foreign bank is a more direct knowledge of and contact with international commercial activities that may prove beneficial to local exporters, importers, and investors. Knowledge of product markets, sources of imports, and money and credit conditions overseas can generally be secured more readily and completely from external banks. Generally, offices of foreign banks have been active in extending commercial and industrial loans to multinational corporations, financing international trade transactions, and providing medium-term loans to borrowers in home countries.

For the state seeking large amounts of investment from foreign sources, the existence of a bank office from the relevant country may prove to be most helpful. Accordingly, from a broad perspective, foreign

---

[7]New York's reciprocity provision (under §202-a) was deleted by the Omnibus Banking Law of 1984 effective October 8, 1984

banks serve as financial intermediaries, a supply of information, and a source of competition that contributes to the efficient use of scarce resources. Further, the direct amount of income and employment generated by foreign banks is likely to be relatively small compared with that generated by the commerce and industry that such institutions may help develop.

Although there are potential advantages of foreign banks to a community or a state, there is also likely to be opposition. Concern may exist in the banking community that outside banks with an interest in a local market are likely to be large institutions that are too competitive for local banks. Empirical evidence suggests that the removal of geographic restrictions against banking would increase competition and result in substantial benefits. Such action, of course, would be to the advantage of consumers and the public.[8]

There are also fears that external banks may not be primarily interested in serving local interests; of particular concern is that local capital deposited in such banks would be drained away to major financial centers, where the rates of return may be greater. Actually, previous studies of domestic banking indicate that there is no evidence that multibank holding companies shift funds from rural areas to urban areas.[9]

Evidence at the international level indicates that there is a two-way flow of funds across national boundaries, usually in response to current market conditions. For example, as far back as 1974, head offices of U.S. banks permitted funds to flow to their overseas branches—overseas offices were net borrowers from the United States-located offices. This pattern continued through 1982, but in 1983 and 1984, the situation reversed as head offices of U.S. banks borrowed from their overseas branches. According to one estimate, for example, U.S. banks borrowed almost $26 billion from their overseas offices in the Caribbean and the United Kingdom in 1983.[10] Thus if offices of foreign banks located in the United States operated in a similar fashion, it could be expected that during some periods they would absorb funds to be channeled for overseas use; during other periods, they would be a source of capital secured from abroad for local use.

[8]Charles Morris, "The Competitive Effects of Interstate Banking," *Economic Review,* Federal Reserve Bank of Kansas City (November 1984), pp. 3-16.

[9]U.S. Department of Treasury, *Geographic Restrictions on Commercial Banking in the U.S.: Report of the President* (Washington: January 1981), p. 141.

[10]See Russell B. Scholl. "The International Investment Position of the United States in 1983," *Survey of Current Business* (Washington: June 1984), pp. 74-78.

FACTORS AFFECTING STATE POLICIES

Although many states have used various techniques and procedures of a protective type, some states also have provisions that are more open or expansive in nature. The position that a state legislature takes with regard to foreign banks depends not only on its attitude toward the existence of outside banks within its borders, but also on the extent to which local banks have an interest in operating abroad. Potential overseas opportunities, of course, are particularly relevant for the state with banks that are either large or have the potential for largeness. A reciprocity provision affords a state some leverage to gain entrance for its banks in external markets and is most likely to be imposed by states attempting to assist local banks seeking to establish abroad.[11] Most of the largest banks in the United States are located in New York, Illinois, and California. These are also included among the states that have, or have had, reciprocity requirements. By 1986, national banks from about two-thirds of the states maintained overseas offices. In terms of numbers, states with the most overseas offices included Texas, Ohio, New York, and Florida.

In contrast, a state may have an interest in developing a financial center or attracting foreign investment. Such a state may form a more lenient position in order to encourage the entrance of foreign institutions.[12]

The state with a firmly entrenched financial community that fears competition from outside is most likely to prohibit foreign institutions completely. However, it is possible that a state's attitude may change over time. In this context, it has been noted that "there is a point in the development of an indigenous banking system at which a foreign banking presence is perceived more as a contribution to banking efficiency than as unwelcome competition."[13] In many states, a relaxation of restrictions against bank concentration has increased the size of local banking organizations and improved their performance.[14] Presumably increased size and better performance would enhance their ability to compete with outside institutions.

[11]See Organization for Economic Cooperation and Development, *International Trade in Services: Banking* (Paris: 1984), p. 15.

[12]See Adrian E. Tschoegl, "The Regulation of Foreign Banks: Policy Formation in Countries Outside the U.S.," *The Monograph Series in Finance and Economics* (1981), pp. 40–44.

[13]U.S. Department of Treasury, *Report to Congress on Foreign Government Treatment of U.S. Commercial Banking Organizations, 1984 Update* (Washington: 1984), p. x.

[14]Charles Morris, "The Competitive Effects of Interstate Banking," *Economic Review*, Federal Reserve Bank of Kansas City (November 1984), pp. 3–16.

ACTION TO CONTROL FOREIGN BANK OFFICES

Most of the state legislatures that permit a foreign banking presence impose provisions and procedures in order to placate local interests and to insure the viability of their own banking systems. In the first place, before a foreign bank can establish an office in the United States, it must secure approval of the appropriate supervisory agency, usually by demonstrating that such establishment would contribute to the needs and convenience of the community being served, that competition and resource allocation would not be adversely affected, and that the applicant has sufficient capital and managerial expertise.

Permission to establish agencies only, a situation which characterizes about a dozen states, reduces the likelihood of capital from local sources being absorbed for transfer abroad, since agencies generally cannot accept local deposits. In addition, the activities of agencies are usually restricted to international commerce.

TECHNIQUES TO PROTECT DEPOSITORS

Some states use asset maintenance or asset deposit provisions to protect depositors in event of failure of an institution. Georgia law (Section 7-1-717) requires that each international banking corporation hold certain specified assets that can be freely converted into U.S. funds in an amount equivalent to 108 percent of the corporation's liabilities.[15] California law (Ch. 14, § 1756.1 b) contains an asset maintenance requirement equivalent to 108 percent of specified liabilities.[16] California law has also required deposits from domestic sources to be FDIC-insured. Thus when FDIC coverage was authorized by the IBA, the branch became a viable type of office. As a result, the number of foreign branches in California increased from two in 1980 to 32 by the end of 1986. Part of the shift was the result of several conversions from agencies to branches.[17] Florida's asset maintenance law (Chapter 663.07) is similar to California's, except that the comparable ratio is 105 percent.[18] These provisions have been used by some states in which state-chartered branches of foreign institutions are not insured by the FDIC. However, all states except three—North Carolina, Texas, and Washing-

[15]GA. CODE ANN. §7-1-717 (1982)

[16]CAL. FIN. CODE §1756.1(b) (West 1968)

[17]Federal Reserve Board, *Foreign Investment in U.S. Banking Institutions* (Washington: various issues), computer printout.

[18]FLA. STAT. ANN. §663.063 (West 1984)

ton—require state-chartered banks to secure deposit insurance as a prerequisite to securing a state charter.[19]

Some states require that offices of foreign banks under their jurisdiction maintain a deposit, usually at an independent bank, equal to a certain percentage of external liabilities. New York law (§202-b-l) requires branches of foreign banks to keep on deposit certain liquid assets equal to five percent of their liabilities (excluding International Banking Facilities' liabilities) to unrelated parties; branches with FDIC-insured deposits are exempted from this requirement.[20] Pennsylvania and Oregon require offices of foreign banks to hold a certain volume of assets on deposit for the purpose of protecting consumer deposits.[21]

Thus both asset maintenance and asset deposit provisions are designed to protect local depositors by making certain the banks have sufficient marketable assets in order to cover the claims of depositors in event of liquidation. In some states that permit agencies only, the asset maintenance provisions are of limited significance if the objective is to protect local depositors. Agencies are typically prevented from holding local deposits, although in some instances they may hold "credit balances." This is the case, for example, in Georgia with the 108 percent provision previously noted.

A key component of some of the asset maintenance provisions is that the assets held be *readily convertible into U.S. dollars.* Such a provision may prevent the local office of an outside bank from making loans to foreign borrowers from countries with exchange controls and inconvertible currencies. At present, the currencies of most advanced industrialized countries are freely convertible. Those of the low-income countries are generally subject to some types of exchange restrictions and presumably are most affected by this provision.[22]

Some foreign countries have been critical of the asset maintenance provisions. Japanese authorities, for example, argue that such requirements are discriminatory, since they place an additional burden on foreign banks.[23]

---

[19]See *12 Code of Federal Regulations* (Washington: January 1, 1987 ed.) Subpart C, 346.16-347.6, Vol. 49, pp. 310-19. See also William Ryback, "Federal Supervision of Branches and Agencies of Foreign Banks," *International Banking: U.S. Laws and Regulations* (Washington: American Bankers Association, 1984), p. 12-11.

[20]N.Y. BANKING LAW §202-b.l (McKinney 1987).

[21]PA. STAT. ANN. tit. 7, Section 105 (b.l) (Purdon 1987); and OR. REV. STAT. ch. 713.025 (1987).

[22]International Monetary Fund, *Exchange Arrangements and Exchange Restrictions, Annual Report 1986* (Washington: 1986), pp. 568-573.

[23]Japanese Ministry of Finance and U.S. Department of Treasury, *Report on Yen/Dollar Exchange Rate Issues* (May 1984), p. 8.

OTHER TYPES OF RESTRICTIONS

Other techniques have been employed by the various states.[24] Alabama law (Comment to 5-1A-4) generally excludes foreign banks but does permit them to establish loan production offices and to participate in the closing of loans.[25] Arkansas does not register foreign banks to do business in the state, but Section 64-1217 permits them to conduct certain activities not considered to involve the transaction of business.[26] Delaware law (Chapter 14, §1403 (c)(2)) requires that agencies of foreign banks operate in a manner and at a location that is not likely to attract customers from the general public to the substantial detriment of existing banking organizations.[27] Texas law (Article 342.1007) authorizes federal agencies of foreign banks only if they select Texas as the home state. In addition, Texas permits agencies (with either a state or a federal charter) to establish only in counties with population size of 1,500,000 or more.[28]

Other states also place geographic restrictions on foreign offices. Louisiana law (R.S. 6:550 B) permits federally licensed agencies in parishes with a population of more than 500,000.[29] Illinois law (S.H.A. Ch. 17, 2710) restricts the location of foreign banking offices to downtown Chicago.[30] Where restrictive practices of this type exist, the foreign offices are typically limited to the urbanized areas, presumably to prevent a drain of funds from the more rural areas and to protect smaller banks located in rural areas.

The ability of states to permit conditional entry has not been clearly established. Although a state may *prohibit* federally chartered offices, the courts have ruled that they cannot place conditions on their entry. Thus the Comptroller of the Currency can authorize a federal branch or agency in a state unless that state prohibits all foreign banks from establishing an equivalent office.[31]

---

[24]A fairly comprehensive, although somewhat dated, description of tax laws of several states relative to foreign banks is provided in Peat, Marwick, Mitchell & Co., *Banking in the United States: A Guide for Foreign Banks* (New York: 1980), pp. 207-284.

[25]ALA. CODE §5-1A-4 (1981)

[26]ARK. STAT. ANN. §64-1217 (1973 Sup.)

[27]DEL. CODE ANN. tit. 5, §1403 (c)(2) (Michie 1986).

[28]TEX. REV. CIV. STAT. ANN. art. 342-1002 and art. 342-1007(i) (Vernon 1988).

[29]LA. REV. STAT. ANN. §6-550.B (West 1986)

[30]ILL. REV. STAT. ch. 17, par. 2710 (1985)

[31]See Laurel C. Williams, "International Banking," *Vanderbilt Journal of Transnational Law*, Vol. 17, pp. 759-771.

TAX CONSIDERATIONS

Taxes can be used either to discourage production and consumption or for revenue purposes. A high tax rate may effectively discourage bank activity; a more moderate tax provides a source of revenue for the imposing political entity. In general, states wishing to exclude foreign bank offices appear to accomplish this objective with direct legislative prohibitions. Taxes are levied on banks, or bank property and income, primarily as a source of revenue.

The nature of tax laws varies from state to state. Because of differences in the tax base, deductions, and other adjustments, a comparison of effective rates is of limited value. However, the tax provisions of the three major host states might be noted. New York law (Art. 32, Sect. 1450-68) imposes a tax on every banking corporation for the privilege of exercising its franchise or doing business in the state. The tax is based on the corporation's net income.[32] California law (Art. 3, Sect. 23181-6) imposes a tax on banking companies for the privilege of exercising a franchise within the state as measured by net income.[33] Illinois law (Ch. 120, Sects. 556-7) assesses and taxes stockholders on the value of shares of the various types of banks located in the state.[34]

Although tax laws vary from state to state, at least three generalizations can be made. First, it is generally concluded that a bank shares tax yields a lower tax burden on a firm than does an income tax.[35] Accordingly, the shares tax can be used to give banks a preference not available to other businesses. Second, it is generally concluded that, from a bank's perspective, U.S. tax laws are more advantageous to the establishment of an agency or branch rather than to an Edge Act Corporation or a subsidiary.[36] Accordingly, if permitted by the state, and depending upon the type of operations to be undertaken, an agency or branch may be the preferred type of office. Third and finally, the temptation of a state to lay a discriminatory tax on a politically powerless foreign bank must be tempered by the constitutional and statutory constraint that such effort entails.[37]

[32]N.Y. TAX LAW §1450-1468 (McKinney 1975).

[33]CAL. REV. & TAX CODE §23181-6 (West 1979)

[34]ILL. ANN. STAT. Ch. 120, par. 556-557 (Smith-Hurd 1970)

[35]Uncertainty remains regarding the circumstances under which a state can impose a bank shares tax on national banks. See *Michie on Banks and Banking* (Charlottesville, Va.: 1971 and 1985 Cumulative Supplement), Vol. 8. This publication also provides an extensive analysis of state powers to tax banks.

[36]See Edward L. Symons, Jr., "State Taxation of Banks: Federal Limitations," *Banking Law Journal*, (October 1982), pp. 817-842.

[37]See Steven M. Lucas and Scott A. Anenberg, "Regulation of Foreign Banks in the United States," *International Banking: U.S. Laws and Regulations* (Washington: American Bankers Association, 1984), pp. 11-42 - 11-45.

FOREIGN OFFICE LOCATION BY STATE

Foreign banks locate offices in particular areas not only on the basis of state laws and regulations but also in response to other factors—the existence of a major financial center, nearness to seaport and export-import activity or to customers of the parent bank, and the size and density of population. An indication of the choice of office locations by state for 1980 and 1987 is provided in Table 6.1. Foreign bank activity is most

TABLE 6.1   Form Of Bank Organization By State, Select Years

	1980	1987
New York		
Holding companies	3	13
Edge Corporations	3	6
Subsidiaries	30	46
Agencies	61	30
Branches	109	235
California		
Holding companies	4	18
Edge Corporations	3	4
Subsidiaries	31	42
Agencies	89	94
Branches	2	34
Illinois		
Holding companies	2	5
Edge Corporations	2	4
Subsidiaries	6	14
Agencies	0	0
Branches	32	50
Florida		
Holding companies	5	16
Edge Corporations	5	12
Subsidiaries	23	24
Agencies	16	44
Branches	0	0
Texas		
Holding companies	1	4
Edge Corporations	2	6
Subsidiaries	4	22
Agencies	0	13
Branches	0	0
Other States		
Holding companies	15	29
Edge Corporations	1	3
Subsidiaries	22	81
Agencies	11	18
Branches	26	32

Source: Compiled from Federal Reserve Board, *Foreign Investment in U.S. Banking Institutions* (Washington: various issues).

heavily concentrated in New York, with significant numbers in California, Illinois, Florida, and Texas. Although much of the growth during the years 1980 through 1987 also occurred in New York, both Florida and Texas are becoming more attractive as host states. The concentration of some types of offices is also evident: branches in New York, subsidiaries and agencies in California, and Edges in New York, Florida, and Texas.

FLORIDA, GEORGIA, AND DELAWARE EXPERIENCE

For the state desiring to take full advantage of the benefits of international commerce, the existence of offices of foreign banks is beneficial. Two states that have opened their doors to foreign banks in the late 1970s are Florida and Georgia. In both cases, deliberate efforts were made to "internationalize" their economies, including the designation of international airports, the establishment of free trade zones, promotion of foreign trade, and the encouragement of financial activities. In 1976, Georgia authorized agencies of foreign banks to enter the state. By the end of 1987, over a dozen offices had been established. Florida shifted to a more liberal approach by authorizing the establishment of agencies or representative offices effective at the beginning of 1978; by the end of 1987, about 45 agencies had commenced operations within the state.[38]

Delaware is another state that has not only authorized agencies of foreign banks, but has also offered a number of important incentives to attract such institutions. Through provisions of its Foreign Banking Development Act (1986), agencies are able to take advantage of a favorable bank franchise tax. The rate applied to foreign agencies as well as all banking organizations in the state is regressive—lower tax rates apply to higher levels of taxable income.[39]

INTERSTATE BANKING AND FOREIGN BANKS

Individual states have had to formulate policies regarding not only foreign banks but also banks from other states. Interstate banking, which involves the production and sale of bank services by a single firm

---

[38]Federal Reserve Board, *Foreign Investment in U.S. Banking Institutions* (Washington: various issues), computer printout.

[39]DEL. CODE ANN. tit. 5, §1403 (c)(2) (Michie 1986). Efforts of Delaware and South Dakota to promote a financial services sector are described in Eleanor H. Erdevig, "New Directives for Economic Development in the Banking Industry," *Economic Perspectives,* Federal Reserve Bank of Chicago (September/October), 1988, pp. 17-24.

in more than one state, has generally been prohibited in the United States. However, some activities are permitted, including interstate credit card operations, correspondent bank activities, and electronic funds transfer networks. The advantage foreign banks held over domestic institutions prior to 1978 was eliminated by the International Banking Act, which restricted the interstate activities of foreign banks by prohibiting the establishment of full service offices in more than one state. However, interstate efforts have been conducted through other avenues. To begin with, "grandfather" provisions permitted some types of multistate networks to remain in force. Second, the IBA authorized the use of limited branches and Edge Act Corporations as vehicles for interstate banking. Third, some approaches, including the use of bank holding companies, have come to be employed more widely.

The grandfather provision of the IBA is an important consideration in interstate banking. Section 5(b) provides that a foreign bank can continue to operate outside its home state any branch, agency, bank, or commercial lending subsidiary in operation on or before July 29, 1978. Even as late as mid-1987, the grandfather provisions of the IBA contributed to a significant component of the interstate structure of foreign banks. By that time, about one-third of the 200 agencies of foreign banks operating in the United States, about 24 percent of 330 branches, and about 13 percent of 85 subsidiaries (those with 25 percent or more foreign ownership) remained grandfathered under the IBA to conduct business in a state other than the designated home state.[40]

Although the IBA prohibited a foreign bank from establishing new full service branches in more than one state, it did authorize them to create limited branches outside a designated home state. In many instances, New York has become the designated home state, with limited branches operating especially in Chicago and major cities in California.

The Bank Holding Company Act permits bank holding companies (BHCs) to acquire or establish subsidiaries in other states if approved by the Comptroller of the Currency and if explicitly permitted by that state. A large number of states have liberalized their laws regarding bank holding companies in recent years. Liberalization has applied not only to holding companies chartered by the states but also to companies chartered by other states. As a result there has been a sharp increase in the number of these companies and the extent to which they control banking assets.

The growing importance of bank holding companies applies to both domestic and foreign-owned firms. By the end of 1987, almost 85

---

[40]Federal Reserve Board, *Structure Data for U.S. Offices of Foreign Banks by Types of Institution as of June 30, 1987* (Washington: 1987), computer printout.

bank holding companies with some foreign ownership were registered for operation in the United States. About 25 percent of these BHCs had established a presence in a second state, in some instances in the form of a subsidiary, in other an Edge Act Corporation.[41]

An interstate presence (first authorized by the IBA in 1978) is also permissible through Edge Act Corporations. The potential interstate expansion with Edges arises in two ways. First, a foreign bank holding company or subsidiary is able to establish an Edge in another state. Second, an Edge itself is able to locate a branch in still another state. Because the activities of Edges are severely restricted, they have come to be selected most frequently as an alternative and perhaps second-choice form of unit in states that prohibit foreign branches and/or agencies. The majority of foreign-owned Edges are located in Florida, which prohibits branches; in Texas, which prohibits branches and restricts agencies; and in Illinois, which prohibits agencies. The most typical arrangement is one in which a New York parent firm establishes an Edge in Houston or Miami.

INTERSTATE BANKING AND REGIONAL RECIPROCITY

Much of the impetus to interstate banking in recent years has been the result of many states authorizing out-of-state bank holding companies to acquire an interest in state banks and usually on a reciprocal basis. The authorization has occurred either by individual states or through regional compacts. The regional banking compacts were placed on a firm foundation in mid-1985, when the U.S. Supreme Court ruled that such compacts were both legal and constitutional.[42] At that time, approximately half of the states had authorized some form of regional arrangements. But an important aspect of the Court decision is that while states can take action that encourages banking activity with other states, they need not open their doors to unimpeded interstate banking. In other words, states can include banks from selected states while excluding those from other parts of the United States or from other countries. By the end of 1987, over three-fourths of the states had authorized some form of interstate banking, usually in the form of

[41]Federal Reserve Board, *Foreign Investment in U.S. Banking Institutions* (Washington: December 31, 1987), computer printout.

[42]"High Court Gives Green Light to Regional Banking Accords," *Congressional Quarterly Review* (June 15, 1985), p. 1161. A summary of interstate banking is provided in Donald T. Savage, "Interstate Banking Developments," *Federal Reserve Bulletin* (Washington: February 1987), pp. 79-92.

liberalization of policies regarding out-of-state multibank holding companies.

The implications for foreign bank offices of the exclusion principles have yet to be fully determined. Foreign banks have expressed concern, for example, regarding the legislative action of North Carolina and Florida, both of which have agreed to regional banking arrangements that expressly prohibit foreign banks from participating. Concern has also been voiced by the Japanese government that Congress will free U.S. banks from various interstate restrictions that continue to apply to foreign institutions.[43] The growth in interstate banking and the opportunity for U.S. offices of foreign banks to participate may be one of the most important sets of conditions affecting the growth of foreign banking in U.S. financial markets.

Another implication of the shift toward interstate banking is that it may facilitate U.S. bank activities abroad. For example, several major east coast banks plan to establish operations in California in the expectation that they can use the location to operate more efficiently in Japan and other Asian countries.

FOREIGN BANKS, REPRESENTATIVE OFFICES, AND LOAN PRODUCTION OFFICES

The policies of governments toward representative offices vary from state to state. Some states prohibit such offices; in others, the law is silent and no effort is made to monitor their activities. In many of the remaining states, representative offices can be established subject to the approval of a regulatory agency. Of the 410 representative offices of foreign banks located in U.S. markets in 1986, about 40 percent were situated in New York City, with most of the rest in Houston, Chicago, Los Angeles, and San Francisco.[44]

Foreign banks also use loan production offices (LPOs) as an alternative to expand into markets outside the home state. Loan production offices are limited service offices used primarily by commercial banks as well as other financial institutions to establish a presence and assist in lending activities away from the home office at either an in-state or out-of-state location. An authorized LPO is able to undertake all of the

---

[43]Japan Economic Institute, "U.S. Financial Markets: Closing the Door to Japan?" *Japan Economic Survey* (May 1988), pp. 5, 12.

[44]U.S. Department of Treasury, *National Treatment Study, 1986 Update* (Washington: 1986), p. 20.

functions associated with the processing of loans except the final approval of the loan and the disbursement of funds; these functions must be performed by the main office of the bank or one of its subsidiaries. In practice, LPOs are able to solicit loans, assemble credit information, prepare loan applications, and seek to have investors contract with the bank for the servicing of loans. The restriction that loan approval and disbursement of funds not be undertaken at the LPO is one of the factors that from a legal perspective differentiates such units from branch offices.[45]

The initial effort to formalize a national policy on LPOs occurred in the 1960s, when the Comptroller of the Currency ruled that such offices were not branches and therefore not subject to the restrictive laws imposed on branches. However, the attitude toward the establishment and use of LPOs by foreign banks varies considerably from state to state.[46]

Some of the more important international banking centers, including California and Illinois, treat LPOs as representative offices. California divides the LPOs licensed by the Superintendent of Banks into two types: those established by foreign banks are licensed as "representative offices"; those established by all others are licensed as "places of business."[47]

The Illinois Attorney General has issued opinions that LPOs are illegal as a result of banking prohibitions. However, under the Foreign Bank Representative Office Act, foreign banks may be licensed to establish representative offices that perform the functions essential to LPOs.[48] Another state, Georgia, also treats LPOs as synonomous with representative offices.[49]

Several states authorize foreign banks to establish LPOs with restrictions similar or identical to those imposed by the Comptroller of the Currency; that is, LPOs cannot provide final approval or disburse funds. This includes New York as well as Kansas, Louisiana, Nevada, New Mexico, Oregon, Texas, and Utah. Michigan permits agencies of foreign banks to set up LPOs. Although a foreign bank cannot establish an LPO in New Jersey, a nonbank subsidiary of a foreign bank or holding company has such authority; the laws of Vermont and Connecticut are similar. Kentucky, Maryland, Montana, South Carolina, and South Da-

---

[45]For a more complete analysis of loan production offices, see Charles W. Hultman, "Foreign Banks and U.S. Loan Production Offices," *International Journal of Bank Marketing*, Vol 5, No. 1 (1987), pp. 55-60.

[46]Comptroller of the Currency, *Interpretive Ruling 1966*; subsequently codified as *12 Code of Federal Regulations*, Section 7.7380.

[47]CAL. Fin Code, Sect. 540 and Sect. 1700 et seq

[48]ILL. ANN. STAT. ch. 17, par. 2851-6 (Smith-Hurd 1987)

[49]GA. Financial Institutions Code of Georgia, Section 7-1-590.

kota authorize loan production offices subject to adherence to state law. Implicit authorization is provided by Ohio law.

Some states have no formalized policy regarding LPOs, and such offices do not exist in those states. They include Arizona and Oklahoma. Others, including Massachusetts and Tennessee, have no policy, but foreign banks have established LPOs within the state. Rhode Island has several "licensed lending offices" operated by a foreign bank holding company.

Most states authorize the use of LPOs under some circumstances but at least a few (West Virginia and Wyoming) prohibit such offices (at least for out-of-state firms) on the basis of established law, regulation, or policy. These states also exclude agencies and branches of foreign banks.

In a few states, LPOs have been established by foreign banks as a result of individualized agreements with state banking authorities; these include North Carolina and Pennsylvania.

SUMMARY AND CONCLUSIONS

The dual system of bank regulation and supervision that characterizes the United States affects foreign banks as well as domestic banks. Many states employ reciprocity provisions, asset maintenance or deposit requirements, and geographic restrictions to control the activities of foreign banks within their borders. Tax laws may also have some influence on the decision of foreign banks regarding the location and type of office. Only a few states pursue an open policy that could be considered equivalent to a national treatment approach.

Despite the differences in the approaches used by federal agencies and the various states, and despite some problems in being able to enunciate a truly national commercial policy for the United States in its negotiations with other banking countries, in fact, the arrangement has worked relatively well if the growth in foreign banking in the United States is used as a criterion. Despite restrictions imposed by some states in what is perceived as a need to protect local interests, there is a fairly high degree of freedom on the part of foreign banks to open offices in U.S. markets, especially in the major financial centers. Yet, although the United States is one of the most open economies regarding foreign bank entry, foreign bank activity along with that of domestic banks is closely restricted, regulated, and supervised.

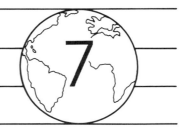

FOREIGN CONTROL AND ACQUISITION—THE TAKEOVER CONTROVERSY

Although the International Banking Act established a national policy for foreign banks operating in the United States, concern continues to be expressed over the outright acquisition by foreigners of large U.S. banks and also the growing share of the U.S. banking industry controlled by foreigners. One proposed Congressional resolution (June 26, 1979) states, "... the Congress finds that the takeover in whole or in part of U.S. financial institutions by foreign interests may constitute a threat to the health of the economy of the U.S." Congress also imposed a temporary moratorium on the foreign acquisition of large U.S. banks (deposits of $100,000 million or more) under Title IX of the Monetary Control Act of 1980.

Does foreign ownership of a part of the U.S. banking industry constitute a "threat to the U.S. economy?" An evaluation of the issue requires an analysis of several basic questions. How significant is direct acquisition and foreign ownership in the U.S. banking sector? What are the potential dangers and/or disadvantages of foreign ownership? What are the possible advantages of foreign ownership?

NATURE OF FOREIGN OWNERSHIP

Most of the concern regarding foreign ownership and control is directed toward the acquisition of existing firms by foreign banks. United States banks can be either established *de novo* (set up as new banks) or secured by acquisition (outright purchase of stock of, or merger with, an existing institution) by foreign buyers (banks, bank holding companies, government agencies, or individuals). During the period 1970-1979, 24 banks were established *de novo* in the United States by foreigners; 80 were purchased outright.[1] This pattern has generally continued. For example, the estimated foreign outlays for U.S. banking businesses amounted to $6.7 billion in 1987; $5.6 billion was spent to acquire existing firms; $1.1 billion, to establish new firms.[2] Outright purchase or merger acquisition is of particular concern not simply because it is the predominant approach to entry, but also because the foreign purchaser secures existing deposits and customers; as a result, a competitive presence is felt immediately. Included in some of the important acquisitions in recent years were the Mitsubishi Bank acquisition of Bank of California; Hongkong and Shanghai Banking Corporation's purchase of Marine Midland which subsequently acquired Crocker National Bank; National Westminster Bank's aquisition of National Bank of North America; and Allied Irish Bank's purchase of First Maryland Bankcorp.

The significance of foreign ownership can be expressed in other ways. For example, about one dozen of the largest 100 banks in the United States have majority control in the hands of foreigners; in addition, by 1987 about 19 percent of the banking assets of the United States-located banks were under control of foreign interests. This portion is relatively high compared with the equivalent ratio in such countries as Austria, Denmark, Germany, Italy, Japan, and Spain; yet it is relatively low in comparison with Belgium, Luxembourg, and the United Kingdom, in which the foreign presence is far more extensive.[3]

A related consideration is that foreign ownership is not widely distributed among a large number of foreign countries. Rather, foreign ownership is concentrated in banks from a small number of foreign

[1]An extensive discussion of the pattern of establishment *de novo* and acquisition is provided by William Longbrake, Melanie Quinn, and Judith Walter, "Foreign Ownership of U.S. Banks: Facts and Patterns," *Staff Papers* (Washington: Comptroller of the Currency, June 1980).

[2]Ellen M. Herr, "U.S. Business Enterprises Acquired or Established by Foreign Direct Investors in 1987," *Survey of Current Business* (May 1988), pp. 50-58.

[3]Federal Reserve Board, *69th Annual Report 1982* (Washington: 1983), p. 172; and R. M. Pecchioli, *The Internationalisation of Banking; the Policy Issues* (Paris: Organization for Economic Cooperation and Development, 1983), pp. 68-70.

countries, particularly Japan. For example, by mid-1987, Japanese banks held about 32 percent of all U.S. banking assets in U.S. subsidiaries controlled by foreign banks, about 54 percent of U.S. assets held by foreign branches in the U.S., and about 55 percent of all foreign agency assets.[4] And by mid-1987, almost half of all U.S. banking assets held by foreign interests were owned by Japanese institutions.

Although foreign ownership is not yet a major component of U.S. banking activity, the industry is one of the more attractive to foreign investors in the U.S. economy. During any given year, as much as one-fourth of the value of all U.S. business enterprises acquired by foreigners has been in the field of banking.[5]

The concern regarding the foreign ownership of United States-located banks relates more generally to the apprehension expressed by some Americans regarding the ownership by foreigners of any major portion of U.S. productive capacity. For example, the 1988 trade bill signed by President Reagan includes a provision authorizing the president to block foreign takeovers of U.S. companies on national security grounds. Whether or not a president will actually use the authority and whether or not national security could be jeopardized by a bank takeover remains subject to question. The point is that there is at least some sentiment in this country against extensive foreign ownership of domestic productive capacity.

United States financial institutions are clearly a prime target for foreign buyers. Foreign interests have been willing to pay a premium in excess of that paid by domestic firms to acquire U.S. banks. A major reason is that foreign interests are seeking diversity in their investments as they enter the U.S. market.[6] Similarly, efforts to reduce risk through overseas diversification characterize the action of U.S. banks. The advantages of diversification of banks assets have become apparent in recent years; for example, a large share of troubled banks in the United States are those that have not achieved sufficient diversification among industries.

---

[4]Percentages derived from Federal Reserve Board, *Foreign Investment in U.S. Banking Institutions* (June 30, 1985), and *Structure Data for U.S. Offices of Foreign Banks By Type of Institution* (June 30, 1987).

[5]R. David Belli, "U.S. Business Enterprises Acquired or Established by Foreign Direct Investors in 1981," *Survey of Current Business* (June 1982), pp. 27-31; and R. David Belli, "U.S. Business Enterprises Acquired or Established by Foreign Direct Investors in 1982," *Survey of Current Business* (June 1983), pp. 21-32.

[6]Thomas Loeffler and William Longbrake, "Prices Paid by Foreign Interests to Acquire U.S. Banks," *Staff Papers* (Washington: Comptroller of the Currency, 1981).

POTENTIAL PROBLEMS OF FOREIGN OWNERSHIP

United States tradition has been to limit foreign ownership in American industries that "affect the public interest."[7] This philosophy is applied to the defense industry and to parts of the communication and transportation system. The banking sector is also considered to be central to the economy and, accordingly, its health and activities are very much in the public interest. Society must have confidence in the money and credit system, which is a key component of the framework within which all market transactions occur. In addition, banks must be responsive to the direction provided by the central monetary authorities if the goals of overall price and employment stability are to be achieved. A basic question is whether or not foreign-owned or -controlled banks would support monetary policies of the Federal Reserve Board if such policies conflicted with those of the country of the parent bank.

Another concern is based on the potential disruptions associated with the purchase of large banks by foreign interests. Although bank takeovers are usually not hostile, negotiations could continue over a lengthy period of time or could subsequently lead to disruption of management. As a result there could be a loss of confidence in the institution.

United States financial interests also argue that it is particularly in the case of bank acquisitions that reciprocity usually is not practiced by foreign governments—that U.S. banks generally are not allowed to purchase a large foreign bank. Of course, most foreign countries have a small number of large banks, so the situations are not completely comparable.

Another concern is that there is a growing trend toward the purchase of U.S. banks by individuals or families rather than by banking organizations. By the end of 1987, over one-half of the foreign-owned United States-chartered banks were held by one or more individuals, many of whom were from Canada and the United Arab Emirates. However, the larger banks are owned by foreign banks, the smaller by foreign individuals; as a result banks hold far more assets than do individual buyers. In addition, most of the foreign banks with a sizable presence in the United States are associated with well-known major banks abroad,

---

[7]For a discussion of the problems associated with foreign ownership, see H. John Heinz III, "Foreign Takeover of U.S. Banking—A Real Danger," *The Journal of the Institute for Socioeconomic Studies* (Autumn 1979), pp. 5-9; Caroline Atkinson, "Foreign Banks in the U.S.," *Europe* (March-April 1981), pp. 36-37; and General Accounting Office, *Despite Positive Effects, Further Foreign Acquisitions of U.S. Banks Should be Limited Until Policy Conflicts Are Fully Addressed* (Washington: August 1980).

which generally have high credit ratings.[8] In part, the concern with foreign individuals appears to relate to the wealth that has been created for some of the families of the OPEC nations and a fear that the acquired banks are even less likely to be operated in the best interests of the United States.

The purchase of U.S. banks by state-owned or -controlled organizations has also raised concerns on the part of the Federal Reserve Board, although it has approved such purchases on numerous occasions. In a 1982 case in which Banca Commerciale Italiana applied to secure 100 percent of the voting stock of LITCO Bancorporation of New York, the Board noted that attention must be given to policy issues involved in government ownership of multiple banks and commercial-industrial enterprises.[9] Similarly, when Banca Commerciale applied to purchase Irving Bank Corporation in 1988, the Board raised questions regarding commercial activities of the parent organization. When there are extensive holdings of firms in banking, commerce, and industry, there is the question of maintenance of a separation of commerce and banking as required in the United States. Countries that become relevant in the matter of government ownership or control include Italy, Spain, France, Greece, Mexico, and Korea.

Another aspect of the problem is that under some circumstances, U.S. laws have permitted a foreign bank to purchase a U.S. bank that could not be bought by another U.S. institution. Historically, the U.S. use of antitrust laws and restrictions on interstate banking has promoted the existence of many small banks, which presumably best serve the needs of local communities. Essentially, U.S. laws that are designed to discourage concentration in banking by prohibiting banks from establishing operations in other states or that prevent small banks from being acquired by large U.S. banks serve to give foreign banks a competitive advantage.

The General Accounting Office (GAO) has concluded that such laws create an inequity with sufficient justification to place a temporary moratorium on future foreign acquisitions of large U.S. banks—those with total assets of $100 million or more. The GAO proposal was not a blanket moratorium, nor was it intended to be permanent. The assumption was that additional time was needed to resolve an apparent inequity in U.S. laws as applied to domestic and foreign banks.[10] One solution

[8]E. Gerald Corrigan, *Statement Before the Committee on the Budget*, U.S. Senate (May 6, 1987). (Mimeo)

[9]See "Legal Developments: Banca Commerciale Italiana," *Federal Reserve Bulletin* (Washington: July 1982), pp. 423-426.

[10]General Accounting Office, *Despite Positive Effects, Further Foreign Acquisitions of U.S. Banks Should Be Limited Until Policy Conflicts Are Fully Addressed* (Washington: August 1980), pp. i-xiii.

would be to relax regulations applicable to domestic banks to eliminate the foreign bank advantage. This has already occurred to an extent with the growth in interstate banking. In addition, the Competitive Equality Banking Act of 1987 gave the FDIC authority to allow an out-of-state bank to acquire a large, failing bank.

Another possible disadvantage relates to disclosure and the availability of financial records required to undertake an investigation of crime and tax evasion. Congress passed the Bank Secrecy Act in 1970 to facilitate the investigative work of authorities, including cases where records of foreign banks were involved. Essentially, domestic banks are required to maintain extensive records and photocopies of certain types of transactions. In order to overcome the inability to secure the records of foreign financial institutions, residents of the United States or those transacting business in the United States who have a relationship with a foreign financial institution must keep a record of the transaction.

Yet concern remains that regulatory agencies are not always able to secure information that may be needed from the foreign owner of a United States-located bank. This applies not only to records needed for criminal investigation but also for those regularly required for examination and supervisory purposes. A related difficulty is that financial standards, accounting practices, and legal definitions used in foreign banks are not always readily available, not always comparable with external institutions, and not easily understood by outsiders. As a result, judging the financial strength of an outside institution applying to buy a U.S. bank may be difficult.

The various reservations regarding the presence of foreign banks in U.S. markets, especially as a result of outright acquisition, contain at least some validity. But an assessment of an appropriate level of involvement also requires consideration of the degree of control maintained by U.S. regulatory agencies over foreign institutions. Equally important, it requires an awareness of the benefits provided by foreign institutions serving the American market.

CONDITIONS FOR FOREIGN ACQUISITION

Foreign banks do not have complete freedom in their purchase of American financial institutions. As provided by Section 3 of the Bank Holding Act, the Federal Reserve considers three factors when it evaluates an application of a foreign bank or holding company to acquire a domestic bank: (1) the financial and managerial capabilities of the applicant bank; (2) the convenience and needs of the affected community; and (3) the effect on competition and resource concentration in the United States. Essentially, it is expected that the purchasing bank will add to the financial and managerial strength of the bank being purchased, that the service provided to the local community will be improved, and that the purchasing bank does not already possess a large share of the local market. Generally, the rules that apply to foreign banks with respect to acquisition are the same as those that apply to U.S. banks.

The applicable standards are slightly different if the foreign buyer is an individual rather than a bank or holding company. These are contained in the Change in Bank Control Act of 1978. The prospective buyer must give the appropriate regulatory agency 60 days notice of intent. Approval is not granted if the effect is to lessen competition substantially, results in a bank monopoly in the United States, places the bank to be purchased in financial jeopardy, or is contrary to the acquired bank's best interests.

One recent study concludes that offices of foreign banks owned by foreign banks and bank holding companies tend to be more domestically oriented than offices under other owners. They hold more state and local government securities and real estate loans; they hold smaller balances with banks in foreign countries than institutions owned by foreign individuals and governments.[11]

Although federal regulators may consider the type of purchaser, they do not consider nationality in making their decision. This is consistent with the Congressional intent of the International Banking Act, which provides for national treatment. In other words, the principle of reciprocity is not a factor that influences the Federal Reserve Board in considering a foreign bank application to acquire a U.S. bank. However, as was noted in Chapter 6, those state agencies bound by a reciprocity provision must consider the nationality of the prospective buyer.

Banks that come to be controlled by foreign interests are supervised as closely as domestic banks. The same standards and regulations are applied by the appropriate regulatory agency at either the state or federal level. Since 1980, all U.S. depository institutions are subject to uniform reserve requirements. Prior to 1980, state-chartered banks (both U.S. and foreign) were usually subject to lower reserve requirements.

---

[11]David R. Meinster and Elyas Elyasiani, "The Performance of Foreign Owned, Minority Owned, and Holding Company Owned Banks in the U.S.," *Journal of Banking and Finance* (1988), pp. 293-313.

BANK HOLDING COMPANIES AND THEIR USE BY FOREIGNERS

One method of acquiring a greater amount of control over resources is through the multibank holding company. Several foreign countries have established and/or controlled offices in the United States through United States-chartered bank holding companies. A bank holding company is defined by the Federal Reserve Board as a company that holds at least 25 percent ownership of a U.S. bank. In some instances the Board may assume that effective control exists with less than 25 percent ownership and, accordingly, presume the firm to be a holding company. Initially, bank holding companies were defined to include companies owning stock of two or more banks. Since 1970, one-bank holding companies have also been included in the definition for regulatory purposes. Bank holding companies are regulated by the Federal Reserve but are established only if permitted by state law; they are also subject to regulation by the Securities and Exchange Commission.

Bank holding companies are usually formed in an effort to achieve managerial control and technological economies of scale for a group of banks. For example, lower cost financing may be available to a subsidiary if it is based on the reputation of the parent firm.

Bank holding companies are also formed to develop an affiliation with companies in activities closely related to banking in order to diversify operations. Permissible activities are determined by legislation and regulation. The Glass-Steagall Act of 1933 requires the separation of banking and commerce. The Bank Holding Company Act of 1956 brought bank holding companies under Federal Reserve control. Section 8 of the International Banking Act made foreign bank holding companies generally subject to the Bank Holding Company Act. Through its Regulation Y, the Federal Reserve Board specifies which financial activities are closely related to banking and are therefore permissible. Regulation Y also lists activities not closely related to banking, including insurance premium funding, underwriting, real estate brokerage, and syndication.

Bank holding companies offer financial institutions potential advantages as a result of other legislative and regulatory changes. For example, as noted in Chapter 13, U.S. banks were authorized in 1987 to participate in debt-to-equity swaps to cope with nonrepayment of debts of Third World countries. However, the securities acquired in such swaps cannot be held by the creditor bank but only by the parent holding company or a nonbank subsidiary.

In addition, consideration is being given to granting U.S. commercial banks additional financial powers especially in the fields of insurance, real estate, and securities underwriting. Some of the proposed legislation would extend the authority to bank holding companies, rather than banks, in order to maintain a separate legal distinction between traditional banking functions and certain other functions perceived as involving greater risk.[12] By maintaining such a separation, banking organizations could participate in new forms of financial activity without jeopardizing the security desired by bank depositors.

Bank holding companies may also be an approach to interstate banking for foreign bank organizations. Over three-fourths of the states authorize some form of interstate banking. In most cases, this involves granting permission to out-of-state bank holding companies to acquire a controlling interest in in-state banks.

In some cases, banks of foreign countries have established bank holding companies in order to increase the number of locations within a given state. This is particularly true of Canada, with a large number of subsidiaries in Illinois and Colorado, and Saudi Arabia, in Texas.

How important or extensive are foreign-owned bank holding companies in the United States? By the end of 1987, 83 banking firms in this country were identified as holding companies with foreign ownership. This represented less than two percent of approximately 4500 companies of this type in the United States. The 83 holding companies with foreign ownership controlled 175 U.S. commercial banks; 60 of these were one-bank holding companies and 23 were multibank.[13] As a result, about 80 percent of the assets of foreign-owned banks in the United States are under the control of foreign-owned bank holding companies. In addition, several of the largest foreign-owned holding companies are included in the top 100 bank holding companies in the United States (in terms of assets). These include First Chicago Corporation (Saudi Arabia), Marine Midland Banks, Inc. (Hong Kong), Republic New York Corporation (Brazil), Union Bancorp (United Kingdom), and Harris Bancorp, Inc. (Canada).

Does the growth of foreign bank holding company activity represent an unusual or unexpected development in U.S. financial markets? Probably not. The rapid increase in the use of holding companies by

---

[12]Organizational structures that may separate traditional banking activity from related financial activities are analyzed in General Accounting Office, *Insulating Banks from the Potential Risks of Expanded Activities* (Washington: April 1987). See also Nicholas L. Deak and JoAnne Celusak, "Bank Holding Companies," *International Banking* (New York: New York Institute of Finance, 1984), pp. 210-222.

[13]For a brief description of the growth of bank holding companies, see Thomas Watkins and Robert West, "Bank Holding Companies: Development and Regulation," *Economic Review*, Federal Reserve Bank of Kansas City (June 1982), pp. 3-13. Data on foreign bank holding companies operating in the U.S. are available in Federal Reserve Board, *Foreign Investment in U.S. Banking Institutions* (Washington: published semi-annually), computer printout.

See also Federal Reserve Board, *Annual Statistical Digest* (Washington: Annual).

foreign interests parallels a similar type of growth on the part of domestic institutions. By the end of 1970, about 50 percent of bank assets of all commercial banks in the United States were also under the control of holding company groups (either domestic or foreign-owned). The equivalent figure for 1987 was about 90 percent. In terms of the impact on the financial sector, the bank holding company movement is particularly significant in connection with other developments in commercial banking, including the erosion of legal restraints on interstate banking. The impact will be even greater if national banks secure freedom to function in insurance, securities underwriting, and real estate.

NATURE OF BENEFITS OF FOREIGN OWNERSHIP

Most of the foreign acquisitions of U.S. banks have occurred in recent years, but there is some evidence of favorable benefits or results. A study by the GAO drew the conclusion that foreign investors usually bought banks under less than average conditions but subsequently strengthened them. Frequently, foreign investors bought institutions with examination ratings assigned by regulatory agencies that were lower than the national average. They also purchased a large share of problem banks and banks that had failed; equally important is that generally the ratings of the banks improved in subsequent periods. The GAO study also included a survey of state banking regulators in states with a major foreign banking presence—New York, Illinois, and California. The responses indicated that the foreign offices were well managed, provided a service to users, and had a positive impact on various areas in the respective states.[14]

California is one of the states that has experienced a substantial growth in the volume of foreign banking activity within its borders. Japan and Switzerland particularly have established facilities in California and banks from many other countries have at least one type of office within the state. A 1974 study by the California Superintendent of Banks concluded, " . . . additional foreign banks, in whatever capacity they are present, have generated increased competition, whether by way of specialized services, more convenient locations, lower costs, or improved communications, which has, so far, been to the unqualified interest of consumers."[15] In addition, California passed legislation in 1987 that

---

[14]General Accounting Office, *Despite Positive Effects, Further Foreign Acquisitions of U.S. Banks Should Be Limited Until Policy Conflicts Are Fully Addressed* (Washington: August 1980), pp. 7-8.

[15]See testimony of John G. Heimann, *Annual Report* (Washington: Comptroller of the Currency, 1981).

affirmed the right of foreign banks to merge with or acquire California banks. In contrast, U.S. banks from the east coast will be unable to do this until 1991, when California becomes open to full interstate banking.

In general, the experience with foreign-owned U.S. banks appears to be favorable. The problems experienced by U.S. banks under foreign ownership have been no greater or more significant than for U.S. banks as a whole.[16] In addition, the rate of earnings of acquired banks increased slightly as compared with the preacquisition period. Several foreign banks also participated as lenders in the solution of the financial difficulties of some of the major U.S. manufacturing corporations, including the Chrysler Corporation and International Harvester.[17] Offices of foreign banks have generally accepted and worked within the regulatory structure.

A major advantage of the presence of foreign banks in U.S. markets is the increased competition, which has been beneficial to borrowers and other users of bank services. From a broader perspective, they have contributed to an internationalization of the U.S. economy, thereby facilitating the flow of goods, services, and capital in and out of the country in accordance with free market forces. By using the U.S. dollar as a base for their transactions, they have contributed to the continued use of the dollar as a trading currency.

SUMMARY AND CONCLUSIONS

Foreign acquisition of U.S. banks may contribute to a competitive environment, assist in the disposition of U.S. banks facing serious financial problems, and reinforce the U.S. position as an international financial center. It may also be consistent with freedom of U.S. banks to participate in overseas markets. Yet U.S. tradition has been to limit foreign ownership in American industries that "affect the public interest," including parts of the communication and transportation system, and defense industries. But U.S. laws that prevented domestic banks from acquiring out-of-state failing banks may actually have enhanced the opportunity for foreign acquisitions. In addition, the monetary and banking system of the country is in a sense its most basic and important sector in terms of the overall well-being of the entire economy; accord-

---

[16]See, for example, Judith A. Walter, "Supervisory Performance of Foreign-Controlled U.S. Banking Organizations," *Staff Papers* (Washington: Comptroller of the Currency, June 1980).

[17]In 1980, the Office of the Comptroller of the Currency published a series of studies that examined several of the major issues associated with foreign ownership of U.S. banks. For a survey of these and related studies, see Judith A. Walter and Steven J. Weiss, "An Evaluation of the Foreign Acquisition Issue," *Issues in Bank Regulation* (Winter 1981), pp. 3-9.

ingly, it is essential that the interests of bank owners be compatible with those of the United States.

Whether or not a substantial amount of foreign ownership is or could become inconsistent with the national interest is a question that ought not be ignored. This question is most likely to surface when a large U.S. bank is acquired by a foreign interest (such as National Bank of North America in 1979, Crocker National Bank in 1981, and Harris Trust Company in 1984) or when serious conflicts develop with foreign governments. Even among U.S. government agencies, there is a disagreement over the appropriate policy regarding foreign acquisition of U.S. banks. The Comptroller of the Currency, the Federal Deposit Insurance Corporation, and the Federal Reserve are generally opposed to major restrictions if specified conditions are met by the purchasing bank. However, the General Accounting Office has concluded that, although there are numerous advantages associated with foreign takeovers, a temporary moratorium should be reinstated under certain circumstances.

Finally, although national treatment may be the proper U.S. approach regarding takeovers by foreign banks, support for its use is diminished by the existence of reciprocity and restrictive attitudes abroad. As described more fully in the following chapter, about 45 foreign governments prohibit any outside ownership of banks in their respective economies. Although many of these represent less developed countries or countries closely aligned with the Soviet Union, it has also included Sweden, Norway, New Zealand, and Mexico. Another group of countries, about 35 in number, have in the past limited foreign participation to less than a controlling interest in domestic banks; included were Australia, Canada, Japan, United Kingdom, and the Netherlands. On balance U.S. policy on bank acquisitions by outside interests is more liberal than that of foreign countries. However, perhaps the important factor to be recognized is that a limitation on foreign acquisition and control may be considered appropriate and desirable in terms of short-term goals but that over time it will come at a cost to the U.S. economy.

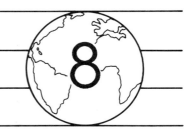

NATURE OF OVERSEAS
OPERATIONS

Although the major growth in U.S. commercial bank activity overseas has occurred since the mid-1960s, some American banks had secured foreign markets for the sale of their services even prior to the Federal Reserve Act of 1913. Much of the initial effort consisted of foreign lending of U.S. dollars by major U.S. banks from their home offices. Banking activity subsequently expanded in connection with the growth of U.S. trade and investment abroad. The Federal Reserve Act permitted U.S. banks to establish branches in foreign countries; legislation in later years increased their freedom to engage in foreign banking operations. By the mid-1920s, U.S. banks had established over 150 branches in various parts of the world. This movement slowed down and actually reversed in the 1930s as a result of world recession and the sharp decline in trade and investment among nations. The disruptions of World War II prevented financial expansion and, even by the early 1960s, the United States had only about 125 branches in foreign countries representing only eight U.S. parent banks.[1] The focus of this chapter is on U.S.

---

[1] Information on early history of bank operations abroad is provided in Martin Mayer, *The Bankers* (New York: Weybright and Talley, 1974); Clyde William Phelps, *The Foreign Expansions of American Banks* (New York: Ronald Press Co., 1927); and Karl Erich Born, *International Banking in the 19th and 20th Centuries*, translated by Volker R. Berghahn (New York: St. Martin's Press, 1983).

banking activities in foreign countries since the mid-1960s, particularly in terms of lending abroad and the establishment of offices in external markets.

FACTORS CONTRIBUTING TO U.S. BANKING ABROAD

A U.S. banking presence of major significance abroad is primarily a development of the years following the mid-1960s. A principal impetus to U.S. activity abroad and international banking was provided by the emergence of the Eurocurrency market and, in 1965, the U.S. government's imposition of controls on international capital movements. The U.S. government and those of most other countries control not only the establishment and basic character of both domestic and foreign banks within their boundaries; they frequently also maintain a regulatory system that directly affects the international operations of their banks. Generally, the regulatory systems of the Organization for Economic Cooperation and Development (OECD) countries have been designed to control the movement of international capital.[2]

The objective of the U.S. government's use of capital controls during the late 1960s and early 1970s was to improve the country's balance of payments situation. Governmental efforts to influence U.S. private capital movements included the Interest Equalization Tax (IET), Public Law 88-563, which placed a levy on borrowings by foreigners in U.S. markets in 1963. The Voluntary Foreign Credit Restraint Program in force during the period 1965-1974 hindered U.S. banks from making overseas loans directly from their home offices. Initially, the assets of foreign branches were not included in guidelines applicable to the parent corporation. As a result, parent banks were able to shift foreign credits to their external branches and still remain within the guidelines. In addition, the Eurocurrency market offered U.S. overseas branches a greater opportunity to secure funds without being subject to domestic reserve requirements and interest rate ceilings. As a result of these developments and a desire on the part of commercial banks to work closely with overseas customers, U.S. banks established foreign offices at an unprecedented rate.

The IET and the Credit Restraint Program were terminated in 1974. One reason was to encourage U.S. banks to expand lending to the developing countries, many of which were experiencing payments prob-

---

[2]Organization for Economic Cooperation and Development, "Regulations Affecting International Banking," *Financial Market Trends* (Paris: June 1981), pp. 1-9.

For an extensive survey of the use of capital controls by the industrialized countries, see Organization for Economic Cooperation and Development, *Controls on International Capital Movements* (Paris: 1982).

lems associated with rising petroleum prices. Since then most of the remaining major industrial countries have also liberalized controls on capital movements across national boundaries. This trend is partially the result of the movement toward floating exchange rates and the reduced pressure on governments to protect foreign exchange reserves in order to peg their exchange values. In addition, experience during this period suggested that controls on capital movements are frequently circumvented; as restrictions are placed on some types or forms of movements, alternative methods to transmit funds to areas of higher return are usually found. Accordingly, the U.S. government no longer directs regulatory action toward control of international capital movements of commercial banks; instead efforts have centered on encouraging prudent lending policies and instituting precautionary methods where risk and the potential for loss are great.

Individual U.S. banks have responded to opportunities in foreign commerce in varying degrees and forms of participation. In some instances, the response is limited to a correspondent relationship with an overseas institution to facilitate financing of export and import transactions. At the other extreme is the relatively small number of American multinational banks, which operate on a worldwide basis through a network of branches, affiliates, and subsidiaries. In addition, these institutions are involved in interbank borrowing and lending transactions with unrelated banks as well.[3] The result is a close interrelationship and interdependency among the larger banks and other international financial institutions of the world.

GROWTH IN BANKING ACTIVITY

An indication of the growing importance of U.S. banking activity abroad is provided in Table 8.1. The figures represent assets abroad of United States-located banks identified in the Department of Commerce's statement of the U.S. investment position in the world economy.[4] The importance of bank investment as a share of all U.S.

---

[3]For a discussion of the world network of banking, see Diane Page and Neal Soss, "Some Evidence on Transnational Banking Structure," *Staff Papers* (Washington: Comptroller of the Currency, September 1980).

[4]U.S. Department of Commerce, *Survey of Current Business* (Washington: various issues).

United States banking assets abroad refer to those assets held by all banks located in the United States and include both short- and long-term claims reported for their own account and for the custody accounts of their customers. They include loans, collections outstanding, acceptances, deposits abroad, claims on affiliated foreign banks, foreign government obligations, and foreign commercial and finance paper. See "Explanatory Notes," *Survey of Current Business* (Washington: June 1978), Part II, p. 14.

TABLE 8.1   U.S. Banking Assets And Total U.S. Assets Abroad (in billions of dollars)

Year	U.S. Banking Assets Abroad	Total U.S. Assets Abroad	Banking Assets as % of Total Assets
1970	$ 14	$ 166	8%
1976	81	347	23%
1978	131	448	29%
1980	204	607	34%
1981	293	720	41%
1982	405	839	48%
1983	434	893	49%
1984	446	898	50%
1985	447	949	47%
1986	505	1068	47%
1987	548	1168	47%

Source: *Economic Report of the President Transmitted to Congress* (Washington: February 1984), and U.S. Department of Commerce, *Survey of Current Business* (Washington: various issues).

investment abroad has grown substantially in recent years—from about eight percent of the total in 1970 to 50 percent in 1984 with a slight relative decline thereafter. In absolute terms, the amount increased from $14 billion in 1970 to about $548 billion in 1987. The growth in banking claims through 1986 has offset a relative decline in private direct investment abroad and in U.S. government lending to foreign governments and institutions.

COMPOSITION OF BANKING CLAIMS ABROAD

As indicated in Table 8.2, Section (a), U.S. bank assets or claims against foreigners amounted to about $530 billion by early 1988. The phrase "claims against foreigners" is broad and vague—what does it mean? Table 8.2 provides a detailed breakdown of the content of the $530 billion. Initially, as indicated in Section (b) of Table 8.2, most of the claims are those owned by the banks themselves; only about seven percent ($39 billion) are claims held by banks for their customers. Second, and as noted in Section (c), most of the banks' own claims are payable in dollars; a small portion ($52 billion) is payable in foreign currencies.

TABLE 8.2   Claims On Foreigners Reported By U.S. Banks, March 1988

(a)	Total claims	$530b	
(b)	Banks' own claims	492	
	Customer claims	39	
	TOTAL		$530b
(c)	Payable in dollars	440	
	Payable in foreign currency	52	
	TOTAL		492
(d)	U.S.-owned bank claims	200	
	Foreign-owned bank claims	240	
	TOTAL		440
(e)	U.S.-owned bank claims:		
	On own foreign offices	98	
	Unaffiliated foreign banks	42	
	Other foreigners	60	
	Foreign-owned bank claims:		
	On own foreign offices	123	
	Unaffiliated foreign banks	75	
	Other foreigners	43	
	TOTAL		440
(f)	Western Europe	128	
	Canada	28	
	Japan	101	
	Other industrialized	4	
	Caribbean banking centers	122	
	Latin America	98	
	Asia	39	
	Other	9	
	TOTAL		530

Source: Data derived from U.S. Department of Commerce, *Survey of Current Business* (Washington: June 1988), p. 58.

Another important aspect of U.S. banks' own claims on foreigners relates to ownership of the U.S. lending banks as reflected in Section (d). The $440 billion claims are claims of *United States-located* banks, but somewhat more than half of the claims are foreign-owned—that is, owned by offices of foreign banks located in the United States.

Section (e) indicates the type of foreign borrowers. As noted, United States-located banks (both U.S.- and foreign-owned) extend a substantial share (about 50 percent) of their loans to their own foreign offices.

Finally, claims in terms of geographic area are indicated in Section (f). A large share of claims are held against borrowers in Western Europe, Japan, and Latin America. A significant share of claims also apply to the offshore banking centers in the Caribbean. As described in Chapter 10, many of these centers are located in the Bahamas, the Cayman Islands, and Panama.[5]

COUNTRY EXPOSURE

One of the best indications of the magnitude of U.S. banking activity abroad and its importance relative to various parts of the world are the cross-border claims. The "Country Exposure Lending Survey," initiated in 1977 and provided on a regular basis since 1979 by the Federal Financial Institutions Examination Council (FFIEC), contains information covering credits to (i.e., claims on) foreign residents held at all domestic and foreign offices of 184 U.S. banking organizations. (Unlike data in Tables 8.1 and 8.2 which reflect lending of United States-located banks, FFIEC's data show lending of major U.S.-owned bank offices regardless of location.) Claims in the tabulation are of two types: *cross-border* lending, defined as the claims resulting from a U.S. bank's office in one country lending to residents of another country, or *cross-currency,* lending in a currency other than that of the borrower's country. In the first case, a United States-located bank might extend a loan to a British importer in any currency; in the second case, a U.S. branch located in Germany might extend a dollar loan to a German firm. The survey provides detailed information on about 100 foreign countries and international organizations by country, type of borrower, and maturity distribution.[6]

---

[5]Detail on both the banking and overall investment position of the U.S. economy is provided by Russell B. Scholl, "The International Investment Position of the U.S.," on an annual basis in *Survey of Current Business,* usually in a midyear issue. See also Russell C. Krueger, "U.S. International Transactions, First Quarter 1988," *Survey of Current Business* (June 1988), pp. 28-69.

A useful guide to lending statistics is provided by Rodney H. Mills, "Foreign Lending by Banks: A Guide to International and U.S. Statistics," *Federal Reserve Bulletin* (Washington: October 1986), pp. 683-694.

Lending statistics of the members of the IMF are published in IMF, *International Financial Statistics* (Washington: published monthly). An analysis of the data is provided by Joslin Landell-Mills, *The Fund's International Banking Statistics* (Washington: International Monetary Fund, 1986).

A more extensive analysis and comparison of different sets of lending statistics is provided by Geoffrey E. J. Dennis, *International Financial Flows* (Lexington, Mass.: D. C. Heath and Company, 1984), pp. 21-63.

[6]The figures used to indicate the volume of banking activity may vary depending upon the items included. The term "claims" is generally used to cover loans, demand and time deposits held by banks, certificates of deposit, promissory notes, acceptances made for foreigners, and items in process of collection.

Figures are provided quarterly in Federal Financial Institutions Examination Council, "Country Exposure Lending Survey," *Statistical Release* (Washington).

As indicated in Table 8.3, by March of 1988, the cross-border claims of U.S. banking organizations amounted to about $260 billion, a figure that does not include foreign currency claims amounting to about $140 billion. Generally, the lending has included interbank lending, short-term private trade financing, long-term loans guaranteed by governments, or long-term loans through syndicates that are not guaranteed.

As might be expected, the great bulk of U.S. bank loans were made to the Group of 10 countries (G-10, which includes Belgium-Luxembourg, Canada, France, West Germany, Italy, Japan, Netherlands, Sweden, and the United Kingdom) and Switzerland. However, a substantial share of U.S. commercial bank lending has been to developing countries in Latin America and Asia.

The volume of claims against the countries of Eastern Europe represents less than two percent of all claims. Of the $3.2 billion total, about 75 percent are claims against Poland and Yugoslavia. With the exception of these two countries, U.S. banks are not an important source of funds for the East European countries as compared with lending institutions of other industrialized countries. Trade, the financing of trade, and investment with these countries is hampered by a lack of the customary financial information, the need to negotiate with a government agency, and restrictions on many types of exports and imports. Generally, their currencies are not freely convertible; as a result, U.S. firms usually require payment in dollars or a hard currency.

Of the approximately $260 billion in loans covered in the survey, about 47 percent was extended to banks, 30 percent to public borrowers, and 23 percent to other private borrowers. To a great extent, these loans are of short-term duration; 67 percent have a maturity of one year or less,

TABLE 8.3　U.S. Commercial Banks Cross-border Claims March 1988 (billions of dollars)

Area	Amount
G-10 and Switzerland	$107.1
NonG-10 developed countries	21.3
Eastern Europe	3.2
OPEC exporting countries	15.1
Nonoil exporting developing countries in Latin America and caribbean	62.2
Nonoil exporting developing countries in Asia; and Africa	19.0
Offshore banking centers	30.2
All other	1.3
Total	$259.5

Source: Federal Financial Institutions Examination Council, "Country Exposure Lending Survey," *Statistical Release* (Washington, July 8, 1988).

indicating the desire on the part of commercial banks for liquidity and also, in part, the large volume of interbank lending. About 16 percent of the loans have a maturity of one to five years; 18 percent, over five years.

The "Country Exposure Lending Survey" provides information not only for the 184 U.S. banking organizations as a group, but also for the nine largest banks and for the next thirteen largest banks. Thus, for example, of the $260 billion in loans outstanding by March of 1988, $164 billion, or 63 percent, was provided by the nine largest banks. The next thirteen largest banks accounted for $43 billion, or 17 percent of the total. Less than two percent of all U.S. banks are involved in international lending to any significant extent.

EXPORT TRADING COMPANIES

United States banking claims and external activity may be expanded as a result of participation with private companies and public bodies in the development of export trading companies (ETCs). The Export Trading Company Act of 1982 authorizes certain specified banking institutions to become equity partners in export trading companies. An export trading company is defined as a company that "is exclusively engaged in activities related to international trade and which is organized and operated principally for purposes of exporting goods or services produced in the United States by unaffiliated persons by providing one or more export trade services."[7] Export trading companies were designed to promote U.S. exports and thus help the U.S. balance of payments position. Title II of the act amends the Bank Holding Company Act to permit bank holding companies, bankers' banks (associations owned by other depository institutions) and certain Edge Act Corporations (those that are subsidiaries of bank holding companies) to participate in such companies. As much as five percent of the capital and surplus of the investing firms can be placed in an ETC. Commercial banks themselves or commercial bank-owned Edge Act Corporations are precluded from investing in an export trading company. The act is particularly important because it departs from traditional banking legislation in that banking organizations are permitted to participate in commercial activities.

The act eliminates the fear of antitrust prosecutions of such companies by establishing a preclearance procedure and prior certification of antitrust exemption. The Federal Reserve Board must be given notice at least 60 days in advance of proposed investment in an ETC. Generally, a

[7]Export Trading Company Act.

request on the part of an institution to participate in a company is approved unless it reflects an unsafe or unsound banking practice, has the effect of reducing competition, or appears to be designed to contribute to the sale of goods or services from the company within the U.S. market area.

The participation of bank organizations in these ventures was expected to facilitate the availability of capital for export financing as well as increase the number of contacts and experience needed for overseas sales. Although commercial banks cannot participate directly, they can be involved indirectly through an affiliated organization that does participate in such a trading company.[8]

The initial opportunity to participate in ETCs coincided with recession in the United States and Western Europe and at a time when U.S. exports were relatively low. As a result, the number of applicants to establish ETCs has remained relatively small. Generally, the first applicants were holding companies, most of which were located in major financial centers. Early efforts of the companies have centered on assisting small- and medium-sized firms to develop an overseas market for their products.

By mid-1986, about 40 bank holding companies had notified the Federal Reserve Board of an intent to invest in ETCs. Although there is an indication of expansion and profitability on the part of some of the companies, about a dozen are no longer operational because of a lack of success. Generally, the overall impact of the ETCs has been disappointing. Some consideration has been given to modifying legislative restrictions on these companies to improve their flexibility and profitability.[9]

FACTORS CONTRIBUTING TO U.S. ESTABLISHMENT OF FOREIGN OFFICES

United States bank involvement in international activity is reflected in the volume of lending and borrowing as well as in the location of offices in foreign countries. The nature and extent of a physical presence in foreign markets has been influenced by U.S. laws that affect interest

[8]For a description of the legislative history underlying export trading companies, see Edward L. Yingling and Diana H. Hill, "New Export Trading Company Act Presents Investment Opportunity for Banking Firms," *American Banker* (October 21, 1982), pp. 4, 7, 10, 12, 13. See also "Export Trading Company Legislation," *International Letter*, Federal Reserve Bank of Chicago (October 22, 1982), pp. 1-2.

[9]See statement by Manuel H. Johnson before the Subcommittee on International Finance and Monetary Policy, reproduced in Federal Reserve Board, *Federal Reserve Bulletin* (Washington: August 1986), pp. 554-559; and Robert McMahon, "What Went Wrong with Export Trading Companies," *The Bankers Magazine* (May-June 1987), pp. 49-53.

rates and international capital flows and also the laws of host countries that determine conditions of entry and operations. United States banks considering establishing an office abroad are affected by the same type of basic economic factors that cause foreign banks to open offices in the United States.

Perhaps the most important factor affecting the establishment of offices in foreign markets is the extent of U.S. investment in those markets. American banks locate in specific places to serve U.S. manufacturing and other firms in the areas. United States direct investment in Western Europe and Latin America has been a particularly important influence on the establishment of U.S. bank offices.[10] The initial impetus was the Voluntary Foreign Credit Restraint Program in 1974, which made it difficult for U.S. banks to service the financial needs of U.S. multinational corporations from their home offices.

Another contributing factor is the desire for diversification. Operations in several overseas markets lower the risk of instability or economic losses associated with a single market. Development of a network of offices on a worldwide scale also permits a bank to take advantage of interest rate and exchange rate differentials on a more comprehensive basis.

Avoidance of taxes, reserve requirements, and restrictive regulations have provided a strong incentive to locate an office abroad. As described in the following chapter, a large number of offshore facilities (usually branches or subsidiaries) have been set up in the Bahamas, the Cayman Islands, Panama, and other areas that are virtually free of restrictions.

Another consideration is that deposits held in overseas branches are not subject to the assessments of Federal Deposit Insurance Corporation (FDIC) insurance premiums. This premium has amounted to 1/12 of 1 percent on domestic deposits covered under the program.

EDGE ACT CORPORATIONS

An important component of U.S. bank involvement in international commercial activity is undertaken through the Edge Act Corporation. Edge Act Corporations (EACs or Edges) were noted briefly in Chapter 5 in connection with their use by foreign banks in U.S. markets since 1978. Edges also afford U.S. banks a relatively high degree of freedom

---

[10]An analysis of locational factors is provided by Douglas Nigh, Kang Rae Cho, and Suresh Krishnan, "The Role of Location-Related Factors in U.S. Banking Involvement Abroad: An Empirical Examination," *Journal of International Business Studies* (Fall 1986), pp. 59-72.

in their international banking and financial transactions. They have come to be used by banks as part of a strategy to establish international banking offices in major financial markets outside the home state; a U.S. bank cannot establish a branch in another state, but it can market some of its services in another state through an Edge Corporation. Edges are supervised by the Federal Reserve System and are all located in the United States. By 1986, there were almost 140 Edge Corporations, which had about 100 branches.[11]

Regulations provide for two different types of Edges—*banking* Edges and *investment* Edges—although since 1963 the differences have diminished. Operations of banking Edges center on trade-related activities, whereas investment Edges function primarily as holding companies by U.S. banks in their control and use of foreign subsidiaries and affiliated firms.

The initial difference between the two types of Edges was based on authorized activities of each. The banking Edge is established by U.S. banks primarily to participate in international financial transactions. This includes the financing of international trade, dealing in foreign currencies, and activities related to the exchange of goods and services with other countries. Banking Edges accept deposits in the United States from nonaffiliated persons, whereas investment Edges cannot accept any deposits. Further, banking Edges can provide credit to any one customer only to a maximum of 10 percent of its capital and surplus, whereas investment Edges can lend to any one customer up to 50 percent of capital and surplus.[12] Many large banks located outside the major financial centers establish banking Edges in the financial centers, particularly New York, to assist in international transactions.[13]

In contrast, the investment or nonbanking Edges are generally holding companies with overseas branches and subsidiaries designed to facilitate foreign investments in a wide range of companies abroad. Although U.S. banks since 1966 can invest directly only in foreign banks, through the use of an Edge Corporation they can invest in almost any foreign company with one exception—investment is not permitted in any foreign firm that does business in the United States.

Regulation K was revised in 1963 to permit both types of Edges to perform international banking and investment functions. Nevertheless, the two types of Edges have tended to retain their initial identities. In

---

[11]Federal Reserve Board, *Annual Report 1986* (Washington: 1987), p. 201.

[12]A useful analysis of Edges is provided in James V. Houpt, "Performance and Characteristics of Edge Corporations, *Staff Studies* (Washington: Federal Reserve Board, January 1981).

[13]Data from Federal Reserve Board table, "Banking Edges and Agreement Corporations," July 19, 1985.

addition, since 1970, U.S. bank holding companies have been permitted to invest in foreign companies, but under guidelines similar to those applicable to investment Edges.

FORMS OF ORGANIZATION

A shift in the approach of the U.S. banking industry is apparent in data reflecting this country's lending in international markets by each of the three types of lenders—U.S. bank offices, foreign branches of U.S. banks, and foreign subsidiaries of U.S. banks. In the early 1960s, the great bulk of U.S. bank lending was undertaken from the home location in this country. In subsequent years, home offices have become a relatively less important source of international loans. Foreign branches of U.S. banks, in turn, have experienced the largest gains as a source of loans.

United States banking organizations have also found it advantageous to participate in joint ventures abroad. Joint ventures involve a noncontrolling share of ownership ranging from 20 to 50 percent of voting stock usually in banking, financial and related activities.

UNITED STATES BRANCH BANKS ABROAD

Establishment of an overseas branch is authorized by the Federal Reserve Act and Regulation K with the approval of the Federal Reserve Board. The Board's decision to grant a bank permission to set up a branch is based on legislative considerations, the financial condition of the bank, and the bank's international experience. A large U.S. bank may find it easier from a regulatory point of view to locate a branch in a foreign country than in the home market, especially if it has already created a presence in that foreign country.

From the perspective of the parent company, branches are able to perform the usual banking functions and are easiest to control. They are an integral part of the U.S. parent company, although most countries require that they be separately capitalized. As a part of the parent company, branches are frequently able to make larger loans than could a subsidiary.

In addition to the usual banking powers, a foreign branch is authorized to undertake a wide range of activities under Federal Reserve Regulation K. These include the guarantee of customers' debts, acceptance of drafts and bills of exchange, investment in securities of government agencies in the host country, and acting as an insurance agent. Branches may also apply for permission to undertake other activities that are consistent with usual banking practices in the host country. The experience gained in the provision of these services as branches and subsidiaries continue to operate abroad will in all likelihood prove valuable to parent companies should geographic and product restrictions be relaxed within the United States.

How extensive is the use of the overseas branch? According to one estimate, there were over 1000 overseas branches of U.S. banks with assets of about $458 billion.[14] Although these are widely spread throughout the world, the largest number have been located in the Bahamas, Cayman Islands, Argentina, Panama, the United Kingdom, Hong Kong, Chile, and Puerto Rico. Branches are concentrated in the economies of the major trading partners and in the offshore centers, which serve as a base for operations elsewhere. For example, of the $458 billion in assets of branches, about 32 percent are held in the United Kingdom, and 29 percent in the Bahamas and Cayman Islands.[15]

Interbank lending represents a substantial part of the activity of foreign branches of U.S. banks. For example, by mid-1988, of the $493 billion dollars in claims, about 21 percent were against the U.S. parent banks; 21 percent were claims against other branches of the parent bank; and 24 percent were claims against all other banks.[16] Much of the activity involves *intrabank* lending—the provision of credit to an overseas affiliate. Although an overseas branch is an integral part of the parent company, from a practical point of view, it is separate in certain respects; thus the parent bank may either lend to or borrow from the overseas branch. In addition, the accounts of a branch must be maintained separately from the home office; they are also periodically examined by the Comptroller of the Currency.

In general, parent banks rely on foreign branches as sources of funds when a restrictive domestic monetary policy prevails. When parent banks have a surplus of funds, they use their foreign branches to loan out part of the excess.[17] High interest rates and tight monetary policies in the United States in the late 1960s encouraged foreign branches to lend their Eurodollar deposits to U.S. parent banks. The restrictive monetary

---

[14]A description of the activities of foreign branches, subsidiaries, and joint ventures of U.S. banks is provided in Victor L. Saulsbury, "Activities of U.S. Banking Organizations Abroad," *Regulatory Review*, Federal Deposit Insurance Corporation (Washington: October-November 1986), pp. 1-13.

[15]Federal Reserve Board, *Federal Reserve Bulletin* (Washington: June 1987), pp. A55-56. The geographic distribution of overseas branches of U.S. banks is provided in *American Banker* (July 29, 1986).

[16]Federal Reserve Board, *Federal Reserve Bulletin* (Washington: October 1988), p. A55.

[17]Sarkis J. Khoury, *Dynamics of International Banking* (New York: Praeger Publishers, 1980), pp. 45-63.

policy also provided an incentive for U.S. banks to set up more branches in foreign markets.

FOREIGN SUBSIDIARIES

The subsidiary offers other types of advantages. In at least a small number of countries, subsidiaries are the only form of office authorized. As a separate legal entity, a subsidiary can perform a variety of functions in many foreign countries that are not open to U.S. banks or their overseas branches because of U.S. laws. A major function is that of securities underwriting, which cannot be undertaken by U.S. banks or their branches.[18] If services are to be provided at the retail level, subsidiaries may be most useful because they can usually be tailored to resemble or to identify more closely with indigenous institutions and the local environment.

In terms of numbers and asset value, subsidiaries are less important than branches for overseas operations. By the end of 1986, about 860 overseas subsidiaries were under the control of U.S. banking institutions and held assets amounting to about $132 billion.[19] A large share of the assets of the subsidiaries were owned by a small number of U.S. banking organizations. These included Citicorp, Chase Manhattan Corporation, BankAmerica Corporation, Manufacturers Hanover Corporation, Continental Illinois Corporation, and J.P. Morgan & Company.

Although a large share of the foreign subsidiaries are commercial or merchant banks, several types of nonbanking institutions are represented, including consumer finance, commercial finance, and leasing companies. As a result, the subsidiaries perform a wide range of services in addition to the standard commercial bank functions—acceptance of deposits and extension of loans. Merchant banks are utilized primarily to underwrite securities; they also carry out certain functions in the host country for the parent company. Many of the nonbanking subsidiaries are engaged in the provision of consumer and commercial credit—personal loans, mortgage financing, and automobile and real estate financing. A large share of the nonbank overseas subsidiaries are under the control of a United States-owned Edge Act Corporation. Some of the larger overseas subsidiaries of U.S. banks include Citibank Savings in the

---

[18]A detailed description of subsidiaries is provided in James V. Houpt and Michael G. Martinson, "Foreign Subsidiaries of U.S. Banking Organizations," *Staff Studies* (Washington: Federal Reserve Board, October 1982).

Permissible activities of overseas subsidiaries of U.S. banks are contained in *12 Code of Federal Regulations*, 211.5(d). (See Appendix A8.1.)

[19]James V. Houpt, "International Trends for U.S. Banks and Banking Markets, *Staff Studies* (Washington: Federal Reserve Board, May 1988), p. 11.

United Kingdom, Citibank AG in West Germany, Manufacturers Hanover Bank Nordique in France, and Saudi American Bank in Saudi Arabia.

BANK CONSORTIA

United States banks may participate abroad with other banks to pool their efforts on particular projects frequently for limited periods of time. Consortium banks are usually defined as joint ventures that are owned and incorporated separately by two or more parent banks with different nationalities. Usually no one bank holds more than a majority of the share of the consortium bank. The consortium banks have come to be used more widely since the mid-1960s and are usually formed to provide a particular service or group of services; in recent years, a major purpose has been to perform various functions relating to the provision of Eurodollar loans. By 1986, U.S. banking organizations were involved in more than 100 joint ventures valued at $680 million.

The consortium arrangement facilitates the accumulation of a larger volume of resources than would be possible with a single bank. It also provides an opportunity for individual banks with limited international experience to participate to a greater extent in an overseas market. Among the institutions in which U.S. banks have participated are European Banks International Company (Brussels), World Banking Corporation (Nassau), and Societe Financiere Europenne (Paris).[20]

INTERNATIONAL BANKING AND THE U.S. TAX REFORM ACT

One of the more complex sets of factors affecting U.S. banking activity in foreign markets relates to the U.S. taxation of such activity. Several important changes have occurred in tax policies as a result of the Tax Reform Act of 1986. These relate to the deferment of foreign income gains until repatriated, the use of the foreign tax credit, the treatment of loan-loss reserves on international loans, and the reduction of the U.S. corporate tax rate.

United States tax laws have been an important consideration affecting the form of overseas offices. Unlike subsidiaries, overseas branches are part of the parent company, and their earnings are included immediately as part of the parent company's income for tax purposes. As a result of the Tax Reform Act of 1986, U.S. banks are no longer able to defer

---

[20]Consortium banking and the post-World War II move to multinational banking are examined in Rae Weston, *Domestic and Multinational Banking* (New York: Columbia University Press, 1980), pp. 285-392.

the U.S. taxation of interest, dividends, and security gains of subsidiaries until such income is repatriated to the United States. The net result of this provision is to reduce the attractiveness of overseas offices, particularly the subsidiary.

Another change pertains to the calculation of tax credits and the avoidance of "double taxation" (by both a foreign government and the U.S. government) of income earned abroad. With the tax credit, banks are able to use tax payments to foreign governments to offset taxes paid to the U.S. government. In the past, banks have been authorized to calculate tax credits by aggregating income from various foreign sources and by aggregating taxes paid to various foreign governments. The Tax Reform Act eliminates the aggregation or averaging of income and of taxes. Instead, restrictions are placed on the calculation of foreign tax credits, which will effectively lower after-tax income of major U.S. banks with international operations.

The Tax Reform Act also affects the establishment of loan-loss reserves for tax purposes. Essentially, as examined more fully in Chapter 12, large U.S. lending banks (assets in excess of $500 million) are no longer able to establish loan-loss reserves as deductions from taxable income in anticipation of uncollectible loans. Instead, creditor banks may deduct loan losses only at the time such losses actually occur.

The favorable part of the 1986 act was the lowering of the tax rate on a corporation's taxable income to a maximum of 34 percent. For example, the taxable income of a bank in excess of $100,000 was subject to a 46 percent rate in 1986. The applicable rate declined to 40 percent in 1987, and to 34 percent thereafter.

The lower maximum tax rate will partially offset the additional costs imposed by the Tax Reform Act. On balance, however, the act is likely to reduce the incentive for large U.S. banks to establish offices and operate in foreign markets.[21]

THE UNITED STATES AS A NET DEBTOR COUNTRY

The changing environment in which U.S. banks operate internationally is evident in several ways, one of the most important being the shift in the U.S. position to a net debtor country in 1985. The growing creditor status of the United States and the subsequent sharp decline to a net

---

[21]The Tax Reform Act of 1986 is analyzed in George E. French, "The New Foreign Tax Rules and Their Significance for Banks," *Regulatory Review*, Federal Deposit Insurance Corporation (February 1987), pp. 1-14; and Stanley Yellin, "Highlights of the Tax Reform Act of 1986," *Bank Performance Annual* (Boston: Warren, Gorham & Lamont, Inc., 1987), pp. 43-55.

debtor was supported or reinforced by changes in U.S. commercial bank claims against and liabilities to foreigners over this same period of time. United States bank claims on foreigners grew substantially in both absolute and relative terms; by 1985, they represented almost half of all U.S. assets abroad. In addition, almost one-third of U.S. liabilities abroad by 1985 were claims against U.S. banks. However, since 1980, foreign claims against U.S. banks have increased more sharply than U.S. bank claims against foreigners (a 100 percent increase versus a 50 percent increase).

A part of the change in the volume of flow was the result of the establishment of International Banking Facilities, which led to a substantial increase in both external claims and liabilities on the part of United States-located banks. In addition, United States-located parent banks, which were net creditors of their overseas branches during the latter part of the 1970s and early 1980s, became net debtors to their branches in 1982. However, on an overall basis, U.S. commercial banks have retained a creditor position.

Although bank capital flows were an important component of the change in the U.S. investment position, it should not be concluded that they were the major causal factor. Merchandise and capital flows are closely interrelated. In some instances, changes in bank claims or liabilities are the result of merchandise trade. In other instances capital flows directly or indirectly influence merchandise trade, especially through their impact on the rate of exchange.

The reversal of the U.S. position in international investment between 1982 and 1985 was offset by a gain in the status of other capital-supplying countries. The major change occurred in the case of Japan, which in the period of a few years became the major net creditor to the equivalent of about $265 billion by the end of 1987. The status of West Germany and the United Kingdom also improved, with net creditor positions of $150 billion and $160 billion respectively by the end of 1987.[22]

While the United States' net debtor status greatly exceeds that of the major Latin American debtor countries, a comparison of potential repayment problems that focuses on the external debt magnitude can be misleading. The U.S. debt to foreigners is but a small share of its productive capacity; for many Latin American countries the external debt is large enough to cause a significant drain on internal resources.

Whether or not the United States remains a net debtor country—borrowing more than what it lends abroad—cannot be readily projected. A creditor status could conceivably return within several years if interest

---

[22]International Monetary Fund, *World Economic Outlook* (Washington: April 1988), p. 89.

rates and the size of the federal deficit were to decline in the United States, if there were a significant increase in the rate of saving, if the dollar were to depreciate in value, and if strong and pervasive economic recovery were to occur in other industrialized countries. From all indications, however, this is not likely to be the case; it is more likely that the debt position of the United States will continue to increase into the 1990s.[23]

Although the United States will continue to be a source of credit for many foreign countries, the share provided by U.S. banks is not likely to continue to expand as was the case during the 1970s; bank credit is likely to continue to be the dominant U.S. source but not a growing source. In particular, there are indications that foreign direct investment may be gaining in importance. There is also evidence that the role of commercial banks in direct international lending is diminishing but that banks are becoming increasingly involved in money and capital markets through off-balance-sheet activities.[24]

SUMMARY AND CONCLUSIONS

An early feature of U.S. bank activity in external markets was the lending to foreigners from United States-located offices. The growth in private direct investment overseas, establishment of Edge Act Corporations, and restrictive bank regulation in the United States contributed to the establishment of overseas offices. By 1986, over 2000 offices with assets in excess of $500 billion were in operation in a wide range of foreign countries. Through home offices and overseas offices, U.S. banks became a dominant force in international lending and related activities. By early 1988, U.S.-located banks held claims against foreigners in the amount of $530 billion, but over half of the total was held by offices of foreign banks located in this country. In addition, because of the current account deficit and large capital inflows, the United States became a net debtor country in 1985.

---

[23]The U.S. debtor position is analyzed in Russell Scholl, "The International Investment Position of the U.S. in 1985," *Survey of Current Business* (June 1986), pp. 26-35; and Reuven Glick, "The Largest Debtor Nation," *Weekly Letter*, Federal Reserve Bank of San Francisco (February 14, 1986), pp. 1-3.

At the end of 1987, foreigners owned $1536 billion of U.S. assets while U.S. residents held $1168 billion in foreign assets. Accordingly, the United States was a net debtor to the extent of $368 billion.

[24]See James Chessen, "Banks' Changing Role in International Financing," *Regulatory Review*, Federal Deposit Insurance Corporation (Washington: August 1986), pp. 1-11; and Bank for International Settlements, *Recent Innovations in International Banking* (Basle, Switzerland: April 1986).

United States bank participation in world capital markets and the establishment of overseas offices depend primarily upon economic conditions. The U.S. banking presence abroad also depends to a great extent on the policies of foreign governments. In the following chapter, the nature of U.S. bank access to foreign financial markets is examined.

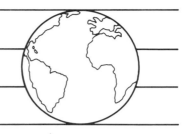

APPENDIX A8.1
PERMISSIBLE ACTIVITIES
IN OVERSEAS OPERATIONS

The Federal Reserve Board has determined that the following activities are usual in connection with the transaction of banking or other financial operations abroad:

1. Commercial and other banking activities
2. Financing, including commercial financing, consumer financing, mortgage banking, and factoring
3. Leasing real or personal property or acting as agent, broker, or advisor in leasing real or personal property, if the lease serves as the functional equivalent of an extension of credit to the lessee of the property
4. Acting as fiduciary
5. Underwriting credit life insurance and credit accident and health insurance
6. Performing services for other direct or indirect operations of a United States banking organization, including representative functions, sale of long-term debt, name saving, holding assets acquired to prevent loss on a debt previously contracted in good faith, and other activities that are permissible domestically for a bank holding company under sections 4(a)(2)(A) and 4(c)(1)(C) of the BHC Act
7. Holding the premises of a branch of an Edge Corporation or member bank or the premises of a direct or indirect subsidiary, or holding or leasing the residence of an officer or employee of a branch or subsidiary
8. Providing investment, financial, or economic advisory services

9. General insurance agency and brokerage

10. Data processing

11. Managing a mutual fund if the fund's shares are not sold or distributed in the United States or to United States residents and the fund does not exercise managerial control over the firms in which it invests

12. Performing management consulting services provided that such services when rendered with respect to the United States market shall be restricted to the initial entry

13. Underwriting, distributing, and dealing in debt and equity securities outside the United States, provided that no underwriting commitment by a subsidiary of an investor for shares of an issuer may exceed $2 million or represent 20 percent of the capital and surplus or voting shares of an issuer unless the underwriter is covered by binding commitments from sub-underwriters or other purchasers

14. Operating a travel agency provided that the travel agency is operated in connection with financial services offered abroad by the investor or others

15. Engaging in activities that the Board had determined by regulation in 12 CFR 225.25(b) are closely related to banking under section 4(c)(8) of the BHC Act

16. With the Board's specific approval, engaging in other activities that the Board determines are usual in connection with the transaction of the business of banking or other financial operations abroad and are consistent with the FRA or the BHC Act.

UNITED STATES BANK ACCESS TO FOREIGN MARKETS

The opportunities available to U.S. banks as they seek to establish offices and conduct business abroad vary significantly from country to country. Some countries are relatively open, while others are virtually closed to outside firms. In this chapter, a summary is provided of the foreign treatment accorded U.S. banks, of U.S. efforts to increase access to foreign markets, and of domestic factors that hinder U.S. bank operations abroad.

FOREIGN TREATMENT OF U.S. BANKS

Although U.S. legislators supported a liberal approach toward foreign banking activity in this country in 1978, they were concerned with the nature of foreign treatment of U.S. banks by governments abroad. As a result, Section 9 of the International Banking Act (IBA) required that a study be made of the policies of foreign governments toward U.S. banks. Of specific interest was the extent to which U.S. banks were denied, whether by law or practice, national treatment in foreign countries. The U.S. Treasury study published in 1979, entitled *Report to Congress on*

Foreign Government Treatment of U.S. Commercial Banking Organizations, was the first major source of information on policies of foreign countries that affect the activity of U.S. commercial banks.[1]

Conditions affecting U.S. bank activity in external markets cannot always be easily determined or quantified. Restrictions may apply either to conditions of entry or to actual operations once entry has been established. The impact of the latter, including restrictions on types of deposits, types of services offered, or access to central bank discount facilities, is most difficult to assess.

In addition, the attitude displayed by foreign governments toward the entry of external banks in their respective economies varies significantly among the 141 countries examined in the Treasury study. At one extreme was a small number of countries mostly characterized by relatively low incomes that permit no external offices of any type. This included Afghanistan, Bulgaria, Cuba, Czechoslovakia, Ethiopia, Guinea, Iraq, Laos, Libya, Madagascar, Nepal, and Somalia. Most of the countries in this group have nationalized banking systems and prohibit the entry of private institutions. They are also countries with which the United States conducts a minimal amount of trade.

The centrally planned economies do not require the services of commercial banks as utilized in the free market economies. Accordingly, Eastern European countries are highly restrictive of foreign banking, including that of the United States. A few countries in this group—East Germany, Hungary, Poland, Romania, and the Soviet Union—permit banks to establish representative offices; Romania permits one offshore branch. Generally, the purpose of these offices is to facilitate the flow of trade, to help multinational clients establish contacts and conduct business, and to assist in provision of short- and long-term credit for trade purposes. Correspondent relationships are also permitted with major Soviet financial institutions.[2]

At the other extreme is a group of countries (about 35 in number) that impose virtually no restrictions on any type of foreign bank entry. This includes many of the smaller countries that have promoted the development of offshore banking centers (described in Chapter 10) such as the Cayman Islands, Jamaica, Luxembourg, Panama, and Switzerland. Also included are such countries as Austria, Belgium, Federal Republic

[1]Department of the Treasury, *Report to Congress on Foreign Government Treatment of U.S. Commercial Banking Organizations* (Washington: 1979). This study was updated in 1984 and 1986.

[2]For a discussion of this trade, see Abraham S. Becker, ed., *Economic Relations With the USSR* (Lexington, Mass.: D. C. Heath & Co., 1983). See also Robert V. Roosa, Michiya Matsukawa, and Armin Gutowski, *East-West Trade at Crossroads* (New York: New York University Press, 1982).

of Germany, Israel, Italy, and Spain. For the most part it is only in this group of countries that a U.S. bank could buy the controlling interest in an indigenous bank and that a national treatment approach prevails.

A major center of location for U.S. banks is London, which, in fact, has been the single most attractive place for U.S. banks to establish foreign operations. Over 40 U.S. banking organizations maintain over 100 branches and about 20 controlled subsidiaries with assets of about $130 billion in the United Kingdom. There are no entry restrictions except that foreign banks cannot acquire a controlling interest in an indigenous commercial bank. In some respects, London is a more important financial center than New York. London's role in the Eurocurrency market, the United Kingdom's importance in world trade and investment, and the use of the pound as a reserve and trading currency attracts not only U.S. financial institutions but also those from other countries.

Few major industrial countries are as open to outside banks as the United Kingdom. Most countries fall into an intermediate group that permits representative offices only, that prohibits bank branches, that limits the degree of control in indigenous commercial banks, or that follows a reciprocity approach. Some of the industrialized countries that have been restrictive include Australia, Japan, New Zealand, Norway, and Sweden, although in some instances attitudes are changing.

In general, foreign countries are somewhat more restrictive in their laws and regulations pertaining to outside banks than is the United States. For example, about two-thirds of the countries permit no foreign branches and/or no controlling interest in indigenous commercial banks. And about 25 countries permit no external commercial banking except representative offices.

CHANGES SINCE THE IBA
AND THE NATIONAL TREATMENT POLICY

The banking laws and regulations of many foreign countries have been changed and are in the process of being changed since the enunciation of the U.S. national treatment policy. Several foreign countries have eased their laws toward foreign banking since 1978, and there is evidence that an extensive use of reciprocity has not been as restrictive as it was assumed would be the case. According to one study, reciprocity has not been imposed in a rigid way by national governments but instead has been used as a bargaining device to ensure that their own banks can participate in international business. As noted by a 1984 Organization for Economic Cooperation and Development (OECD) study, ". . . considerations of reciprocity have had the effect in practice of opening up more domestic markets to foreign banks."[3] The OECD study also concludes that although some significant barriers remain regarding the right of establishment, most OECD countries accord national treatment to established foreign banks.

The financial relationship with Canada has been important to the United States. Canada did not allow foreign commercial bank branches or controlling interests in indigenous banks. However, under the Canadian Bank Act of 1980, entry by foreign banks as full service banks is authorized; by mid-1985 almost 60 external banks had offices in Canada.

An important change for this country occurred with the ratification of the U.S.-Canada Free Trade Agreement following the Conservative victory in Canadian elections in November of 1988. This agreement, signed by President Reagan and Prime Minister Mulroney in January 1988, will affect much of the trade between the two countries, including financial services. It will greatly relax although not eliminate Canadian restrictions on activities of U.S. banks. Canada will provide U.S. nationals and companies treatment as favorable as persons of Canada with respect to the ability to purchase shares of Canadian-controlled financial institutions. United States banks will not be subject to a 25 percent limit on total domestic assets of foreign bank subsidiaries in Canada. The United States will offer Canadian financial institutions the same treatment accorded U.S. institutions with respect to various types of banking and financial legislation.[4] Banks will also be affected by the freer flow of goods and services between the two countries; in response to a shift in the pattern of commerce, new opportunities will be created in the financing of trade and direct investment.

Other instances of liberalization since 1984 characterize Portugal and Norway. West Germany has eased restrictions pertaining to types of activities open to outside banks.[5]

The Department of Treasury's *National Treatment* (1986 Update) indicates that several important trading countries with restrictive bank-

---

[3]Organization for Economic Cooperation and Development, *International Trade in Services: Banking* (Paris: 1984), p. 15.

[4]Canadian Government, *Canada-U.S. Free Trade Agreement: Elements of the Agreement*, 1988, pp. 21-22; and U.S. Congress, *United States-Canada Free-Trade Agreement* (Washington: July 26, 1988), pp. 500-505. See also Jeffrey J. Schott and Murray G. Smith, eds., *The Canada-United States Free Trade Agreement: The Global Impact* (Washington: Institute for International Economics, 1988).

[5]J. David Germany and John E. Morton, "Financial Innovation and Deregulation in Foreign Industrial Countries," *Federal Reserve Bulletin* (Washington: October 1985), pp. 743-753.

ing policies had taken significant steps to open their markets.[6] For example, Australia granted full banking service to 16 foreign banks in 1985; Norway allowed nine external banks to establish full service subsidiaries in 1985 and 1986; and Sweden opened its doors to foreign banks for the first time in 1986.

United States bank access to a major overseas market will also be affected by the continuing financial integration of the European Economic Community (EEC, or simply the European Community) with the adoption of a set of proposals contained in the Second Council Directive. Under existing EEC rules, the principle of reciprocity applies in the establishment of bank offices. In addition, a subsidiary of a U.S. bank located in one member country can establish a branch in a second member country, but the branch is subject to the authorization, supervision, and restrictions imposed by the host country. Under the Second Banking Coordination Directive signed by the finance ministers of the 12-nation bloc in mid-1988, the remaining barriers to freedom of establishment in the banking sector would be removed. Commercial banks—including externally owned banks—licensed by any member state of the Community would be free to establish branches and offer services freely throughout the Community by 1992 (which, incidentally, includes underwriting and trading in securities).[7] The Directive also provides for community-wide reciprocity. As a result, outside banks from some countries may still be unable to secure a license to establish in the EEC if those countries prohibit or restrict EEC banks. Presumably existing banks will be able to locate and provide services throughout the Community as long as their home countries afford full reciprocity to Community banks. However, whether the Community decides to apply the reciprocity principle in a rigid or in a liberal fashion remains uncertain.

Banks will also be affected by a free flow of goods and services throughout the European Community as various nontariff barriers are relaxed or removed. Much of this will be accomplished with the adoption of common business standards which, at least initially, appeared to work to the disadvantage of nonEEC companies. Although the concept of a single market has been sought in Europe since the 1950s, the likelihood of it becoming a reality has become apparent only since the mid-1980s.

---

[6]U.S. Department of Treasury, *National Treatment Study, 1986 Update* (Washington: 1986). The 1986 Update provides an extensive summary of developments in several countries that have been somewhat restrictive toward external banks.

[7]Commission of the European Communities, *Proposals for a Second Council Directive* (Brussels: February 16, 1988). See also Serge Bellanger, "Toward an Integrated European Banking System: 1992 and Beyond," *The Bankers Magazine* (July-August 1988), pp. 54-59; and David D. Whitehead, "Moving Toward 1992: A Common Financial Market for Europe?" *Economic Review*, Federal Reserve Bank of Atlanta (November/December, 1988), pp. 42-51.

As a result, major companies and banks are developing plans and procedures to function in a huge, closely integrated market.

U.S. banks already located in the Community will be required to develop an organizational structure and sales strategy consistent with a community-wide, rather than the narrower nation-wide, market. Although new opportunities will appear, competition from European banks is likely to be more intense. West German bankers are expected to provide the most competition; they have been able to conduct both commercial and investment banking and are able to own common stock. In addition, the West German economy is the strongest in the Community. Competition from British banks is also expected to increase, particularly if Britain decides to participate in the European Monetary System.

The Community encompasses a population of 320 million people, about 25 percent greater than the United States, with a gross national product roughly equal to that of this country. The European Community is the major trading partner of the United States, accounting for more trade than either Japan or Canada.

Important changes are occurring in other parts of the world. A major step toward normalization of commercial relationships with the People's Republic of China (PRC) occurred in late 1978 under the terms of an agreement of the Joint Communique. The United States agreed to recognize the PRC as the sole legal government of China, and relationships with Taiwan were placed on an unofficial basis. In addition, the United States in 1980 liberalized its export policy pertaining to the sale of military support and dual use technology equipment to China. United States-PRC trade has increased since that time, and the United States has become one of the three or four major trading partners. In addition, numerous U.S. firms have set up production facilities in China following the PRC's Law on Joint Ventures. China has become active in both the IMF and the World Bank, and has applied for full participation in the General Agreement on Tariffs and Trade. As a result, there is a possibility of expanded banking opportunities with mainland China either in terms of loans for trade and investment and/or the establishment of representative offices or branches to facilitate commercial activity. Initial indications suggest a degree of uncertainty in U.S.-PRC commercial relationships depending particularly on political developments and U.S. policies toward Taiwan.[8]

---

[8]See Anant R. Negandhi, ed., "China's Trade with Industrialized Countries: Socio-economic and Political Perspectives," *Research in International Business and International Relations* (Greenwich, Conn.: JAI Press, 1986).

THE JAPANESE POSITION

Japan has made dramatic gains in the international financial community but has been reluctant to open her domestic market to outside banks in a commensurate fashion. However, Japan is introducing some changes in its policies toward external banking and has agreed to pursue a more liberal approach. Japan's 1982 Banking Law established the principle that foreign bank branches be extended equal treatment with indigenous banks. In the *1984 Report on Yen/Dollar Exchange Rate Issues*, Japan restated its intent to pursue measures to provide equal treatment of foreign financial institutions under Japanese banking and financial regulations.[9] About 20 U.S. banks have offices, primarily in Tokyo, but like other external firms have found it difficult to penetrate the Japanese market.[10] Some external banks find it difficult to compete against the more structured Japanese banks. In addition, Japanese corporate customers tend to be loyal to their banks.

In the retail field, Citibank is the only U.S. bank with some success in capturing a share of the Japanese market. Citibank's operations include several branches, a credit card business, and other activities related to consumer financing. Although the growth in per capita income in Japan provides a basis for a strong retail market, uncertainties in the market and the high cost of establishing operations have generally discouraged other external financial institutions.

The extensive presence of Japanese banks in the United States, coupled with the problems American banks have encountered making inroads into Japanese markets, have contributed to a protectionist sentiment in the U.S. Congress. One provision of the 1988 Omnibus Trade and Competitiveness Act authorizes the U.S. President to block takeovers of U.S. companies by foreign firms. Another provision bars foreign firms from performing as primary dealers in U.S. government securities unless reciprocity is provided by their governments. Although two Japanese firms (Daiwa Securities and Nomura Securities International Inc.) were authorized as primary dealers of Treasury securities in 1986, U.S. companies have not secured equivalent privileges in Japan.

---

[9]Japan Ministry of Finance and U.S. Department of Treasury, *Report on Yen/Dollar Exchange Rate Issues* (May 1984).
[10]Reuven Glick, "Foreign Financial Institutions in Japan," *Weekly Letter*, Federal Reserve Bank of San Francisco (April 24, 1987), pp. 1-3. See also General Accounting Office, *Implementation of the Yen/Dollar Agreement* (Washington: June 1986); General Accounting Office, *Competitive Concerns of Foreign Financial Firms in Japan, the United Kingdom, and the United States* (Washington: June 1988); and Leon Hollerman, "Banks—Facing Inward and Outward," *Japan, Disincorporated* (Stanford, California: Hoover Institution Press, 1988), pp. 50-92.

A presence in Japan is considered important because of the size of the financial market. In addition, major multinational banks require an office in the three major time zones that include Tokyo, London, and New York.

GATT AND SERVICE TRADE

Because national treatment and competitive equality have not been universally adopted, and because of the growing importance of service exports in the U.S. balance of trade, an effort has been made by the United States to encourage the reduction, on a multilateral basis, of various restrictions on such transactions. Obstacles to the flow of invisible trade in the banking and finance area include restrictions or prohibitions on establishment of branches or subsidiaries, debt to capital ratios that favor indigenous banks, limits on capital transfers in and out of the country, delays in obtaining foreign exchange permits, and various other service and operational restrictions. However, the major barriers include restrictions on remittances, convertibility limitations on various currencies, and restrictive regulatory and administrative procedures.[11]

The U.S. interest in easing of restrictions is based to a great extent on the rapid growth in U.S. service trade and the apparent comparative advantage it has developed in this type of activity. In its early commercial history, the United States had a comparative advantage in world trade in raw materials, agricultural and other primary products. Eventually, with continuing capital formation and technological change, the advantage shifted to industrial products, which provided an important source of growth for the U.S. economy. But merchandise exports are now declining somewhat in relative terms with a corresponding gain in service trade. For example, in 1972, U.S. service exports amounted to $52 billion, with a net surplus (service exports less service imports) of about $4.5 billion. By 1986, U.S. exports in this category amounted to $149 billion with a net surplus of $20 billion. Commercial bank activities are an important component of overall service efforts. Since 1984, interest received on bank claims against foreigners has amounted to about 25 percent of all balance of payments service receipts; interest paid on bank liabilities, about 20 percent of service payments.[12]

---

[11] A survey was taken of U.S. banking institutions by the U.S. International Trade Commission to determine, among other things, the nature of obstacles to service trade. Results of this survey are presented in U.S. International Trade Commission, *The Relationship of Exports in Selected U.S. Service Industries to U.S. Merchandise Exports* (Washington: September 1982), pp. 167-198.

[12] Russell Krueger, "U.S. International Transactions, Fourth Quarter 1987," *Survey of Current Business* (March 1987), p. 39.

During the years just preceding 1981, the U.S. merchandise trade account was in deficit with the rest of the world. The difference was more than offset by the service surplus in turn leading to a favorable overall trade account. But since 1981, the favorable service balance has failed to offset the merchandise gap. As a result, the United States has experienced an unusually large current account deficit since that time. In order to alleviate this situation, the United States has sought to reduce overseas barriers to service as well as merchandise trade. A liberalization of restrictions on service trade is not expected to lead to a major short-term improvement in the U.S. current account position.[13] Benefits are likely to be more long term in nature and may be more closely associated with the transfer of technology and other benefits that accompany such flows. In addition, it is suggested that trade in goods and services is interdependent, that merchandise trade may be restricted unless service trade is relatively unrestricted.

Much of the U.S. effort has centered on action within the General Agreement on Tariffs and Trade (GATT) with its broad membership and capacity for multilateral negotiations. GATT has been encouraged to expand its jurisdiction to include the invisible trade pertaining to activities of the banking, insurance, telecommunications, and shipping sectors. A "GATT for Investment" would provide a framework for the multilateral removal of obstacles to investment and service flows in much the same way that GATT has helped reduce and eliminate barriers on merchandise trade flows. A proposal of this type was one of several major items of discussion in the November 1982 GATT meetings.

The 1982 GATT meetings failed to reach an agreement on an acceptable approach to the liberalization of restrictions on invisible transactions. As a compromise measure, a recommendation was made that the participating countries with a major interest in service trade undertake a national examination of the implications of the issue.[14] Generally, the multilateral discussions of liberalization of trade in banking services did not prove fruitful. As a result, the United States has resorted to bilateral efforts directed particularly at Canada, Japan, Taiwan, and Korea to gain access for U.S. banks.

[13]Office of Technology Assessment, U.S. Congress, *International Competition in Services* (Washington: 1987), pp. 70-73.

[14]"GATT Ministers' Meeting," *IMF Survey* (December 13, 1982), p. 385 ff.

A description of the problems apparent in negotiating a liberalization of restrictions in service trade is provided by Michael P. Blackwell and Robert W. Ley, "International Trade in Services is Under Study in Various Forums," *IMF Survey* (May 21, 1984), pp. 145, 156-158.

An analysis of the difficulties involved in determining comparative advantage is provided in H. W. Arndt, "Comparative Advantage in Trade in Financial Services," *Banca Nazionale del Lavoro Quarterly Review* (March 1988), pp. 61-78.

The liberalization of impediments to invisible trade is more complex and difficult than that of reducing restrictions on merchandise trade. It is not certain that items pertaining to service trade can be subjected to the same GATT rules of commerce as those applicable to merchandise trade. The language and concepts in GATT apply to "goods," although nothing in the agreement excludes services. Some member states argue that GATT has no legal right to negotiate in services. In addition, some participants argue that in banking and certain other service sectors, a local presence is required if outside firms are to compete with domestic firms; accordingly, the development of an investment policy is more appropriate than the development of a trade policy.[15]

However, multilateral efforts at the liberalization of service barriers have not been abandoned. At the Uruguay Round of GATT, which commenced in late 1986, negotiations are being conducted on service trade. If progress is achieved in methods to free service trade during the planned four-year session, proposals will be merged with those developed for merchandise trade, and the Ministers of the Member States will attempt to accept all recommendations.[16]

In addition, the United States has made comprehensive proposals for liberalizing restrictions on insurance, transportation, telecommunications, computer and data processing, as well as banking. These proposals call for reducing restrictions on cross-border movements of services and establishing foreign operations to deliver services to the host country. In line with the U.S. International Banking Act, they also call for national treatment—that foreign and domestic service firms be regulated identically.[17]

DOMESTIC OBSTACLES TO BANKING ABROAD

The Federal Reserve Act of 1913 authorized U.S. banks to establish foreign branches. Since that time, U.S. banks have generally been encouraged to participate in overseas activities. Authority to establish foreign offices is governed by the Federal Reserve's Regulation K. In general, U.S. banks are required to secure Federal Reserve Board ap-

---

[15]H. P. Gray, "A Negotiating Strategy for Trade in Services," *Journal of World Trade Law* (September-October 1983), pp. 377-388.

[16]For a discussion of the Uruguay Round, see Pierre-Louis Girard, "The New Multilateral Trade Negotiations: The Opportunities and the Challenges," *EFTA Bulletin* (April-June 1987), pp. 3-7. See also Part II, "Negotiations on Trade in Services," *Ministerial Declaration on the Uruguay Round*, 1986.

[17]See Paul Gibson, "United States Proposes Services Framework," *International Economic Review*, U.S. International Trade Commission (January 1988), pp. 4-5.

proval to establish only the first of each type of office in each foreign country; for additional offices, banks are simply expected to notify the Board of subsequent actions. Thus in terms of specific enabling regulations, restrictions are minimal.

In other respects, and in an indirect way, the U.S. regulatory framework may impede U.S. banking opportunities abroad as a result of at least two factors: (1) reciprocity requirements on the part of some states; and (2) state and federal laws that limit the geographic and product diversification of banks. State restrictions on the operations of foreign banks have some effect on the treatment accorded U.S. banks that attempt to establish offices abroad. Governments of some foreign countries also apply a reciprocity provision as a condition for external bank entry. As noted, for example, in the 1979 U.S. Department of Treasury study, restrictive features of state laws that characterize the U.S. dual banking system, along with other considerations, work to the disadvantage of U.S. banks attempting to operate in countries that employ some variation of the reciprocity principle.[18] For example, until 1985, Japan would not allow a bank from the state of Texas to establish branches within the country because Texas prohibited external branches.

A possible obstacle that may be more difficult to overcome relates to the various U.S. laws and regulations that restrict the domestic activities of commercial banks. Although (as noted in Chapter 8) some domestic restrictions provide the incentive for banks to establish offices abroad, it is also argued that other types of restrictions make competing on a global scale difficult.[19] Thus it is argued that historically and within domestic markets, federal laws have tended to encourage the existence of a large number of banks. But they discourage and even prohibit geographic expansion and product diversification into certain major areas of financial activity.

Among the activities not generally open to banks (particularly national banks) in domestic markets are securities underwriting, real estate, and insurance. Many banks overseas are involved in investment banking, which includes origination, underwriting, and distribution of new security issues. Participation in securities underwriting, for example, would permit United States-located commercial banks to produce note issuance facilities (NIFs), one of the fastest-growing innovations in world financial markets.

---

[18]Department of Treasury, *Report to Congress on Foreign Government Treatment of U.S. Commercial Banking Organizations* (Washington: 1979).

[19]A statement of this concern is provided by the Comptroller of the Currency, Robert L. Clarke, in "The Choice is Yours To Make (A speech to the American Bankers Association, San Francisco, October 27, 1986). A discussion of bank competition with other financial institutions is provided by Karen D. Shaw, "Bank Regulation—Why Be a Bank?" *The Bankers Magazine* (March-April 1987), pp. 70-72.

The continuing importance attached to product diversification was reflected in the Competitive Equality Banking Act of 1987, in which Congress placed a temporary moratorium on authorization of new powers for commercial banks. In certain respects, the laws of some states have become more liberal than federal laws in terms of both product and geographic activities; however, most state-chartered banks are not involved to a great extent in international banking.[20]

Yet there has been a strong interest on the part of major commercial banks in investment banking and the power to underwrite and deal in corporate securities. At least three major banks (Citicorp, Chase Manhattan Corporation, and J. P. Morgan & Company) have applied for permission to participate in corporate securities. The proposed investment in Goldman, Sachs & Co. of New York on the part of Sumitomo Bank Ltd. is an indication of the foreign interest in U.S. security firms. There is some evidence that in the absence of Congressional action, the Federal Reserve Board will ultimately grant security powers, under restricted circumstances, to commercial banks.[21]

Another advantage of foreign banks is that in some foreign countries nationwide branching is permitted. This is not the case in the United States, where branching across state lines, and frequently across county lines, is prohibited. In fact, in several unit banking states, no branching is allowed. Presumably, the limited domestic base imposed on United States-located banks also limits their potential for overseas expansion.

In addition, nonbanking companies are prohibited from owning banks. Banks from many foreign countries (and even some U.S. thrift institutions) are not as severely restricted. The net result is that U.S. banks are perceived as less able to acquire the experience, capital, and domestic operational network needed to compete globally. Such domestic limitations on U.S. bank activity presumably impose an even greater burden as money and capital markets become increasingly integrated and impervious to national boundaries.

A 1987 study by the Office of Technology Assessment (OTA) concluded that U.S. regulatory authorities need to be more concerned with the competitive implications of their actions, and that data collected on international banking services were inadequate. The OTA proposed that Congress might consider several options to enhance the competitiveness of American banks in world markets, suggested the creation of an agency to monitor federal and state agency actions affecting competition, and

[20]See Victor L. Saulsbury, "State Banking Powers: Where Are We Now?" *Regulatory Review*, Federal Deposit Insurance Corporation (Washington: April/March 1987), pp. 1-16.

[21]With the exception of the United States, Japan, Canada, Greece, and Turkey, most Organization for Economic Cooperation and Development (OECD) countries authorize underwriting of securities by commercial banks. See R. M. Pecchioli, *Prudential Supervision in Banking* (Paris: OECD, 1987), pp. 57-66.

advised an improvement in the government collection of data for use by the financial services sector. The OTA also recommended a closer coordination of international bank regulation and supervision, particularly through the Basle Committee (which includes regulatory agencies of the United States and ten other industrial countries).[22]

Disagreement exists among U.S. government agencies and the major financial associations over the appropriate role and function of commercial banks. The Reagan Administration and the U.S. Treasury (and the Comptroller of the Currency) have been supportive of larger banks that are diversified in their activities. The Federal Reserve Board has favored a closely supervised system of banks with a well-defined set of authorized activities. The Board has concluded that the repeal of the Glass-Steagall Act, which restricts commercial banks from dealing in corporate securities, would increase competition in the investment banking industry, lower customer costs, and increase the availability of security underwriting services. The Board recommends that, to protect bank depositors and avoid conflicts of interest, the activities should be undertaken not by banks but by separate subsidiaries of bank holding companies.[23] The Board is also supportive of insurance agency activities by banks and bank holding companies.[24]

Finally, Alan Greenspan, Chairman of the Federal Reserve Board, favors some forms of interstate banking and the concept that bank organizations be authorized to perform certain nonbank functions although in a manner that does not jeopardize depositor safety. However, he does not believe that U.S. banks have to be larger to compete internationally.[25]

United States bank operations overseas have generally expanded since the 1960s. However, some major institutions have curtailed their foreign efforts since the early 1980s. Chase Manhattan, First National Bank of Chicago, and other institutions have closed some of their overseas facilities especially in retail activities. Factors contributing to the decline in the foreign presence include increased competition from foreign banks, the lingering Third World debt problem, and profit opportunities in domestic financial markets.

[22]Office of Technology Assessment, U.S. Congress, *International Competition in Services* (Washington: July 1987), pp. 348-352.

[23]Alan Greenspan, "Statement Before the Subcommittee on Monopolies and Commercial Law," *Federal Reserve Bulletin* (Washington: November 1988), pp. 746-751.

[24]H. Robert Heller, "Statement Before the Subcommittee on Commerce, Consumer Protection, and Competitiveness," *Federal Reserve Bulletin* (Washington: November 1988), pp. 743-746.

[25]Alan Greenspan, *Testimony Before a House Subcommittee on Telecommunications and Finance*, U.S. House of Representatives (Washington: October 5, 1987).

SUMMARY AND CONCLUSIONS

An increasing comparative disadvantage in many types of merchandise production in the United States has been offset by a comparative advantage in invisible exports, including banking services. Foreign markets for services remain somewhat closed, although it is difficult to quantify since regulations apply to market entry, type of office, type of service performed, tax laws, and the like. The degree of access to foreign markets by U.S. banks varies considerably from country to country. The governments of many of the industrialized countries have been relatively open, employing either a national treatment approach or a reciprocity approach that is not applied in a rigorous fashion.

Several of the markets that were partially or completely closed in the past have been opened somewhat since 1978. Pressure has been applied through GATT to liberalize trade in services, but bilateral negotiations have been more successful in securing gains for banking and financial services. Major market areas that have been liberalized include Canada, Japan, Korea, Norway, Sweden, and Taiwan.

Finally, while the doors to some overseas markets, such as Japan and Australia, have been opened, U.S. banks have frequently found they are not easily penetrated. In part, this simply reflects the difficulty associated with establishing operations in a different cultural, legal, and economic framework. But it may also stem from the restrictive geographic and product base imposed on U.S. banks by federal and state laws. Commercial banks in many foreign industrialized countries participate in a wide variety of financial activities, frequently are not limited geographically, and, as a result, may hold an advantage over U.S. banks.

OFFSHORE CENTERS
AND INTERNATIONAL
BANKING FACILITIES

The activities of commercial banks are affected significantly by tax laws and by other regulatory measures designed to insure prudent business practices and to retain public confidence in the monetary system. Yet these same measures may make it more difficult for United States-located banks to compete in world markets. In this chapter, two institutional arrangements designed to enhance commercial banking opportunities in overseas areas are examined—offshore banking centers and International Banking Facilities (IBFs). Operations in offshore banking centers were initiated by U.S. banks to facilitate overseas business activity. International Banking Facilities were authorized by the Federal Reserve Board to facilitate overseas business activity from domestic locations. In both arrangements, operating costs are reduced for U.S. banks because legal reserve requirements are waived or avoided.

OFFSHORE CENTERS

A significant share of external lending activities of U.S. banks are channeled through offshore banking centers (OBCs). *Offshore banking* is frequently defined to include the operations of banking offices in the

Caribbean, the Near East, and Southeast Asia. The IMF defines an offshore banking center as a country where the banking system acquires substantial external accounts beyond those associated with economic activity in the country concerned.[1] Activities of the bank offices involve the acceptance of deposits and granting of loans in currencies other than that of the host country in which the branch or subsidiary is located. Usually, the banking operations are conducted totally or almost totally free of government regulations of the host country. *Foreign banking*, in contrast, reflects borrowing and lending primarily in the currency of the country in which the branch or subsidiary is located, generally in the larger economies.

In some respects, the activities of the OBCs are not significantly different from those of the "full service" centers. London, for example, affords many of the advantages associated with favorable reserve requirements and taxes, but is not included as one of the offshore centers. A major difference is that such traditional centers as London and New York encompass important sources and uses of funds rather than simply serving as a location for financial intermediation. Banks operating in the offshore centers borrow from depositors outside the center and make loans to nonresidents; generally, the transactions involve one of the Eurocurrencies.[2]

Offshore banking facilities are organized either as branches or subsidiaries and are located in various parts of the world. In some instances, location in a particular time zone is an advantage in terms of facilitating international transactions. More importantly, however, offices are located where their presence is encouraged by a government that imposes minimal taxes and restrictions.[3] Yet while bank operations are largely unregulated by the host government, prudence and safety are usually inherent in such activities, because generally entry is limited by the host government to the large reputable international banks.

Part of the impetus to the growth in offshore centers was a Federal Reserve authorization in the late 1960s to U.S. banks to establish "shell" branches in the Bahamas and the Cayman Islands. The objective was to

---

[1] The IMF applies the term "major offshore banking center" to the Bahamas, Bahrain, Cayman Islands, Hong Kong, the Netherlands Antilles, Panama, and Singapore. In each case, the ratio of deposit bank external assets to goods and service exports is more than three times the world average. See Joslin Landell-Mills, *The Fund's International Banking Statistics* (Washington: International Monetary Fund, 1986), p. 46.

[2] A comprehensive analysis of the use of offshore centers by U.S. and British banks is provided in R. A. Johns, *Tax Havens and Offshore Finance* (New York: St. Martin's Press, 1983).

[3] Information relating to public records and taxation for 28 "tax haven" countries is provided in Department of Treasury, Internal Revenue Service, *Tax Haven Information Book*, Document 6743 (Washington: 1982).

permit small banks that could not afford a location in a European money center an opportunity to gain access to the Eurodollar market. Operations could be established by simply maintaining a post office box in the Caribbean region, with the business actually conducted at the home office. At the end of 1985, there were about 135 branches of U.S. national banks located in the Bahamas (population, about 235,000) and Cayman Islands (population, about 20,000)—two major and two of the oldest offshore centers. Another 27 branches were located in Panama; 18 in Singapore; and 65 in Hong Kong.[4] Subsidiaries of U.S. banks also operate in offshore centers, but in terms of numbers they are not as important as branches.

Some of the offshore banking centers are also referred to as tax havens; this has a broader connotation to include areas in which the host government levies low or zero tax rates on some or all categories of income and property. Tax havens also offer banking and commercial secrecy, which frequently enhances their attractiveness.

Although tax havens are sometimes associated with a wide range of illegitimate activities, their major function is to provide a base for sound, legal activity and income.[5] Some banks, for example, have established branches in a tax haven to take advantage of a lower reserve requirement, or have established a subsidiary to gain a tax advantage. In some instances, virtually all of the work is undertaken in the parent bank office, with the OBC office simply a shell to meet the legal requirements of a physical presence. However, the attractiveness of the centers has been affected by provisions of the U.S. Tax Reform Act of 1986; it appears that there are no longer any legal ways to avoid taxes through the use of an overseas tax haven. United States banks are no longer able to defer the U.S. taxation of interest, dividends, and security gains of subsidiaries until the income is repatriated. The ability to defer such income has provided an important incentive for some types of investment abroad.

Another feature common to many offshore centers is the condition of bank secrecy. In most countries, banking laws require banks to keep customer transactions confidential. As a result, the centers are attractive to external depositors as well as banks. Generally, however, banks must provide information about customers as required by the courts or for

---

[4]Comptroller of the Currency, *Quarterly Journal* (Washington: September 1986), pp. 187-188.

[5]A detailed treatment of tax havens and their use by Americans primarily from a tax and legal perspective is provided by Richard A. Gordon, *Tax Havens and Their Use by United States Taxpayers—An Overview* (Washington: 1981).

A detailed description of banking havens, and the technique and principles of banking secrecy are provided in Edouard Chambost, *Bank Accounts: A World Guide to Confidentiality* (New York: John Wiley & Sons, 1983). Bank secrecy is presumed to be provided to afford depositors greater security as well as the opportunity for both tax avoidance and evasion.

purposes of governmental investigation. The Federal Reserve Board requires U.S. banks establishing shells in the Caymans and Bahamas to maintain records for inspection purposes at the home office in this country. United States authorities also have had some success in the use of the subpoena to secure offshore bank records, particularly if it is served on U.S. soil. The most serious problems arise when the court system of a tax haven bars a U.S. bank from releasing information as required by a U.S. court.

Switzerland has traditionally maintained an extreme position, offering numbered bank accounts and making a breach of secrecy by bank employees a criminal offense punishable by fine or imprisonment. Austria, which has become increasingly active in facilitating East-West trade, has also enacted a rigid set of secrecy laws. Some of the offshore centers, particularly Panama and the Cayman Islands, are equally reluctant to make disclosures of customer activities. Confidentiality is conducive to some transactions and assures that the offshore centers will remain permanent havens for certain activities.

Although the offshore banking centers are generally grouped together for purposes of convenience in analysis, there are wide variations in their nature and the services they provide. Panama, for example, has promoted the development of a financial service sector in an aggressive fashion only since the early 1970s. Although Panama has not allowed shell operations, generally it is the most receptive to offshore lending activity; its laws are most favorable to outside interests, and its secrecy provisions are most stringent. Some centers, such as the Bahamas and the Cayman Islands, impose a small annual license fee but assess no other taxes or levies. Because of a tax treaty with the U.S. government, the Netherlands Antilles has been a major Eurobond center for U.S. firms.

Offshore centers are utilized not only by U.S banks but by those of other major financial countries. The Bahamas, for example, were hosts for about 265 offshore banks by 1979, with about 30 percent accounted for by U.S. institutions. The Cayman Islands, another choice location, provides facilities for almost 300 banks; Hong Kong accounts for 200 offshore banks. Other offshore banking centers include Anguilla, Jersey, Netherlands Antilles, New Hebrides, Seychelles, and United Arab Emirates.

In some respects, the activities of the offshore centers and the "full service" centers are not dissimilar. The distinction between the offshore and the more traditional centers is likely to become even more blurred as a result of the establishment in the United States of International Banking Facilities.

INTERNATIONAL BANKING FACILITIES

The International Banking Facility (IBF) is largely the result of the rapid growth in U.S. branch and subsidiary activity in foreign markets and a desire by the government to return part of that activity to the United States. Because of domestic banking regulations and tax considerations, U.S. banks found it advantageous in the 1960s and 1970s to conduct an increasing share of their international business at locations outside the United States. The external locations frequently permit transactions to occur in a relatively unrestricted environment. Deposit liabilities may require minimal or no reserves, and favorable interest rates and tax considerations are provided. As noted previously, restrictions placed on United States-located banks contributed to the development of the Eurodollar market and the offshore centers in the Caymans, Bahamas, Panama, and other financial centers that offered low taxes, limited restrictions, and other concessions.

In an effort to recover and to retain activity of this type in the United States, New York state enacted legislation in 1978 that permitted banking facilities engaged primarily in international transactions to be exempt from city and state taxes. However, to be more effective in encouraging such activity, Federal Reserve Board action was necessary to exempt foreign deposits from reserve requirements and from the Regulation Q provision that specified the maximum interest payable on deposits.

After extensive study and analysis, the Federal Reserve Board authorized the establishment of International Banking Facilities in December of 1981. A basic reservation in establishing an IBF or similar type of arrangement involved the need for such monetary control instruments as required reserves against deposit liabilities. Legally required reserves and, in the past, interest rate limitations have been imposed by the Federal Reserve in its role as a central bank to implement an appropriate monetary policy and to help assure prudent lending policies on the part of individual banks. The problem faced in authorizing IBFs was a possible dilution of the effectiveness of monetary controls as a result of a shift of funds and business from the regulated types of activity into the relatively unregulated operations. This problem was resolved in part by insulating U.S. monetary activity from IBF transactions.

Essentially, the authorization permits U.S. banks to establish special adjunct facilities to accept deposits from foreigners free of reserve requirements and interest rate limitations. However, regulations limited the acceptance of IBF deposits to non-U.S. residents and other IBF holders. Furthermore, all deposit transactions must be a minimum amount of at least $100,000, and nonbank deposits require a minimum two-day maturity. Loans can be made only to foreigners with the added restriction that foreign-based, United States-controlled firms transacting business with IBFs must agree that these deposits or loans are used only for foreign activities. In addition, IBFs are exempt from insurance coverage and assessments pertaining to the Federal Deposit Insurance Corporation. Facilities may be established by any U.S. depository institution, Edge or Agreement Corporation, or U.S. office of a foreign bank. In practice, they are able to undertake business with foreigners on essentially the same basis as an offshore branch.

At the time the IBFs become operational in late 1981, an estimated 150 banks located in the United States—including both domestic and foreign-owned—applied to the Federal Reserve Board to establish the facilities. The IBFs expanded during the early years of operations, reaching a level of assets of $253 billion by May 1988, an indication of the strong interest in this new opportunity. Of the total assets, about 80 percent were held by IBFs located in the state of New York; about 20 percent, in the remaining states.[6] Thus the pattern of distribution of the new IBFs among states closely resembles the distribution of international financial activity already in existence.

LEGISLATIVE ACTION BY VARIOUS STATES

The legislative response to the opportunity created by the Federal Reserve Board varied somewhat among the different states. In many states additional legislation was not required to permit the operation of an IBF. Federal provision was also made for banks to establish an IBF through an Edge Act Corporation that they may own in another state. This was presumed to be beneficial particularly for banks that wish to establish a facility in a major financial center.

Several states have enacted laws to encourage the use of the facilities by exempting them from state and local tax laws; along with the federal concessions, facilities are made even more attractive with such exemptions. New York, the first state to provide tax concessions to IBFs, uses a complex formula to determine the extent to which taxes are reduced in connection with IBFs.

Georgia authorizes banks having capital funds of $25 million to operate an IBF subject to the approval of state authorities. Banks must be registered to operate a facility that is not subject to any tax or license fee in the state.

[6]Federal Reserve Board, "Monthly Report of Assets and Liabilities of Large International Banking Facilities" *Statistical Release* (Washington: issued monthly).

California law specifies that, for purposes of allocation of income relating to taxes, an international banking facility maintained by a bank within California is considered located outside the state. Illinois permits the income of an IBF to be reduced by a "floor" amount, which is based largely on the relative importance of foreign loans. Florida law requires that the State Department of Banks and Banking promulgate rules that create an environment conducive to the conduct of an international banking business in the state. Connecticut law permits the gross income attributable to an international banking facility to be deducted from an institution's gross income in deriving net income for tax purposes. Some IBFs exist in Kentucky, although they have not been specifically authorized by new legislation nor do they enjoy a special tax status.

The location of the 535 IBFs in operation in September of 1988 as well as the type of office to which they are attached are indicated in Table 10.1. Although the facilities have been established in about half the states, most are concentrated in the major financial centers.

The importance of IBFs to U.S. offices of foreign banks is also partially reflected in Table 10.1. The 535 offices include the agencies and branches of foreign banks, which hold about 70 percent of all IBF deposits. Some of the banks, savings and loans institutions, and Edge Corporations included in Table 10.1 are also foreign-owned.

The type of organization in which the IBFs are established is partially a reflection of the nature of international banking, as well as of legislative specifications and related factors. For example, the large number of IBFs set up by agencies and branches, especially those located in New York and California, is to a great extent the result of non-U.S. banks taking advantage of the use of such facilities. That is, a large share of the facilities are in United States-located agencies and branches of *foreign* banks. And, of course, with many of the foreign banks focusing their efforts in the financial centers, concentration is most likely to develop in New York and California.

The use of a facility by an Edge Act Corporation is based largely on legal considerations. A U.S. commercial bank generally cannot establish a branch or an agency across state boundaries. However, a U.S. bank (or bank holding company) can generally set up an Edge Act Corporation in another state in which an IBF can be established. In addition, a large share of the IBFs established by Edges in several states are owned by foreign banks, an ownership made possible by the International Banking Act of 1978.

The large number of IBFs in Edges located in Florida reflects to a great extent that state's recent and dramatic growth in international banking activity. Since the early 1970s, Florida has emerged as a specialized Latin American banking center. Many out-of-state financial institu-

TABLE 10.1   IBFs By State, September 30, 1988

State	Banks and Savings & Loans	Agencies and Branches	Edge Corpora-tions	Total
New York	46	193	16	255
California	17	68	8	93
Florida	25	29	24	78
Illinois	7	19	2	28
Texas	10	0	4	14
District of Columbia	7	3	1	11
Pennsylvania	5	2	1	8
Washington	3	4	0	7
Georgia	4	2	0	6
Ohio	6	0	0	6
Massachusetts	3	1	1	5
New Jersey	5	0	0	5
Connecticut	2	0	0	2
Delaware	2	0	0	2
Kentucky	2	0	0	2
Michigan	2	0	0	2
North Carolina	2	0	0	2
Virginia	2	0	0	2
Arkansas	0	0	1	1
Colorado	1	0	0	1
Hawaii	1	0	0	1
Louisiana	1	0	0	1
Rhode Island	1	0	0	1
South Carolina	1	0	0	1
Wisconsin	1	0	0	1
	156	321	58	535

Source: Data from Federal Reserve Board "Table of International Banking Facilities for September 30, 1988."

tions have set up Edges and IBFs in Miami and elsewhere in Florida to service this market.

As a broad generalization, the legislation of the various states appears to be more specific and detailed where IBF activity could be expected to be greatest. In general, the states tend to fall into one of three major categories. In the first group, with extensive IBF activity, the relevant state legislation provides a substantial amount of detail on the methodology by which state taxes on banks are lowered or eliminated through the use of an IBF. This is particularly true of New York, California, and Illinois.

In a second group of states in which the IBFs are moderately important, state legislation simply specifies in one of several ways that activity pertaining to IBFs is not subject to state taxation. Finally, in a third group of states in which IBFs have been established but only to a very limited extent, no provision has been made for exempting the facility from state taxation. These states are at a disadvantage in attracting the facilities as compared with states offering tax concessions.

A substantial share of the assets of the IBFs takes the form of commercial and industrial loans, and loans to foreign banks and foreign governments, most of which are denominated in U.S. dollars. Less than three percent of assets and liabilities is denominated in terms of currencies other than the U.S. dollar. Additional detail on the major assets and liabilities of the IBFs is presented in Table 10.2.

Furthermore, IBFs are likely to be established by other countries. In late 1986, the Japanese Finance Ministry authorized banks located in Japan to hold foreign deposits free of reserve requirements. The authorization is restricted to deposits and loans but is expected to be particularly attractive to those Japanese banks lacking overseas branches yet interested in participating in international finance.

TABLE 10.2   Major Assets And Liabilities Of International Banking Facilities, May 1988 (in billions of dollars)

Assets		Liabilities	
Gross claims on non-U.S. offices of establishing entity	$ 73.2	Gross liabilities due to non-U.S. offices of establishing entity	$123.6
Loans and balances due from other IBFs	43.2	Loans due to other IBFs	44.3
Commercial and industrial loans to foreigners	23.4	Amounts due banks in other countries	60.9
Loans to banks in foreign countries	28.6	Amounts due foreign governments and official institutions	12.6
Loans to foreign governments and official institutions	25.6	Amounts due other non-U.S. addresses	7.8
Total assets other than claims on U.S. offices of establishing entity	253.4	Total liabilities other than due U.S. offices of establishing entity	271.1

Source: Derived from Federal Reserve Board, "Monthly Report of Assets and Liabilities of International Banking Facilities for May 31, 1988." Washington, pp.1-3.

LOCATIONAL IMPACT OF IBFS

An important consideration of the IBFs is the extent to which banking business is attracted to New York and other states that permit the Facilities, and accordingly the extent to which such business is reduced in foreign centers. In fact, in their early efforts to secure legislation and Federal Reserve approval of IBFs, supporters emphasized the favorable impact on U.S. employment in banking and related service activities. Although the extent to which a transfer occurs cannot be readily quantified, it was expected that the shift would depend upon whether the foreign center was a "full service" or a functional center, such as those in London and other major European cities, or if it was a "shell" or "paper" operation such as those in the Bahamas and the Caymans. Generally, it was believed that the greatest impact would be on the shell operations, which have been almost as important in provision of international loans as United States-based banks.[7]

The initial evidence suggests that during the first year of operations the IBF did not contribute to a substantial amount of new business. Rather, there was either a shifting of assets and liabilities from the establishing institution to the IBFs, or had the IBFs not existed, the business would have been placed with the establishing agency.[8] For example, the asset claims of foreign branches of U.S. banks in the Bahamas (in the same time zone as New York-based IBFs) declined from $104 billion at the end of 1981 to $84 billion by early 1987.[9] Part of the decline was due to a slowdown in international lending activities, but part was due to a shift in U.S. bank activities from overseas branches to the domestic IBFs. Recent evidence also suggests that the greatest share of the growth in IBFs did not come primarily at the expense of the shell branches. Rather, the greatest decline occurred in the full service centers in the major overseas financial markets. One reason that some foreign residents may prefer to hold deposits in the Bahamas, Cayman Islands, or other offshore centers in preference to a United States-located IBF is

---

[7]Some aspects of the relationship between IBFs and the offshore banking centers are discussed in Hang-Sheng Cheng, "From the Caymans," *Weekly Letter*, Federal Reserve Bank of San Francisco (February 13, 1981), pp. 1-3.

[8]For an extensive discussion of early efforts of IBFs, see Sydney Key, "International Banking Facilities," *Federal Reserve Bulletin* (Washington: October 1982), pp. 565-577. See also Russell B. Scholl, "The International Investment Position of the United States: Developments in 1981," *Survey of Current Business* (Washington: August 1982), pp. 42-47; and George W. Trivoli, "The International Banking Facility—Threat or Opportunity?" *The Bankers Magazine* (September-October 1981), pp. 12-16.

[9]International Monetary Fund, *International Financial Statistics* (Washington: June 1987), pp. 100-101.

the fear of seizure of assets in IBFs if a confrontation developed between their government and the United States.

Other studies have concluded that the competitive position of the United States in international banking has improved following the establishment of the IBFs. For example, dollar loans and other dollar-denominated claims on foreigners held as assets by United States-located banks have increased more rapidly since late 1981 than have comparable assets held by banks outside the United States.[10]

OTHER ASPECTS OF IBFS

Over the years, the Federal Reserve eased restrictions on offshore operations through the authorization of overseas shell activities. However, the cost of establishing an offshore office was prohibitive for many small U.S. banks. Because the IBFs permit a bank to undertake shell-type operations in their domestic office without establishing a foreign branch, a cost reduction occurs that permits smaller institutions to participate in certain types of international transactions for the first time. At least initially, a number of small banks indicated an intention of establishing IBFs.[11] The inclusion of over 500 offices with such facilities suggests that many regional banks are participants.

An essential factor leading to the development of the IBFs was the willingness of legislators and government agencies to reduce the amount of regulation in order to attract or retain financial activity in the United States. This action to deregulate the activity in the financial sector is consistent with legislation of the early 1980s and corresponds with the trend toward reduced government involvement in economic activity.

International Banking Facilities are thus a recent development in an already changing and dynamic financial environment. The IBFs and the recently modified Edge Act Corporations, in conjunction with U.S. banks, will be operating within a legislative framework provided as the International Banking Act of 1978 and the Depository Institutions Deregulation and Monetary Control Act of 1980 come to be implemented.

---

[10]General Accounting Office, *International Banking Facilities Have Improved the Competitive Position of Banks in the United States* (Washington: August 7, 1984).

[11]"The Establishment of International Banking Facilities," *International Letter*, Federal Reserve Bank of Chicago (June 19, 1981), pp. 1-3.

SUMMARY AND CONCLUSIONS

For the major commercial banks participating within an international network, offshore centers have been utilized extensively to compete in world money and capital markets. International Banking Facilities have been authorized only since December of 1981, but by 1987 were already in use in about half of the states.

The rapid growth in the offshore banking centers provides support to the thesis that the expansion of international banking is to a great extent the result of the advantage available to banks in nondomestic efforts as compared with domestic efforts.[12] In contrast, the IBFs represent a decision to extend to banks the same advantages for nondomestic functions but within the domestic setting. This is also consistent with the thesis that since banking is both a "footloose" and a global industry, bank regulators in various countries will compete to establish an attractive environment that minimizes the degree of regulation.[13]

Although offshore banking centers and IBFs are useful for several purposes, a major advantage of both arrangements to the parent banks is the reduction or even elimination of the legal reserve requirement against certain types of deposits. Accordingly, bank management gains flexibility in operations in international transactions. This does not mean, of course, that banks are free to pursue imprudent policies. Ultimately, it is in the bank's own interest to maintain sufficient reserves and the degree of liquidity essential for ease of operation and confidence of depositors. Commercial banks in many European countries, for example, are not required by law to maintain a specified level of reserves against deposit liabilities, although in fact some holdings are a practical necessity.

[12]See Herbert Grubel, "Towards a Theory of Free Economic Zones," *Review of World Economics* (1982, Bank 118, Heft 1), pp. 39-61.
[13]Deborah Allen and Ian Giddy, "Towards a Theory of Interdependence in Global Banking Regulations," *Eastern Economic Journal* (December 1979), pp. 445-452.

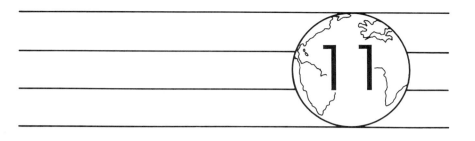

INTERNATIONAL LENDING
AND RISK

Unquestionably one of the major concerns in the area of international finance is the additional risk associated with transactions that involve participants in two or more countries. The two major risks that are of particular relevance to international banking are the exchange rate risk (analyzed in Chapter 2) and risk associated with lending. The lending risk relates to the possibility that certain developments or conditions in a foreign country may interfere with or interrupt the servicing by either public or private borrowers of their external obligations. The purpose of this chapter is to examine the general nature of this risk and to identify the related factors contributing to uncertainty in international lending.

NATURE OF LENDING RISK

Part of the risk faced by a lending bank depends upon the nature of the debtor and the ability to use loan proceeds to earn sufficient revenue for servicing obligations as they fall due. This is sometimes called the *basic* or *credit* risk, a term applied especially to private borrowers, and pertaining to domestic as well as foreign borrowers. One difference is that

generally it is more difficult to secure full and accurate credit information on a foreign borrower for use in comparison with domestic lending
opportunities.

In coping with the basic risk in the extension of loans to private
borrowers, the lending institution must investigate the credit experience
of the potential borrower, including the ability to use loan proceeds in a
productive fashion, the conditions under which debt servicing can be
undertaken, and the procedure to be followed in event of default. The
terms of the loan, including the interest rate, grace period, and the length
of loan must then be constructed to accommodate the borrower in an
appropriate and realistic manner.

Banks participating in international lending must also assess the
country risk because of the involvement of a foreign government and
country. Country risk includes *sovereign risk,* which is based on a variety
of factors within the economic, political, and social structure of a country
that influences or determines the likelihood of debt repayment. It refers
to risk assumed by a lender that a sovereign borrower (government or
government agency) or private borrower with a publicly guaranteed
loan will be unwilling or unable to make repayments. Country risk also
includes the *transfer risk* (or currency risk) in which the borrower has
earned sufficient revenue to discharge his or her obligations but for
whatever reason is not permitted to convert local currencies into the
appropriate foreign currency. Transfer risk is also related to changes in
currency values and is applicable to most international loans, since
repayment is usually made in a currency other than that of the borrowing
country.

The political dimension of country risk may arise for a number of
reasons. A new government assuming power in a debtor country may
attempt to disassociate itself from obligations created by a previous
administration. Or a decision may be made to nationalize or expropriate
foreign property and repudiate foreign debt. Another possibility is that
internal strife, such as continuing and widespread labor unrest and
strikes or political disturbances, may weaken the debtor country's productive capacity and ability to earn foreign exchange through export
sales.

MAGNITUDE OF THE DEBT PROBLEM

A borrowing country is able to use foreign exchange proceeds from the
loans to expand its productive capacity, which in turn enables it to meet
servicing obligations as they fall due. However, it may be unable to
repay with an appropriate currency because of inadequate foreign

exchange earnings. A foreign exchange shortage in turn may be the result of a decline in export prices, a rise in import prices, internal political or social instability, or even world recession. If, for whatever reason, foreign currencies cannot be earned by increased exports (or saved as a result of reduced imports), the debtor country is likely to encounter serious balance of payments problems and difficulty in meeting its servicing obligations.

Serious repayment problems characterize most of the developing countries, which in net terms are also the major borrowers. According to recent figures, the external debt of the 133 countries included by the International Monetary Fund (IMF) as developing countries amounted to about $1095 billion and was projected to reach $1223 billion by the end of 1988 (Table 11.1). This figure includes loans from all sources—banks, governments, and other lenders, as well as government guaranteed loans; it also includes short-term credits—those with a maturity of less than one year.

A large and growing share of the debt is owed by Western Hemisphere developing countries. Among the major debtor countries are Brazil, Mexico, Venezuela, and Argentina. The distribution of debt growth during the 1970s was not uniform among borrowers. An increasing share continued to be held by a relatively few countries (Brazil, Mexico, Algeria, Indonesia, Iran, South Korea, and Venezuela).

The growth in the absolute size of the external debt noted in Table 11.1 does not necessarily by itself imply a weakened position for the borrowing countries. If the loan proceeds are used for productive purposes, if the borrower enjoys a strong market for its export items, or if it is able to initiate a successful program of import substitution, it may be

TABLE 11.1 External Debt Of Developing Countries,* Select Years (billions of dollars)

	1979	1982	1986	1988
Total Outstanding Debt	$533.4	$849.6	$1094.9	$1222.9
Short-term	107.2	203.5	177.2	187.5
Long-term	426.3	646.1	917.7	1035.4
By Area				
Africa	84.8	122.2	156.3	175.3
Asia	114.4	184.2	272.3	313.9
Europe	81.0	106.8	138.2	149.3
Middle East	65.2	102.8	144.8	166.5
Western Hemisphere	188.0	333.5	383.2	417.9

Source: International Monetary Fund, *World Economic Outlook* (Washington: 1987), p. 181.
* Includes 133 countries classified by the IMF as developing countries.

able to service external obligations with little or no strain on its balance of payments and exchange position.

A more meaningful measure of potential payments problems can be derived by relating the debt servicing obligation to the capacity of the borrower to make such payments. One of the most widely used statistical measures is the debt service ratio—the ratio of interest and amortization payments to exports of goods and services. A second measure, the debt/GDP ratio, shows the ratio of the value or volume of external debt to gross domestic product. A third, the debt/export ratio, relates the value of debt to exports of goods and services.

The statistical measures are applied either to individual countries or to groups of countries. An indication of the magnitude of the values involved in aggregate terms for the developing countries for the years 1979, 1982, 1986, and 1988 is provided by the following ratios:[1]

Indicators	1979	1982	1986	1988
Debt-service ratio	14.1	19.5	22.4	20.0
Debt/GDP (percentage)	24.7	32.0	39.8	39.7
Debt/exports (percentage)	90.8	120.1	167.5	160.7

These figures reflect the change in the relative external position of the developing countries over time; for the years under consideration they suggest an unfavorable trend at least through 1986.

Ratios of this type applied to individual countries are a first reflection of the potential debt situation for that country. However, ratios must also be used cautiously and in connection with other factors for a meaningful evaluation. All other things remaining equal, a country borrowing from abroad is least likely to experience difficulties in servicing the debt when the initial investment inflow is employed in projects that are either foreign-exchange earning (expansion of exports) or foreign-exchange saving (reduction of imports); the initial grace period and the total repayment period are relatively long; the exchange reserves held by the debtor country are relatively large; the tariff and import policy of the creditor country is relatively liberal; and the debtor country's exchange earnings are relatively stable over time. The fact is that especially since

[1]International Monetary Fund, *World Economic Outlook* (Washington: 1987), pp. 186-188.

Data on the volume of external debt of developing countries and international bank lending are provided by the International Monetary Fund, the Bank for International Settlements, and the Organization for Economic Cooperation and Development. See Rachel Weaving, "Measuring Developing Countries' External Debt," *Finance and Development* (March 1987), pp. 16-19.

1982, many debtor countries, including some of the larger borrowers, have not been able to meet their external obligations.

The concern of possible default or payment delays on international obligations has intensified in recent years.[2] At the end of 1986, 57 countries were identified by the IMF as having external payments arrears or being behind schedule in meeting external financial commitments. The amount in arrears was SDR 40 billion (the equivalent of about $45 billion).[3] The payments delays were related to several types of transactions—servicing of long-term debts, remittance of profits and dividends on foreign investments, and undue delays in provision of foreign exchange for approved import transactions. Because several debtor countries were able to secure an extension of maturity dates and other concessions on external debts through a restructuring agreement, the number in arrears was lowered somewhat.

The number of debtor countries that have requested debt restructuring has also increased significantly in recent years. As described in Chapter 13, restructuring has provided debtor countries with at least temporary relief from the burden of heavy interest and amortization obligations.[4]

UNITED STATES LENDING CONTRIBUTION

As noted in Chapter 8, cross-border claims of U.S. banks amounted to about $260 billion by early 1988. United States commercial bank lending accounts for about one-third of all bank lending to developing countries. United States banks have directed a large share of their lending activities toward Latin American countries (Table 11.2). This concentration is the

[2]Default commonly refers to a creditor declaration that the borrower has failed to comply with the loan agreement. The repudiation of a loan is an explicit refusal of a borrower to pay interest and/or principal according to the agreement.

These terms are examined in Jonathan Eaton and Mark Gersovitz, "Poor-Country Borrowing in Private Financial Markets and the Repudiation Issue," *Princeton Studies in International Finance* (Princeton: Princeton University, June 1981), pp. 1-7.

A brief history of international banking and debt crises going back to ancient Babylonia is provided in Benjamin J. Cohen, "So What's New?" *In Whose Interest? International Banking and American Foreign Policy* (New Haven, Conn.: Yale University Press, 1986), pp. 83-118.

[3]Countries in payments arrears at the end of 1986 included Argentina, Bolivia, Brazil, Central African Republic, Chad, Costa Rica, People's Republic of the Congo, Dominican Republic, Ecuador, Egypt, El Salvador, The Gambia, Ghana, Guyana, Haiti, Honduras, Jamaica, Liberia, Madagascar, Mali, Nigeria, Paraguay, Peru, Poland, Senegal, Somalia, Sierra Leone, Sudan, Tanzania, Uganda, Venezuela, Vietnam, Zaire, and Zambia. Information on countries in arrears is provided in International Monetary Fund, *Exchange Arrangements and Exchange Restrictions, Annual Report* (Washington: 1987), pp. 18-19.

[4]See E. Brau and R. C. Williams, *Recent Multilateral Debt Restructurings With Official and Bank Creditors* (Washington: International Monetary Fund, December 1983).

TABLE 11.2   Major Countries Borrowing From U.S. Banks, March 1988 (billions of dollars)

Country	Amount of Debt
Newly-Industrializing Countries	
Mexico	$21.6
Brazil	20.6
Argentina	8.8
Korea, South	4.1
Taiwan	3.9
Spain	3.0
Greece	1.9
Yugoslavia	1.9
Middle Income Countries	
Chile	5.8
Philippines	4.6
Colombia	2.0
OPEC	
Venezuela	8.3
Ecuador	1.8
Indonesia	1.4
Offshore Banking Centers	
British West Indies	8.6
Hong Kong	8.5
Singapore	5.4
Bahamas	3.6
Panama	1.3

Source: Data from Federal Financial Institutions Examination Council, "Country Exposure Lending Survey," Statistical Release (Washington: July 8, 1988); country classification is based on Organization for Economic Cooperation and Development, *External Debt of Developing Countries, 1982 Survey* (Paris: 1982).

result of the relatively large volume of trade with Latin America, the high level of activity on the part of other U.S. firms in the Latin American economies, as well as their nearness to the United States. Table 11.2 indicates several categories of nonindustrialized countries that owed U.S. banks $1 billion or more by early 1988. It is apparent that the great bulk of U.S. bank lending is to the newly industrializing countries, with lesser amounts to the middle-income countries and OPEC members.

United States bank lending to a large group of low income countries (defined as those with a 1980 gross national product per capita of less than $600) is minimal. The low-income countries include India, El Salvador, Bolivia, Egypt, and many of the nations of Africa. In none of these countries do U.S. banks have investments of more than $1 billion. Many of the countries in this group depend upon loans at concessional terms from various international agencies.

Many of the countries listed in Table 11.2 have experienced balance of payments strains related to debt servicing in recent years. Most have also requested debt restructuring in recent years, including Mexico, Argentina, and Brazil, the three largest international borrowers among the developing countries.

The extent to which major U.S. banks hold investments in countries experiencing payments deficits varies not only from country to country, but also from bank to bank. For example, of the ten largest U.S. banks lending to three Latin American countries (Mexico, Brazil, and Venezuela), the largest volume of loans outstanding of one bank to one country was $4.36 billion; this amount represented about 5.1 percent of that bank's total outstanding loans. Generally, however, for this group of banks, the portion of loans outstanding to a single country was about 3.5 percent.[5]

FACTORS CONTRIBUTING TO REPAYMENT PROBLEMS

The large volume of U.S. bank loans and subsequent repayment problems have raised questions regarding the wisdom of lending during the 1970s and early 1980s. Was the debt burden the result of unforeseen adverse economic conditions? Or did U.S. commercial banks overextend themselves in their loans abroad? The argument has been made that banks failed to adopt prudent lending policies during the 1970s, especially with respect to the developing countries. But it can also be argued that banks played an essential role in recent years in providing resources that would otherwise have been required of national governments or international institutions.[6]

Many of the developing, borrowing countries were seeking to open their economies to world trade and investment during the 1970s. Many were able to achieve high rates of economic growth during the first part of that decade. During the entire period, the losses of U.S. commercial banks on foreign credits were lower than on domestic lending, providing banks with the incentive to expand their foreign lending despite the additional types of risk they encountered.

---

[5]"Big Bank Problems—Nation Loans Exceed Equity," *American Banker* (March 17, 1983), pp. 1-6.

[6]For a discussion, see F. John Mathis, "Lessons Learned from International Debt Rescheduling," *The Journal of Commercial Bank Lending* (January 1983), pp. 15-25.

The reasons for the debt servicing problem experienced by countries since the early 1980s vary from country to country but are associated with several basic and somewhat interrelated elements. Perhaps the most important was the need to use loan proceeds and other available foreign exchange to secure essential petroleum imports; these were used for balance of payments purposes for which there was little or no productive capacity generated that would facilitate debt repayment. A second contributing factor was the declining terms of trade for primary producing countries. The relative decrease in prices of primary commodity exports lowered the foreign exchange earning capacity of many of the borrowing countries. This condition, in fact, also applies to at least a few of the oil-exporting countries, including Mexico, which borrowed heavily from abroad in anticipation of a growing market for high-priced petroleum exports. A related element was the low rate of growth of many European countries and subsequent weak demand for primary imports.

Another aspect contributing to repayment difficulties was the imposition of a variable interest rate on loans which, in connection with worldwide inflation, resulted in higher interest rates and an expanding interest expense. "Capital flight"—short-term speculative capital outflows—which absorbed foreign exchange that might have been used for debt servicing, also has had an adverse impact. Such flights were particularly large for Argentina, Mexico, and Venezuela during the late 1970s and early 1980s.[7] In a few countries, political unrest sharply reduced the export potential and also increased import needs. Finally, in at least some cases loans were made that reflected less than prudent practices.

Perhaps the major factor contributing to uncertainty in international financial markets during and since the 1970s relates directly or indirectly to petroleum. Since the OPEC action in 1973, many oil-importing developing countries experienced growing balance of payments deficits. These countries found it necessary to continue importing oil, capital goods, and other items, part of which was financed directly or indirectly out of the cash surplus of the OPEC countries.

After the end of 1973, the commercial banking sector played a major role in these transactions. Official institutions, including the IMF and the World Bank, made a much smaller contribution to the alleviation of the deficit problems of the oil-importing countries.[8] Commercial banks participated in the "recycling" process by serving as an intermediary—channeling payments surpluses of certain countries, including OPEC nations,

---

[7]See John T. Cuddington, "Capital Flight: Estimates, Issues, and Explanations," *Princeton Studies in International Finance* (December 1986).

[8]For a discussion of the role of commercial banks, see *International Financial Cooperation: A Framework for Change*, ed. Salah Al-Shaikhly (London: Frances Pinter, Publishers, 1981).

to the deficit countries. However, these same banks also faced serious consequences as the borrowing countries, while benefiting from the proceeds of the loans for use in continued importation, also acquired the burden of a growing external debt and found it difficult or impossible to make repayments. Banks generally were not discouraged in their recycling efforts by their respective governments, and serious international financial problems were averted or at least postponed. But the subsequent decline in petroleum prices and OPEC cash surpluses, the increased frequency of debt restructuring, and the perception that some banks may not have followed prudent lending policies placed a damper on this type of banking effort by 1983. And while many borrowing countries became increasingly dependent upon external funding, lending banks have become increasingly reluctant to make it available.

Debt servicing problems of developing countries were intensified as a result of higher interest rates, especially as the use of a variable or floating-rate debt became widespread. Under these arrangements, the basic rate is tied to some publicized rate such as the London Interbank Offer Rate (LIBOR) with a premium added depending upon the borrower and the terms of the credit. The rate is also adjusted periodically to reflect movements in the LIBOR. This arrangement permits lenders to provide loans of an extended maturity at a charge near the current rate of interest. While it facilitates access to capital during periods of inflation and rising interest rates, it also results in increased servicing costs for borrowers. The interest rate paid by developing countries on floating-rate debt has been about double that on fixed-rate debt. For example, the respective rates were estimated by the Organization for Economic Cooperation and Development to be 17.5 percent and 7.9 percent for 1982.[9] A shift in the variable rate also has a significant impact on the financial position of lenders and borrowers. For example, with a floating-rate debt of $400 billion, an increase or decrease of one percent in the rate alters annual interest payments by $4 billion.

A low rate of economic growth in some of the industrialized countries and a decline in the growth rate of world trade, along with deteriorating terms of trade for the commodity-producing countries, have also had a serious impact on most of the developing debtor countries. For example, the IMF's terms of trade index for the nonfuel-exporting developing countries has declined by an average of one percent to two percent during most of the years between 1979 and 1986, although some improvement has occurred since the beginning of 1987. The sharpest decreases occurred in 1980 and 1981, in turn contributing to serious repayment

[9]Organization for Economic Cooperation and Development, *External Debt of Developing Countries: 1982 Survey* (Paris: 1982), p. 11.

problems in subsequent years.[10] Thus the developing countries have found that, as a result of the decline in the relative value of their commodity exports, it became increasingly difficult to earn the foreign exchange needed to secure essential imports as well as to service their debts.[11]

OIL-EXPORTING DEBTOR COUNTRIES

Although attention during the 1970s centered on debt problems of the oil-importing debtor countries, new attention has also been directed toward several oil-exporting countries that had anticipated a growing demand and favorable petroleum prices. Some of these countries, especially Mexico, Nigeria, Venezuela, and Indonesia, incurred large external debts, which presumably would be partially serviced out of petroleum exports. However, a decline in petroleum prices caused by a reduction in world demand, the inability of OPEC to maintain production controls, and an increase in energy production in other parts of the world have had a serious impact on the current account position and the ability of this particular group of countries to meet interest and amortization obligations. Other oil-exporting countries that are major borrowers include Algeria, Ecuador, Egypt, Malaysia, and Peru.

Mexico's debt restructuring effort in 1982 illustrates the culmination of events that has led to concern about some of the oil-exporting countries. The discovery of new oil reserves in 1977 provided the incentive for a substantial growth in Mexican government expenditures, part of which was financed by short-term external borrowings. The worldwide recession of 1982-1983, combined with a disagreement among OPEC countries on price and marketing policies, led to a weakening of oil prices and a deterioration in Mexico's balance of payments position. Although Mexico's merchandise exports in 1982 amounted to about $20 billion, the annual interest on external debt had increased to almost $10 billion. Action on the part of the IMF, the U.S. and Mexican governments, and several major creditor banks averted a serious crisis in 1982, which conceivably could have damaged the entire international banking system.[12]

[10]International Monetary Fund, *World Economic Outlook* (Washington: 1987), p. 147; and International Monetary Fund, "Commodity Prices Rise Sharply in 1987," *IMF Survey* (May 30, 1988), pp. 161, 166-167.

[11]A useful survey of the debt problem is provided by Leelananda Silva, "The Debt Dilemma," *Development Issue Papers for the 1980s* (New York: United Nations Development Programme, February 1985).

[12]"Mexico's International Debt," *International Letter*, Federal Reserve Bank of Chicago (December 17, 1982), pp. 1-4.

ADVERSE IMPACT ON BANKS
AND THE FINANCIAL SYSTEM

Although balance of payments strains and debt rescheduling have become common in international finance, no major banks have failed as a direct result of international loan losses since this type of lending expanded in the late 1960s and 1970s. Three major international banks have failed in recent years, not as a result of international loan losses, but of a combination of other factors, including mismanagement and losses in foreign exchange dealings: I. D. Herstatt in 1974 (Germany), Franklin National Bank in 1974 (United States), and Banco Ambrosiano in 1982 (Italy). However, as a result of the increased frequency of requests for debt restructuring, the country risk factor is now considered to be a potential contributor to insolvency of creditor commercial banks. In addition, many creditor banks have found it necessary to make significant profit and loss and balance sheet adjustments to reflect a realistic financial position. As noted in the following chapter, many U.S. creditor banks did not alter the value of their claims to reflect market conditions until 1987. Accordingly, the earnings statement of many banks reflected significant losses in 1987.

What is the potential impact of default on the part of one or more major debtor countries? Could the international financial system, including the commercial community, readily absorb the shock of major defaults? Or would it, in fact, trigger a crisis that would weaken the entire international banking system? The most serious situation would occur if the volume of defaults were large enough that it precipitated a financial disturbance that threatened the entire international banking system.

One analyst writing in 1980 suggests that defaults by developing countries, even if they occurred on a widespread basis, would not necessarily seriously threaten the stability of the international financial system. Default would adversely affect some banks and private lenders and force some into bankruptcy. Such losses could be absorbed, however, and there need not be grave damage to the Eurocurrency market or to national financial systems. However, debt default should be avoided, but the technique used should be primarily to promote development assistance to some of the debtor countries.[13]

Recommendations from the International Commission on International Development Issues reflect the concern of a potentially serious problem; they also call for major changes if world economic collapse is to be avoided. This commission, established in 1977 to study the global

---

[13]See Peter B. Kenen, "Debt Relief as Development Assistance," *Essays in International Economics*, ed. Peter B. Kenen (Princeton: Princeton University Press, 1980), pp. 388-415.

issues arising from disparities within the world community, offered several major recommendations during a 1982 meeting, some of which were rather drastic. The commission urged that IMF resources be increased to expand world liquidity and to aid the developing countries; that efforts of the World Bank be increased to assist in world development; and that government creditors waive all official debt owed by the least developed countries. The commission noted that such measures represent a minimum to be undertaken given the severity of global economic conditions.[14]

Outright repudiation by a major debtor country such as Mexico or Brazil in all likelihood would lead to an international financial crisis. But the nature and impact of a serious crisis in international banking cannot be projected readily. According to a study for the IMF, a crisis in international banking could lead to a disruption of the international payments mechanism, be disruptive of some types of banking services, and sharply reduce the levels of financial intermediation at the international level.[15]

Because of the variability of conditions relevant to extensive default, it is difficult to anticipate the overall impact. The dimensions and repercussions of a total default on debts would depend upon the magnitude of losses, the extent to which private commercial banks are affected and prepared to cope with losses, political considerations, and the extent to which public institutions are prepared to react to the situation. Although widespread default is not anticipated, as noted in the following chapters the concern is sufficiently serious to cause governments of the major industrial countries to consider additional precautionary measures.

The concern with possible widespread default on debts and the subsequent impact on commercial banks and the international financial system has been intensified by several other situations that have contributed to financial uncertainty in recent years. These include the rapid growth in the Eurocurrency market, severe and worldwide inflation, uncertainty that may have arisen with the shift to floating exchange rates, significant changes in the international value of the dollar, and in part perhaps the large number of commercial banks that have entered the

---

[14]"Brandt Commission Issues a Set of Proposals Directed to Averting World Economic Collapse," *IMF Survey* (February 21, 1983), pp. 61-62; see also D. T. Llewellyn, "Avoiding an International Banking Crisis, *National Westminster Bank Quarterly Review* (August 1982), pp. 28-39.

An analysis of three stages of serious international problems—a credit crunch, mild financial crisis, and severe crisis—is provided in Wharton Econometric Forecasting Associates, "The World Economy at a Crossroads: International Financial Crunch, Crisis or Crash?" *Wharton Special Report* (Washington, February 1983).

[15]G. G. Johnson and Richard Abrams, *Aspects of the International Banking Safety Net* (Washington: International Monetary Fund, March 1983).

world financial market for the first time. Another contributing factor is the unusually high U.S. bank failure rate since 1983, stemming largely from losses on domestic loans to agriculture, real estate, and the energy sectors. Finally, the apparent insolvency of an estimated 500 thrift institutions in the United States has added to uncertainty in the financial markets.

Inflationary pressures and balance of payments strains contributed to instability in the international payments system during the 1970s. Another aspect of the uncertainty is based on the rapid growth of the Eurocurrency market, although, as noted previously, the potential for monetary expansion and inflation may not be as great as initially expected. The collapse of the pegged exchange rate system led to some uncertainty in the foreign exchange markets in the mid-1970s, although the markets have since at least partially adjusted to the new system that gradually came to be established. Yet the sharp appreciation of the U.S. dollar from 1980 through early 1985 and its subsequent depreciation, coupled with a massive current account deficit, has resulted in new protectionist pressures, a situation that could be damaging to the debtor countries.

External debts and debt-related austerity programs of the developing countries have contributed to a negative impact on U.S. trade balances with these countries. Many of the debtor countries have restricted imports in order to be able to finance interest and principal repayments abroad. United States exports to the debtor countries have declined in relative terms especially in motor vehicles and equipment, primary iron and steel manufactures, and chemicals.[16]

The concern with commercial banks' external debt has also been intensified by the large volume of doubtful loans of banks against domestic borrowers, especially in the agricultural, energy, and real estate sectors. As a basis for comparison, by the end of 1987, the 4624 reporting *national* banks identified total loans and leases past due as follows:[17]

Domestic	$53.4 billion
Foreign	$ 8.5 billion

The United States has experienced an unusually high number of bank failures since 1982, but most have been related to domestic loan losses. Nevertheless, the failures have placed an additional strain on the entire U.S. banking system.

---

[16]See International Trade Commission, *The Effect of Developing Country Debt-Servicing Problems on U.S. Trade* (Washington: March 1987).

[17]Comptroller of the Currency, *Quarterly Journal* (Washington: June 1988), p. 169.

SUMMARY AND CONCLUSIONS

Although commercial bank activity at the international level has increased dramatically in recent years, the level of uncertainty and degree of risk also appear to have increased. Much of the uncertainty in world financial markets relates to the debtor countries, who greatly expanded their external obligations during the 1970s and early 1980s, and to their current inability to continue servicing external obligations. During the years 1979 to 1986, the interest payments of the developing countries increased from about \$35 billion to about \$74 billion each year. An increasing share of this amount is owed to commercial banks; the difficulties encountered by the borrowing countries in earning foreign exchange for repayment purposes coupled with the growing number of countries in payments arrears and seeking debt rescheduling have placed many large creditor banks in an uneasy position.

The debt repayment problem may be the most serious international financial problem, but it is only part of the development and change in international finance. The shift to floating exchange rates, major changes in the relative value of the dollar, yen, and mark, the large number of banks with limited experience in world commerce, and deregulation of U.S. financial institutions are also part of the framework within which the system is evolving. But another part of the change includes efforts on the part of individual banks, governments, and international institutions to reduce the degree and type of risk.

Are the commercial banking community, central banks, and international financial institutions properly equipped to avoid or to cope with widespread default on international obligations or with major bank failures? An answer to this question requires an examination of the various methods of reducing risk and adjusting to nonpayment of claims—by banks, governments, and international institutions. These efforts are examined in the following chapters.

COPING WITH RISK
AND REPAYMENT
PROBLEMS IN
INTERNATIONAL LENDING

During the 1970s, the role of commercial banks in facilitating the flow of short- and long-term flows across national boundaries became increasingly significant. United States banks were the most important participants in these activities; by early 1988, the major domestic and foreign offices of U.S. banking organizations held cross-border claims of $267 billion. However, over one-fourth of this amount applied to countries that were in payments arrears or had experienced repayment problems to the extent that rescheduling had taken place. Because of the large number of banks and the volume of capital involved, a variety of techniques and procedures have been devised: **(a)** to avoid and to alleviate risks associated with international commercial bank lending; and **(b)** to cope with situations in which repayments are not being made on schedule. Actions have been initiated by the banks themselves and supplemented by efforts of the government. The purpose of this chapter is to examine methods used by U.S. banks and the U.S. government to cope with risk and nonpayment in international lending, particularly to developing countries.

Commercial banks are a major source of funds to the developing countries, but as quasi-private institutions they must appraise the debt burden faced by the borrowing countries in terms of the potential impact on their own liquidity, profitability, and solvency.[1] Given the rate of return on their lending operations, banks must seek to minimize the degree of risk associated with transactions.

COUNTRY DIVERSIFICATION

One important method of risk reduction is accomplished by extending loans to a large number of borrowers. When individual banks diversify their lending among several countries, they are able to limit their country exposure—the total amount of loans outstanding to a country as a portion of the capital of the bank. Loan diversification requires a greater amount of information and knowledge than is the case with a more concentrated exposure. Yet diversification of lending is particularly essential among developing countries because of their heavy reliance on one or a few primary commodities, the consequent instability of foreign exchange earnings, possible political instability, and other factors.

For the small- or medium-sized bank, diversification is accomplished most easily through participation in syndicated loans. Another possible advantage of syndicated loans is that a large lead bank assumes initial responsibility for securing information on the risk associated with potential borrowers.

For a given bank, diversification requires that attention be given to the entire loan portfolio, not only in terms of geographic and industry coverage, but also in terms of the spread of loan maturities. Essentially the portfolio must reflect a blending of income maximization, risk reduction, and asset liquidity.

QUANTIFICATION OF COUNTRY RISK

Perhaps the most important preventative measure that can be undertaken by the lending bank is to assess as carefully as possible the likelihood of the public or private borrower earning and/or securing the foreign exchange needed for repayment purposes. In the case of the private borrower, the information needed for a full assessment may not be readily available. In the case of government (or government agency)

---

[1]An analysis of methods used by commercial banks to reduce lending risk is provided by Janice Westerfield, "A Primer on the Risks of International Lending and How to Avoid Them," *Business Review*, Federal Reserve Bank of Philadelphia (July/August 1978), pp. 19-28. See also Laurie S. Goodman, "Can Risks in LDC Lending Be Diversified?" *Business Economics* (March 1982), pp. 12-19; and William R. Cline, *Mobilizing Bank Lending to Debtor Countries* (Washington: Institute for International Economics, June 1987).

borrowers, an evaluation of the economic and political viability of the country in terms of the factors that may affect its balance of payments position becomes necessary.

Assessing the country risk includes examining various types of information that can be readily quantified, but it also requires consideration of equally important factors that are not readily quantifiable—political instability, likelihood of nationalization of property, the possibility of economic sanctions being imposed on the country, or other related developments.

One of the systems for assessment of this risk uses the marketplace as a reflection of uncertainties that arise in international lending activities. This rating system, developed by the Euromoney Syndication Service and published regularly in *Euromoney*, considered each country's loans in terms of the volume of loans, spread, and maturity.[2] Specifically

$$\text{Average weighted spread } (\%) = \frac{\Sigma \text{ volume} \times \text{spread} \times \text{maturity}}{\Sigma \text{ volume} \times \text{maturity}}$$

Spread is identified as the margin between the applicable interest rate and some interbank rate. It is used as an indication of the degree of risk; a wide (narrow) spread reflects a borrower with a weak (strong) credit rating.

Euromoney has modified its approach on the assumption that the cost of funds alone is not an adequate indication of a country's credit standing. Criteria used in the revised country credit rating include market indicators (the borrowing country's access to markets and trade finance, and "selldown," which is defined as a measure of oversubscription), credit indicators (difficulties in rescheduling of loans), and analytical indicators (political risk, and economic indicators based on specified external debt ratios). In its assessment of countries in mid-1987, *Euromoney* ranked Switzerland, Japan, the United States, and West Germany as low-risk countries. At the other extreme, high-risk countries included Lebanon, Iraq, Libya, Swaziland, and Uganda.[3]

Another approach to evaluation of creditworthiness of countries and the likelihood of debt default is provided on a semiannual basis by *Institutional Investor*. *Institutional Investor*'s country credit ratings are judgmental in nature; a confidential survey is made of 75 to 100 of the world's leading bankers, who are requested to rank each country on a

[2]"The Country Risk League Table," *Euromoney* (February 1980), pp. 40-46.

[3]Quek Peck Lim, "The Euromoney Country Risk Ratings," *Euromoney* (September 1986), pp. 364-365; and Matthew Barrett, "The Euromoney Country Risk Ratings," *Euromoney* (September 1987), pp. 353-357.

scale of zero to 100. The responses are then weighted according to an *Institutional Investor* formula to develop the country's financial ranking.

In an assessment of 109 countries in early 1987, Japan, West Germany, Switzerland, the United States, and the Netherlands were ranked by *Investor* as low-risk countries. At the other extreme, the high risk calculations applied to Sudan, North Korea, Nicaragua, and Uganda.[4]

Frequently there have been significant ranking differences between *Euromoney* and *Institutional Investor*, in part because of the approaches used. The disparities indicate that bankers' attitudes and decisions do not always reflect what might appear to be objective market information. Second, both approaches must weight the statistical inputs to develop a final index. Regardless of how carefully the weighting system is constructed and undertaken, some bias is likely to develop. A third possible reason for the difference between the rankings of the two services could be attributed to the reference point or period of time; unexpected political instability in a particular country, for example, may not be reflected in one index, yet may appear in the second. Variations in rankings also suggest the imprecise nature of risk assessment.

Other approaches have been developed to assess the likelihood of nonrepayment of external obligations. The increasing availability of debt and economic data to creditors has prompted an interest in the use of statistical models to predict the likelihood of debt crises on the part of borrowing countries. These models typically include statistical indicators of debt and trade as independent variables: the debt service ratio, which indicates a country's capacity to cover debt service payments out of current export earnings; the amortization rates, which reflect the average repayment period or bunching of maturities; and the import/exchange reserve ratio. Success in the use of statistical methods has been limited by definitional problems, unavailability of data, and the difficulty of quantifying some relevant determinants. And there is the self-fulfilling prophecy difficulty—a country may experience a debt crisis if one is expected.[5]

The limited success of the statistical methods indicates the need for improved techniques or approaches to assess and reduce the degree of risk. It also raises the question of whether, even after private banking institutions have made every effort to reduce the degree of lending risk, there is still a need for public institutional arrangements at either the

---

[4]"Country Credit Ratings," *Institutional Investor* (March 1987), pp. 267-270.

[5]Summaries of statistical methods for predicting debt rescheduling are provided by E. M. Manfredi, "Predicting Debt Reschedulings in Developing Countries," *Agricultural Economics Research* (April 1981), pp. 26-30; and Rainer Erbe and Susanne Schattner, "Indicator Systems for the Assessment of the External Debt Situation of Developing Countries," *Intereconomics* (November-December 1980), pp. 285-289.

national or international level to forestall or cushion the impact of potential country default.

OVERSEAS PRIVATE INVESTMENT CORPORATIONS

Commercial banks may find the risk of nonrepayment sufficiently high to warrant securing some type of guarantee. United States banks, along with firms from other types of industries, are able to cope with certain risks through the government-owned Overseas Private Investment Corporation (OPIC). Through this corporation, U.S. companies pay a premium generally ranging from 0.3 to 0.6 percent for coverage of new investments against losses due to currency inconvertibility, expropriation, and war, revolution, or insurrection. An insured U.S. bank can then file a claim for reimbursement if it is not permitted by a foreign government to convert foreign currency earnings into dollars, or if its overseas property is expropriated, or incurs wartime damage.

Since it was first authorized under the Economic Cooperation Act in 1948, the insurance program has been implemented under different U.S. agencies. Coverage is limited to about 100 low-income countries and areas with which the U.S. government has established an implementing agreement. Although most of the users of OPIC have not been banks, at least a few large U.S. financial institutions with major overseas holdings, including American Express Bank Limited, BankAmerica, and Citicorp, have utilized the provisions of the corporation. In addition, U.S. banks have been awarded settlement payments because of war damage in the Dominican Republic, inconvertibility in the Philippines and Vietnam, and expropriation in Chile.[6]

The U.S. Export-Import Bank also provides guarantees for U.S. commercial banks on loans designed to promote American export sales abroad. Coverage is available for export loans only where there is a reasonable prospect of repayment. The Bank paid claims by private U.S. banks in 1983 against delinquent loans of Mexican buyers; the loans were not in default but were 30 to 90 days in arrears following the Mexican government's devaluation of the peso and imposition of stringent foreign exchange restrictions.[7]

---

[6]Subcommittee on International Economic Policy, House of Representatives, *Extension and Revision of Overseas Private Investment Corporation Programs* (Washington: 1981); Overseas Private Investment Corporation, *1986 Annual Report* (Washington: 1986).

[7]Export-Import Bank, *Annual Report* (Washington: 1982).

An analysis of insurance schemes is provided by Henry C. Wallich, *Insurance of Bank Lending to Developing Countries* (New York: Group of Thirty, 1984).

Provision of such guarantees, of course, is not limited to the U.S. government. The use of some type of guarantee by the government of either the lending or the borrowing country is relatively widespread among trading countries.

ASSET VALUATION AND LOAN-LOSS RESERVES

The use of loan-loss reserves is a standard practice for commercial banks in anticipation of some noncollectible loans. The level of loss reserves and decisions relating to asset valuation are of greater significance as a growing number of debtor countries experience payments arrears and request debt restructuring. United States banks are generally required to place loans receivable on a "nonperforming" basis when doubts arise regarding their collectibility—usually 90 days after a debtor fails to meet an interest payment. Interest received on nonperforming loans can be recorded only when received.

The restructuring of loans (examined more fully in Chapter 13) also poses problems relating to asset valuation and liquidity. Restructuring occurs either by refinancing (replacing existing loans with new ones with better terms) or rescheduling (extension of maturity dates of existing loans). Frequently, troubled debt restructuring consists of altering the terms of credit to reduce required payments in the short run in an attempt to help the debtor improve its position and discharge its obligations in the long run. The extension of maturity dates may reduce the liquidity position of banks holding the loans. In some instances, rescheduled loans must be considered as substandard, especially in comparison with those for which interest and amortization payments are made on schedule.[8] Thus creditor banks must determine the value of nonperforming and rescheduled loans, how they should be treated for balance sheet purposes, whether or not they should be considered in a nonaccrual status, and the level of reserves to be set aside to cover possible losses.

The Financial Accounting Standards Board (FASB), established in the United States in 1973, has the major purpose of developing generally accepted accounting principles in the United States. The FASB has a strong and pervasive influence on accounting practices followed by U.S. businesses, including banks and other financial institutions. Accounting policy relating to debt restructuring and the occurrence of troubled debt

---

[8]The Securities and Exchange Commission requires each bank either to list all nations to which it has lent more than one percent of loans outstanding, or to disclose loans to countries that they determine have liquidity problems. See Securities and Exchange Commission, *Staff Accounting Bulletin* (October 1986).

is included in Financial Accounting Standards No. 15. Troubled debt restructuring occurs if a creditor, for economic or legal reasons related to the debtor's financial situation, grants a concession that would not otherwise be provided. Creditors are required to account for troubled debt to accurately reflect the quality of assets and potential for income in a way carefully prescribed by FASB guidelines. The FASB also prescribes the accounting procedures for losses associated with troubled debts.[9]

Commercial banks were permitted for a time by law to prepare for possible loan losses with appropriate amounts charged against operating income; the amounts set aside for anticipated loan losses were tax free. The authority to maintain a tax deductible reserve has been controversial. Banks argue that such provisions reflect a prudent policy and a recognition that some loans will not be repaid. Yet the provisions are criticized by others, who argue they are a tax shelter and that loan losses should be deducted from income only when they occur.

For several years, banks were authorized to maintain a tax deductible reserve against bad debts equivalent to 1.8 percent (1970-1975) and 1.2 percent (1976-1981) of outstanding eligible loans. The permissible rate was reduced to 1.0 percent for tax year 1982, and to 0.6 percent for the tax years 1983 through 1987. As an alternative, a bank could choose to maintain a loss reserve equivalent in amount to the actual losses experienced during the current and five preceding years. For the years following 1987, banks are required to base the bad debt deduction on their own actual experience for a six-year period. They are permitted to maintain a higher level of reserves, but the excess amounts are not deductible for tax purposes; rather, they are a transfer from equity capital to reserve for bad debts.[10] They may also be required to maintain special loss reserves related solely to value-impaired international loans.

The Tax Reform Act of 1986 made changes that affect the calculation of losses on bad debts. Beginning January 1, 1987, large commercial banking organizations—those with assets over $500 million—must use a specific charge-off approach rather than the reserve method. In effect, large banks are not allowed the advantage of tax deductions until loans

---

[9]Financial Accounting Standards Board, *Financial Accounting Standards* (Stanford, Conn.: 1980), pp. 937-948.

[10]A brief description of the provision for loan losses is provided in Oliver G. Wood, Jr. and Robert J. Porter, *Analysis of Bank Financial Statements* (New York: Van Nostrand Reinhold Company, 1979), p. 13.

Provisions for establishing loan-loss reserves were included in the Tax Reform Act of 1969. For a more complete description, see Commerce Clearing House, *Federal Tax Guide 1983* (Chicago: 1983), pp. 1667-1668, and Richard E. Wilson, "Bank Accounting and Reporting: Current Status and Outlook," *Bankers Desk Reference 1982 Yearbook,* ed. Edwin B. Cox (Boston: Warren, Gorham & Lamont, Inc., 1982), pp. 109-140. See also Jane Baird, "How Good Are Bad Loan Reserves?" *Institutional Investor* (April 1983), pp. 165-167.

are actually written off. Provisions are also made for including the balance in existing reserves in taxable income.[11]

COUNTRY EXPOSURE
AND A SUPERVISORY SYSTEM

Another approach to lending risk and repayment problems, described as a country risk examination system, was initiated by the U.S. monetary authorities in an effort to provide improved information and a better understanding of overseas lending practices of commercial banks. Because of the growing involvement of U.S. banks in world money and capital markets, the Federal Reserve System surveys and analyzes bank lending to ensure that foreign activities of U.S. banks do not lead to serious and extensive defaults and thus jeopardize the domestic monetary system. The supervisory system adopted by the Federal Reserve, the Comptroller of the Currency, and the Federal Deposit Insurance Corporation is under the direction of the Interagency Country Exposure Review Committee (ICERC). This system went into effect in 1979 but has been modified to comply with guidelines contained in the International Lending Supervision Act of 1983.[12]

One objective of the country risk examination system is to encourage and accommodate banks to achieve sufficient investment diversification among countries to reduce lending risk. To accomplish this, ICERC attempts to identify countries with actual or potential problems in servicing external obligations, to inform the creditor banks of problem countries, and to evaluate the exposure management systems of such banks.

The Review Committee uses survey data contained in the semiannual report entitled "Country Exposure Lending Survey Statistical Release" as a basis for evaluating country risk trends and exposures. The data cover all U.S. banks with substantial foreign operations (approxi-

---

[11]See Stanley Yellin, "Highlights of the Tax Reform Act of 1986," *Bank Performance Annual* (Boston: Warren, Gorham & Lamont, Inc., 1987), pp. 43-55; and Yolanda K. Henderson, "The Taxation of Banks: Particular Privileges or Objectionable Burdens," *New England Economic Review*, Federal Reserve Bank of Boston (May/June 1987), pp. 3-18. A useful summary of the implications of bank loans to foreign countries with respect to revised U.S. tax laws is provided by George E. French, "The New Foreign Tax Rules and Their Significance for Banks," *Regulatory Review*, Federal Deposit Insurance Corporation (February 1987), pp. 1-14.

[12]A summary of the supervision of country exposure is provided in Comptroller of the Currency, *Annual Report* (Washington: various issues). See also Roger Kubarych, "Country Risk Analysis for Supervisory Purposes," *Research Paper*, Federal Reserve Bank of New York (March 1981).

mately 185 in number). They include claims against individual countries by type of borrower (bank, public, and other private), by maturity structure (one year and under, over one year to five years, and over five years), and by country guarantor. The condition of about 75 debtor countries is monitored in this process. The major statistical indicators applied to each country reviewed are

1. Current account balances as a percentage of goods and services exports.
2. Three-year cumulative current account balance as a percentage of 3-year average goods and services exports.
3. Net interest payments as a percentage of goods and services exports.
4. Net interest payments as a percentage of international reserves, excluding gold.
5. Debt service payments as a percentage of goods and services exports. An effort is also made to incorporate information relating to social and political stability, country studies, and any other relevant data into the analysis.

The debtor countries are then grouped by the ICERC into one of seven categories:

1. *Strong.* No perceivable repayment concerns.
2. *Moderately strong.* Potential repayment difficulties, but not a major concern.
3. *Weak.* Repayment problems, but likelihood of correction.
4. *Other transfer risk problems.* Repayment problems, but efforts being made to correct.
5. *Substandard.* Repayment difficulties and no evidence of corrective efforts.
6. *Value impaired.* Prolonged debt service arrearages and no definite prospects of repayment.
7. *Loss.* Loans considered uncollectible.

The ICERC designations in Categories 4, 5, 6, and 7 are disseminated to banks with applicable exposures. Country exposure information in Categories 5, 6, and 7 must be used by the appropriate regulatory agencies in the evaluation of a bank's asset quality and capital and reserve adequacy during the periodic examination process.

Banks may be required by the federal banking agencies to establish special reserves called allocated transfer risk reserves (ATRRs) for assets against countries in the "value impaired" category (Category 6). This occurs if there is a possibility that an asset cannot be serviced because of a lack of foreign exchange or restraints on the use of foreign exchange on the part of the debtor country—usually if there are prolonged debt servicing arrearages. Prolonged arrearages are reflected in the failure of the debtor country to make full interest payments, to comply with terms of any restructured indebtedness arrangement, to comply with IMF conditions or other adjustment programs, or where there are no definite prospects for an orderly restoration of debt service. The ATRRs are usually set initially at 10 percent of value-impaired exposures. In subsequent years, required reserves may be raised to 15 percent.

For accounting purposes, ATRRs are established by a charge to current income and must be maintained separately from other allowances for possible loan losses. Furthermore, they cannot be included as part of the bank's capital or surplus. Noninclusion in the capital accounts adversely affects banks from a regulatory perspective, since capital-to-asset ratios are not improved. As an alternative to creating an ATRR, a bank may write down the value of the specified asset by an equivalent amount.

Exposures in the loss category (Category 7) must be written off completely by the creditor banks. Such loans are assumed to be uncollectible.[13]

An illustration of the significance of ICERC classification and the dilemma faced by creditor banks is provided in the case of Brazil in 1987. Brazil discontinued making interest payments on loans in early 1987, and difficulties arose in subsequent negotiations to establish a repayment program acceptable to Brazil and her major creditors. Some consideration was given by the ICERC to requiring U.S. creditor banks to downgrade Brazilian loans from "substandard" (Category 5) to "value impaired" (Category 6); however, an agreement was subsequently reached whereby Brazil would commence interest repayments in exchange for additional bank loans.[14] As a result, U.S. banks were not required to establish the 10 percent ATRRs, but they were expected to increase their Brazilian exposure through the extension of additional loans.

Although ICERC credit ratings have traditionally not been publicized, information was obtained in 1988 on some debtor countries. Nine countries (Argentina, Chile, Ivory Coast, Mexico, Morocco, Philippines, South Africa, Venezuela, and Yugoslavia) were reported to be included in Category 4 (transfer risk). Six countries (Costa Rica, Dominican Re-

---

[13]General Accounting Office, *Bank Examination for Country Risk and International Lending* (Washington: September 1982); and General Accounting Office, *The Framework Underlying Risk in International Lending* (Washington: September 1986); and General Accounting Office, *Supervision of Overseas Lending is Inadequate* (Washington: May 1988).

Guidelines regarding the ATRR are provided in P. 211.43 of the Regulations of the International Lending Supervision Act of 1983. See also Federal Reserve Board, "Rules Regarding International Lending Supervision Act," *Federal Reserve Bulletin* (Washington: February 1984), pp. 109-110; and Federal Reserve Board, "Fees on International Loans: Adoption of Rules," *Federal Reserve Bulletin* (Washington: April 1984), pp. 331-332.

[14]Warren Tam, Christopher Arnold, and Beth Lewis, eds., *Bank Notes*, Federal Reserve Bank of Boston (November 13, 1987), p. 4.

public, Ecuador, Nigeria, Panama, and Romania) were reported to be included in Category 5 (substandard). Two countries (Bolivia and Peru) were included in Category 6 (value impaired).[15] As noted previously, countries in the value-impaired category are those with prolonged debt service arrearages and no definite prospects of repayment; allocated transfer risk reserves may be required against loans to these countries. Generally, it appears that ICERC country rankings correspond closely with rankings provided by *Insitutional Investor* and with prices quoted in the secondary market for Third World debt.

Banks with large Third World debt loans also face a further problem in the form of a downgrading by rating agencies of the asset-backed securities they guarantee. Rating agencies have come to scrutinize more carefully the condition of major creditor banks with extensive loans to developing countries as a factor in rating decisions.[16] The large debt exposure to developing countries has also depressed the stock prices of some creditor banks.

SECONDARY DEBT MARKET AND LEVEL OF LOAN-LOSS RESERVES

The tendency to resort to debt arrearages and the frequency of restructuring implies a weakness in the quality of assets and the asset structure of creditor banks. The deterioration is evident in the secondary market for the purchase and sale of troubled debt of Third World countries, which involves discounts ranging from 25 percent to more than 50 percent of the book value of the claims. The market value has varied over time and particularly from country to country; Argentine debt was offered for sale in 1986 at 63 cents on the dollar; Bolivian debt, 7 cents on the dollar; Brazilian debt, 76 cents on the dollar.[17] As a result, the discounted value of sales in the market cast doubt on the stated value of loans held by major banks.

---

[15]See Ed Paisley, "US to Release Credit Ratings for 15 Debtor Countries," *American Banker* (November 15, 1988), pp. 2, 17.

[16]Ann Monroe, "Moody's May Downgrade $6.3 Billion of Mortgage, Asset-Backed Securities," *Wall Street Journal* (December 9, 1987), p. 50.

As an illustration, a listing of short- and long-term debt of 33 major banks of the world for February 1987 by Moody's and Standard & Poor's is provided in "As Others See Them," *The Economist* (London: March 21-27, 1987), p. 61.

[17]Rudiger Dornbusch, "International Debt and Economic Stability," *Economic Review*, Federal Reserve Bank of Kansas City (January 1987), pp. 15-32.

Secondary market prices for bank loans to developing countries are frequently quoted in financial papers. For example, quotations provided by Salomon Brothers are included in "LDC Debt," *American Banker* (August 10, 1988), p. 18.

The Third World debt market was started in 1982 on a small scale and used primarily by European banks. Although the size of the market has grown, it was initially largely avoided by major U.S. banks. Regional banks, however, have used it to reduce their loans to Latin American countries and other countries experiencing repayment difficulties. With continued development, the market has come to be used more extensively by large commercial banks, investment banks, and some large multinational corporations that trade in loans of troubled debtor countries.

Through 1986, U.S. creditor banks generally valued most of their foreign debt at book value or 100 cents on the dollar. In 1987, major U.S. banks took a more realistic approach in their accounting procedures with their addition of billions of dollars to loan-loss reserves. Citibank was the first major bank to take action with a $3 billion addition to loss reserves. Several other major banks followed Citibank's lead, including Manufacturers Hanover, Chase Manhattan, Chemical New York, and Bank of America. As a result, many of the major banks posted large accounting losses for the second quarter of 1987.[18] In general, the losses experienced during the early part of 1987 roughly equalled additions to loan reserves.

Even so, the U.S. General Accounting Office (GAO) concluded in early 1988 that the value of loans to Third World countries in the secondary market is more realistic and that U.S. banks were overstating the true worth of such loans by about $28 billion. The GAO also recommends that ATRRs be required not only against value-impaired loans (Category 6), but also in the case of other transfer risk problems (Category 4) and substandard loans (Category 5). The Federal Reserve Board has disagreed with the GAO conclusions; essentially, the Board believes that secondary market sales are conducted on an expedited basis and provide little useful information about the expected maturity value of such claims.[19]

INTERNATIONAL LENDING SUPERVISION ACT

Potential problems in international commercial bank lending were apparent as early as the late 1970s. As a result, various types of efforts were initiated by U.S. regulatory agencies, including the establishment of the Interagency Country Exposure Review Committee, to monitor more

---

[18]Peter Truell, "Banks' Reserve Action May Make Debt Crisis Even More Vexatious," *The Wall Street Journal* (July 2, 1987), pp. 1, 11.

[19]General Accounting Office, *Supervision of Overseas Lending is Inadequate* (Washington: May 1988).

closely the exposure of U.S. commercial banks to foreign countries with potential external debt problems.[20]

However, the U.S. Congress sought to introduce a more rigid regulatory element into the overseas lending of U.S. commercial banks. In an effort to ensure that the international money and capital markets are not threatened by "imprudent lending policies or inadequate supervision," Congress in November of 1983 passed the International Lending Supervision Act (ILSA, Title IV of Public Law 98-181). Under the ILSA, Congress authorized a SDR 5,310,800,000 increase ($8.4 billion) in the IMF quota. But it also mandated that the U.S. regulatory agencies promulgate rules to increase bank safety and to regulate U.S. bank lending abroad. In general terms, the key provisions of the act were as follows:

1. Federal banking agencies are to require banks to establish special reserves to be charged against current income (the ATRRs described previously) if it appears that the bank's assets have been or are impaired by loans to borrowers in foreign countries.
2. Federal banking agencies are given authority to establish minimum capital requirements as deemed appropriate for commercial banks.
3. Feasibility evaluations are to be undertaken by banks for projects involving loans in excess of $20,000,000.
4. Banking institutions are not allowed to charge fees for the restructuring of international loans that exceed administrative costs unless such fees are amortized over the life of the loan.
5. United States banking agencies are to consult with supervisory authorities of other countries to reach agreement on measures designed to achieve effective and consistent supervisory policies regarding international lending.

Several regulatory changes have been introduced to implement the ILSA. In 1984, the Federal Reserve Board established two rules applicable to restructured loans. First, banks may not charge a restructuring fee that exceeds the actual administrative cost of the restructuring effort. Second, other fees associated with international loans are to accrue as income over the entire life of the loan rather than as front-end income. Other regulations relate primarily to the provision of additional international loan information. In addition, and as described in Chapter 14, U.S. regulatory agencies have worked with supervisory authorities of other counties to establish uniformity of capital requirements among financial institutions.

Other changes have been made with regard to the accounting for nonrefundable fees and costs associated with lending activities. In 1986, the FASB issued Standard Number 91, which stipulates that loan acqui-

[20]The International Lending Supervision Act of 1983 is Title IX of PL 98-181. Related provisions pertaining to the International Monetary Fund are contained in Title VIII of this act.

sition fees associated with performing loans are to be recognized over the life of the loan as an adjustment to the yield of the loan. This differs from earlier practice, in which part or all of such fees were treated as front-end income.[21]

DEVELOPMENTS IN BANK EXPOSURE AND CAPITAL

What has been the impact of bank and government actions to cope with repayment problems? Empirical evidence suggests that U.S. bank lending patterns have altered somewhat in recent years. Table 12.1 (Part A) indicates the volume of loans extended by the nine major money center banks (a) to nonoil-exporting countries of Latin America and the Caribbean, and (b) to all countries; it also indicates the total capital holdings for these banks. (The nine money center banks are Bank of America, Citibank, Chase Manhattan Bank, Manufacturers Hanover, Morgan Guarantee, Chemical Bank, Continental Illinois, Bankers Trust, and the First National Bank of Chicago.) Data reflect three different points in time: June of 1982, just prior to the debt situation crisis; December of

TABLE 12.1   Capital Status, Amounts Owed To Nine Largest And All U.S. Banks, Selected Years

A. Nine Money Center Banks

	June 1982	December 1983	March 1988
Nonoil-Exporting Countries Latin American and Caribbean	$ 39.7b	$ 42.6b	$ 41.4b
All countries	209.5	207.1	163.6
Bank capital	27.1	31.5	52.4

B. All Reporting Lending Banks

	June 1982	December 1983	March 1988
Nonoil-Exporting Countries Latin American and Caribbean	$ 68.1b	$ 71.7b	$ 62.2b
All countries	349.3	357.3	259.5
Bank capital	66.2	79.3	130.9

Source: Figures derived from Federal Financial Institutions Examination Council, "Country Exposure Lending Survey," *Statistical Release* (Washington: various issues).

---

[21]FASB Standard No. 91 appears to be consistent with the ILSA.

1983, at the time the ILSA was enacted; and March of 1988, subsequent to balance sheet changes introduced by major banks.

Figures indicate that the volume of loans to Latin American and Caribbean countries by the nine banks has remained almost constant over the entire period, despite the debt problems experienced by almost all of the countries since the early 1980s. Maintenance of the volume of loans may be surprising, given the seriousness of the repayment difficulties. It may be the result of pressure from U.S. officials to maintain and even expand loans as well as successful restructuring efforts. However, loans by the nine banks to all foreign countries have declined significantly since the end of 1983.

Of particular interest in Part A of Table 12.1 is the increase in the total capital (the net worth of banks as reflected in total assets less total liabilities) held by the nine banks, especially since December 1983. As a result of the increase in total capital, the capital/foreign loan ratio has increased from 15 percent at the end of 1983 to about 32 percent at the early of 1988. This increase is an indication of bank efforts to improve their strength and safety.

Data for all U.S. reporting banks (which cover approximately 185 lending banks—including the nine large banks—that provide information on a regular basis) are included in Part B, Table 12.1. The trend is relatively similar to that of the nine large banks. Loans to Latin American and Caribbean countries declined slightly, but loans to all foreign countries dropped sharply since December of 1983. In addition, the capital/foreign loan ratio increased from 22 percent to 50 percent—again a reflection of creditor bank efforts to strengthen their financial structure.

OTHER EFFECTS OF THE ILSA

The 1983 act also authorized an $8.4 billion contribution to the IMF. As a result of enlarged resources, the IMF has been able to increase its credit to countries "with recent debt servicing problems" from $7.6 billion during the three-year period 1980-1982 to $13.6 billion during the three-year period 1983-1985.[22]

Restructuring fees of lending banks have also been reduced significantly. According to one estimate, the fees associated with restructuring involving the use of new money declined from about 1.25 percent in 1983 to about 0.50 percent in mid-1986.[23]

---

[22]International Monetary Fund, *World Economic Outlook* (Washington: April 1986), p. 241.

[23]William Taylor, "Statement to Congress," *Federal Reserve Bulletin* (Washington: August 1986), pp. 565-568.

The ILSA also encourages U.S. regulatory agencies to cooperate with their counterparts in other countries to create a more effective approach to supervision of international lending. The Basle Concordat, examined more fully in Chapter 14, is the major framework for cooperative efforts in bank supervision. The Concordat provides guidelines for assigning regulatory authority over bank activity in three areas: liquidity, solvency, and foreign exchange positions. International lending falls within the solvency area.

THE OMNIBUS TRADE AND COMPETITIVENESS ACT OF 1988

In 1988, Congress passed trade legislation containing several provisions that were somewhat protectionist in nature. Several other provisions were included in the act, including one that related to Third World debt. Specifically, the provision (Section 3111) mandated that the Treasury Secretary open discussions with other countries in an effort to create a special debt facility to acquire Third World debt, dispose of it through swaps or conversion into securities, or in other ways to take action to reduce the developing countries' debt burden. However, discussions are not required if an interim study concludes that the effect of such a facility would reduce the value of the debt, cause serious problems in debtor-creditor relationships, or otherwise create greater problems than it resolved.

The ultimate impact of this provision remains uncertain. An interim study may conclude that an international debt facility would prove beneficial; alternatively, it may conclude that existing techniques and procedures are adequate. Whether or not a special debt facility is established will depend upon the attitude of the executive branch and the Treasury; it will also depend upon the short-term ability of creditor governments, banks, and the debtor countries to cope with the situation, or if, in fact, changes evolve that appear to pose a threat to the international financial system. In any event, the provision does indicate a continuing Congressional concern over the debt situation.

OTHER PROPOSALS

Several proposals have been offered by members of Congress to affect bank lending to foreign countries or to force changes in bank accounting for nonperforming loans.[24] One proposal would encourage, although not require, creditor banks to either lower the stated value of doubtful loans receivable or to sell them at a discount. A second proposal would require banks to undertake an annual 10 percent write-off of the difference between the market and book value of Third World debt. Although many of the large U.S. creditor banks started to increase loss reserves and to write down loan values in early 1987, a significant gap remains between book and market values.

A somewhat more comprehensive proposal (the Bradley Plan) would lower by three percentage points the interest rate charged by U.S. banks to 15 Latin American countries. In addition, three percent of the loan principal would be forgiven each year for three years. The debtor countries would be expected to make certain trade concessions and to initiate specified internal changes that would encourage economic growth. Implementation of a policy of this type would generally ease the balance of payments burden of developing countries.

Another financing plan suggested by the U.S. government specifically for Mexico would involve the sale of U.S. Treasury bonds to the Mexican government at a fraction of their stated value. Mexico, in turn, would issue peso-denominated bonds, backed by the U.S. securities, to its external bank creditors in exchange for claims held by creditor banks. Although creditor banks would have to sell existing claims at a discount, they would acquire new claims backed by a U.S. Treasury guarantee.

Commercial banks have also initiated techniques to cope with the situation. The exchange of claims held against debtor countries for their commodities has been considered. Chase Manhattan Bank, for example, negotiated with Peru over a debt-for-products exchange. Chase would secure a variety of primary commodities and manufactured products from Peru to cover a specified portion of Peru's debt.[25] Although the payment-in-kind transactions may ease the payments problems for some countries and some creditor banks, they are not likely to have a major impact on the overall debt situation. The major reason is that such exchanges may simply become a substitute for regular commercial transactions that might otherwise occur. In conjunction, they may have the effect of lowering commodity prices and/or export earnings for the debtor countries.

---

[24] A brief discussion of several plans is included in Brian Kettell and George Magnus, *The International Debt Game* (Cambridge, Mass.: Ballinger Publishing Company, 1986), pp. 163–187.

[25] Sam Zuckerman, "Chase May Swap Peru Debt for Products," *American Banker* (December 23, 1987), p. 3.

Whether or not any of these or other proposals are implemented voluntarily or mandated by Congress depends on continuing developments in the capital and commodity markets. The decision by U.S. banks to expand their loss reserves beginning in 1987 and to accept reduced earnings, as well as the strengthening of their capital positions, may forestall further Congressional action not widely accepted by creditor banks. Equally important perhaps is the ability of debtor countries to return to a more acceptable repayment situation. An improvement in the debtor countries terms of trade, a reduction in the number of countries in payments arrears, and, more generally, a strengthening of the payments position of several of the major debtor countries would likely allay Congressional fears of extensive debt repudiation. Finally, Congressional action in 1988 trade legislation to require the Treasury to study the impact of a Third World debt facility may be a substitute for other types of remedies.

SUMMARY AND CONCLUSIONS

United States banks and the U.S. government have devised a variety of techniques and procedures in an effort to avoid international lending losses and to cope with the impact of such losses. This action has become increasingly important and necessary as commercial banks have begun to assume a major role in the capital needs of Third World countries.

United States supervisory actions in 1977 and subsequent action of several other creditor countries included efforts to secure comprehensive data on commercial bank lending activities and to assess country exposure for their respective banks. The early evidence suggests that loan diversification across countries may reduce some of the risk attached to lending activities.

Statistical indicators provide a basis for assessing the degree of risk associated with potential borrowers. However, in many instances, the ability of a debtor country to service external debt depends upon conditions beyond its control, especially the terms of trade and the market for its export products. The growing number of countries in payments arrears, the increased use of debt restructuring, and the continuing possibility of debt repudiation have resulted in accounting problems for banks in their efforts to place a value on such claims and to make provisions for possible losses. The federal regulatory agencies instituted a system to monitor bank lending activities, but Congress mandated a more rigid regulatory procedure with the International Lending Supervision Act of 1983. This act established guidelines regarding special loan-loss reserves, restructuring fees, and capital requirements. Commercial banks have been authorized to maintain a tax deductible reserve against bad debts; change occurred with the Tax Reform Act of 1986, which specifies that large institutions must use a specific charge-off approach rather than a reserve approach.

Commercial bank lending exposures and capital positions have also been modified. Since mid-1982, at which time Mexico stopped making interest payments on external obligations and the debt situation was perceived as reaching "crisis" proportions, lending by U.S. banks to Latin America has remained relatively constant; lending to other countries has declined significantly. Equally important is that since the crisis occurred, lending banks have increased their capital/foreign loan ratio, an indication of an effort to improve their financial strength and safety.

In general, commercial bank lending has become a relatively less important source of resources for the developing world. In 1980, banks provided about 38 percent of all financial resources available to the developing countries; by 1986, this share had declined to six percent. The decline was largely offset by an increase in direct investment and in official development finance provided by the industrialized countries.[26]

The debt situation has prompted action not only on the part of the U.S. government and U.S. banks on a bilateral basis, but also by international agencies and other governments and banks. Multilateral efforts to cope with repayments problems are examined in the following chapter.

[26]International Monetary Fund, "Total Net Resource Flows to Developing Countries," *IMF Survey* (February 22, 1988), p. 61.

MULTILATERAL ACTION
ON DEBT PROBLEMS

Although U.S. banks have borne the heaviest burden of debt repayment problems of developing countries, banks from other countries, especially Western Europe and Japan, have been adversely affected. In addition, repayment problems appear to have stifled the investment programs of many debtor countries[1] and, at least in part, contributed to financial uncertainties and protectionist tendencies. As a result of the global implications, multilateral efforts have been initiated to cope with repayment problems. The most extensive approach involves the restructuring of debts, usually under the auspices of the Bank for International Settlements (BIS), the International Monetary Fund (IMF), or the Paris Club.

DEBT RESTRUCTURING

In general, debtor countries that experience balance of payments difficulties as they attempt to service externally held obligations are reluctant to discontinue making payments to their creditors. A more likely

---

[1]Richard N. Cooper, *Symposium on the Causes of the U.S. Trade Deficit* (Washington: General Accounting Office, May 1987), pp. 14-15.

sequence of events is a delay in payment and/or the restructuring of debt obligations to the lenders. Lending institutions may accept renegotiations and restructuring of loans in an effort to minimize losses by improving the circumstances under which debtor countries can continue to discharge their responsibilities.

A restructured international loan is defined by the Federal Reserve Board as one that meets the following criteria: (1) The borrower cannot service an existing loan and is a resident of a foreign country experiencing a generalized inability to service external debt due to the lack of foreign exchange in the country.   (2) Either the loan terms are amended to reduce stated interest or extend the schedule of payments, or a new loan is made to or for the benefit of the borrower, enabling the borrower to service or refinance the existing debt.[2]

A growing number of developing countries have been forced to delay debt payments as well as to secure a restructuring of their debts. The number of countries that have restructured debts, including those to both commercial banks and governments, increased from an annual average of two or three in the 1970s to about 30 by 1983, although it has decreased since that time. The total dollar amount renegotiated multiplied from an annual average of about $2 billion in the early 1970s to over $100 billion during some recent years.[3]

Rescheduling of both government and commercial loans is not a new or recent type of effort. For the post-World War II period, rescheduling goes back as far as the late 1950s. The process attracted more attention and caused more concern in the late 1970s and early 1980s because it included three countries with which the U.S. has significant commercial ties—Argentina, Brazil, and Mexico. In addition, a large share of the external debt of these countries, both in relative and absolute terms, was held by U.S. commercial banks, and there was a fear that nonpayment of debts could force some financial institutions into insolvency.

Many other debtor countries have experienced payments problems. Creditor banks have found it necessary to restructure loans to Bolivia, Chile, Colombia, Peru, Philippines, Poland, Romania, Turkey, Venezuela, and Yugoslavia. As a result of the use of restructuring,

---

[2]See Board of Governors, *Federal Reserve Bulletin* (Washington: April 1984), pp. 331-32.

[3]An extensive analysis of debt restructuring is provided in E. Brau and R. C. Williams, *Recent Multilateral Debt Restructuring With Official and Bank Creditors* (Washington: International Monetary Fund, December 1983).

For a list of terms and conditions of bank debt restructurings for the period 1978 through 1986 for about 35 debtor countries, see Maxwell Watson, et al., *International Capital Markets: Developments and Prospects* (Washington: International Monetary Fund, December 1986), pp. 125-140. See also The World Bank, "Recent Developments in Debt Relief Negotiations," *World Debt Tables*, Volume I (Washington: 1988), pp. xxxii-xlii.

outright defaults have been avoided and, at least until early 1987, creditor commercial banks have not experienced major or serious losses in the post-World War II period.

PARIS CLUB RESTRUCTURING

Rescheduling of official and officially guaranteed loans has frequently involved meetings of the loosely organized Paris Club (so-called because it is chaired by the French Treasury), an approach that includes the joint efforts and agreement of the governments of the affected creditor countries. This multilateral approach used by official creditors can be traced as far back as 1956, when representatives of several European countries met in Paris to renegotiate Argentina's external debt obligations. Since that time over 60 reschedulings have been undertaken. Other multilateral debt renegotiations have been initiated under the auspices of the World Bank or the Organization for Economic Cooperation and Development. Generally, these arrangements have attempted to alleviate serious liquidity problems on the part of the debtor countries by providing a more generous grace period and by extending the period of repayment of the loan principal.

Although the nature of Paris Club renegotiations varies, depending upon the countries and the conditions, there are several features which, although not formalized, have emerged as the practice continues and becomes an accepted part of the workings of the international financial system. For example, the Club requires an IMF standby arrangement (an agreement by the IMF to provide financial assistance) with the debtor countries as a prerequisite to rescheduling.[4]

A second feature is that because of variations in the structure and financial requirements of the debtor countries, rescheduling occurs on a case-by-case basis. However, a common approach is employed to assure that rescheduling terms for similar types of debt do not differ significantly among creditors and among debtors.

Within the Paris Club framework, a distinction is made between renegotiation designed to alleviate a debt problem and assistance for developmental efforts. The reason is that renegotiations are expected to alleviate debt and balance of payments problems rather than serving as a technique for providing developmental aid. Generally, however, renegotiations include debt assistance within a broad framework that also

---

[4]Paris Club negotiations are described in Jean-Claude Trichet, "Official Debt Rescheduling," *External Debt Management*, ed. Hassanali Mehran (Washington: International Monetary Fund, 1985), pp. 126-136. See also "The Paris Club," *IMF Survey* (August 11, 1986), pp. 246-247.

requires the debtor country to institute austerity measures and a stabilization program. The program generally requires the recipient to pursue monetary, fiscal, and balance of payment policies designed to facilitate future servicing of debt obligations. In some instances, the austerity measures have proved difficult to implement.

OFFICIAL DEBT RESCHEDULING BY THE UNITED STATES

The role and impact of U.S. governmental action is significant in most debt rescheduling decisions. The U.S. government has participated in numerous sets of negotiations, generally through the Paris Club. The U.S. approach to a particular instance of repayment difficulties is formulated by the National Advisory Council; participants include the major government lending agencies that are creditors, and involves lengthening of maturities generally on principal repayments. The Advisory Council considers the possibility of a rescheduling of official loans only under certain circumstances: the debtor country must be at the point of imminent default; the negotiations must be through the creditor club (Paris Club) mechanism; the debtor country must agree to initiate corrective internal policies; and no creditors, either private or public, are to receive preferential treatment. The U.S. position is that debt rescheduling is not a form of developmental assistance, but rather a financial procedure that will maximize the likelihood and amount of repayment.

The United States participated in the renegotiations of debt with Brazil in 1964, at which time about $45 million of loan obligations to the United States were rescheduled. Since that time, rescheduling with other countries has occurred with growing frequency—from about one or two each year to as many as eight or nine each year. It has most frequently involved Latin American countries but has also included Turkey on several occasions and India, Indonesia, Pakistan, and Poland. The U.S. Treasury estimates that the debt relief provided by the U.S. government during the eight years 1974 through 1981 may have amounted to $2.3 billion.[5]

The policy of the U.S. government on rescheduling the official debt of countries experiencing balance of payments crises has important implications for commercial bank creditors. In some instances, the rene-

[5]An analysis of U.S. government policy and practice regarding rescheduling of debt obligations is provided in U.S. General Accounting Office, *U.S. Development Efforts and Balance-of-Payments Problems in Developing Countries* (Washington: February 14, 1983).

gotiations include commercial creditors as well as government creditors. Second, and perhaps more important, is that to the extent that U.S. governmental action alleviates a debtor country's repayment problems, the greater the likelihood that commercial creditors will be reimbursed ultimately by the debtor country.

Does the restructuring of debts represent a sufficient concession on the part of creditor governments to alleviate balance of payments strains for the debtor countries? In most cases other balance of payments factors must be considered. The ability of debtor countries to earn foreign exchange for debt servicing purposes may also require a commercial policy on the part of creditor countries that is consistent with or permits a trade deficit. For example, during 1982 and 1983, the United States experienced bilateral trade deficits with several Latin American debtor countries, including Brazil, Mexico, and Venezuela, three of the largest debtors. To an extent, the U.S. deficit occurred as the Latin American countries restricted imports to conserve foreign exchange as part of their programs designed to adjust to the external debt situation. Yet, a continuation of the relatively large trade deficit has not been acceptable to the United States because of its adverse impact on domestic employment. Thus, successful efforts by the United States to reduce its trade deficits may create an even greater balance of payments strain on debtor countries insofar as their export markets are diminished.

COMMERCIAL DEBT RESTRUCTURING

Although much of the debt restructured in recent years has involved official creditors, since 1982 an increasing number of debtor nations have negotiated for debt relief with commercial banks and other private creditors (sometimes referred to as the "London Club"). In terms of volume, restructured bank debt increased from an annual average of $1 billion to $2 billion in the late 1970s to a peak of over $100 billion in 1984.

Restructuring of commercial bank debt is even less formalized than the procedures in official debt negotiations. Typically, the government of a debtor country approaches the creditor banks with the greatest exposures to seek relief from a debt servicing burden. An advisory committee is formed representing the major banks (frequently part of the syndicate that extended the original loans) to establish guidelines and procedures for negotiations, to minimize commercial disruptions, to inform all creditor banks of developments and progress, and to ensure that all creditor banks are treated equitably. Decisions are made with regard to which debt is to be considered; excluded debt typically involves short-term credit, secured debt, interbank deposits, and debt to multilateral organizations. The actual rescheduling requires the construction of a package that is acceptable to the debtor government in terms of its ability to resume debt service payments given the existing political and economic conditions; it must also be acceptable to the participating banks on the basis of realistic expectations of ultimate repayments. Negotiations must result in easing the immediate and short-term strain to facilitate eventual repayment. Usually an agreement requires a lengthening of the grace period and total repayment time; it may also include additional bank lending.

In some instances debt restructuring undertaken by groups of commercial banks has paralleled, although negotiations have not been a part of, the Paris Club decisions. In other instances they have been undertaken without Paris Club involvement. Frequently, the restructuring process entails formidable organizational problems with as many as 300 commercial banks from several countries participating; negotiations may last well over a year, especially if new loans are required. Frequently, the IMF participates in some capacity; in some cases rescheduling occurs within the context of a Fund-supported adjustment program. The Bank for International Settlements may also be involved. Typically the Bank provides "bridge" financing to prevent short-term disruptions that might otherwise develop.[6]

Ultimately the creditor banks must accept and implement the terms of the new agreement. In some instances, the smaller regional banks are reluctant to support a new agreement, especially if it includes new loans and increases their exposures. There is evidence that these banks are subject to substantial pressure from the money center banks, state and federal regulators, and others to cooperate in debt restructuring.[7]

MEXICO'S DEBT RESTRUCTURING

Mexico is an illustration of a recent debt restructuring. Mexico's situation is of particular interest as a result of the Mexican government decision to suspend interest payments on an estimated $80 billion

[6]Difficulties associated with restructuring are discussed in Benjamin J. Cohen, *Banks and the Balance of Payments: Private Lending in the International Adjustment Process* (Montclair, New Jersey: Allanheld, Osum & Co., Publishers, Inc., 1981), pp. 105-111; Chris Carvounis, "The LDC Debt Problem: Trends in Country Risk Analysis and Rescheduling Exercises," *Columbia Journal of World Business* (Spring 1982), pp. 15-19; Declan Duff and Ian Peacock, "Refinancing of Sovereign Debt," *The Banker* (January 1978), pp. 69-75; "Debt Rescheduling: What Does It Mean?" *Finance and Development* (September 1983), pp. 26-30; M. S. Mendelsohn, *Commercial Banks and the Restructuring of Cross-Border Debt* (New York: Group of Thirty, 1983).

[7]See, for example, John P. Caskey, "The IMF and Concerted Lending in Latin American Debt Restructurings: A Formal Analysis, *Research Working Paper*, Federal Reserve Bank of Kansas City (July 1988).

external debt in mid-1982—a decision that precipitated the "debt crisis." Shortly thereafter, the U.S. government provided financial support to Mexico in cooperation with the central banks of several other industrial countries. Mexico had experienced several years of prosperity; borrowing by the government and private sector increased the country's external debt from $18 billion in 1975 to $60 billion at the end of 1980. But domestic inflation, worldwide recession, and a decline in world demand for oil reduced Mexican exports and the foreign exchange earnings needed to service the growing volume of external debt.

Under a multilateral agreement, the United States committed itself to provide about half of a total of $1.85 billion available to Mexico from the participating governments, the Bank for International Settlements, the IMF, and several major international banks. Mexico, in turn, established a two-tiered exchange rate system, one of which was permitted to float with the expectation that it would facilitate exportation. Various types of monetary action were also taken to control inflation and monetary growth in an effort to restore stability and confidence in the financial system of the country.[8]

One phase of the rescheduling process for Mexico involving commercial banks and covering about $11 billion in loans culminated in mid-1983. An estimated 500 creditor banks accepted the rescheduling agreement, which essentially converted short-term debt into debt with an eight-year maturity date and a four-year grace period.

Another major rescheduling occurred in 1984 and, for a period of time, it appeared that Mexico was succeeding in improving its debt servicing capability. As a result of internal changes and other favorable developments, the country was able to shift its current account deficit of 1981 to a sizable surplus in 1983 and 1984. But conditions changed again and, by 1986, the Mexican debt crisis reappeared. Debt restructuring with commercial banks was again completed in 1987. The major changes included a significant lengthening of maturities and a reduction in interest rates. The Mexican government also relaxed restrictions on external investment within the country. Mexico has come to depend on crude oil exports for as much as three-fourths of her export earnings. Accordingly,

---

[8]"A Two-Tiered Exchange Rate System for the Mexican Peso," *International Letter*, Federal Reserve Bank of Chicago (August 13, 1982), pp. 1-2. See also Teresa Carson, "With Much Pomp, Mexico, Hanover Reschedule Loans," *American Banker* (August 29, 1983), p. 2. An analysis of the 1982 Mexican debt crisis and the impact on bank securities is provided by Robert F. Bruner and John M. Simms, Jr., "The International Debt Crisis and Bank Security Returns in 1982," *Journal of Money, Credit and Banking* (February 1987), pp. 46-55.

A more comprehensive analysis of Mexico's situation is provided in Joseph Kraft, *The Mexican Rescue* (New York: Group of Thirty, 1984).

An analysis of difficulties experienced by Brazil and Chile is provided in P. N. Snowden, *Emerging Risk in International Banking* (London: George Allen & Unwin, 1985).

the country's internal progress depends largely upon high oil prices and other favorable developments in the international economy.

The action of the United States and other foreign governments to assist Mexico and numerous other countries, especially in 1982 and subsequent years, raises some key questions regarding official responsibility when a debtor country appears likely to default on its debt responsibilities. To what extent can or should the banking community depend upon governmental action to alleviate balance of payments and debt repayment problems of debtor countries? Does such action essentially amount to "bailing out" creditor commercial banks? In the case of Mexico, the debt to commercial banks of the industrial countries amounted to about $57 billion. A default on the part of Mexico would have seriously affected many private banks, including not only direct creditors but also other banks related through interbank deposits and correspondent associations. And yet a presumption by private banks that governmental assistance will be available to avoid widespread default may induce the banking community to pursue a less prudent lending policy.

Many members of Congress believe that banks have frequently failed to apply proper banking standards; they have been particularly sensitive to charges that action on the part of U.S. government agencies or international financial institutions are designed primarily to "bail out" creditor banks. For example, in the U.S. International Lending Supervision Act of 1983, Congress mandated, "The economic health and stability of the U.S. and the other nations of the world shall not be adversely affected or threatened in the future by imprudent lending practices or inadequate supervision." Further, a provision entitled "Opposing Fund Bailouts of Banks" was added that requires the U.S. Executive Director to the IMF to oppose loans to countries if the purpose is to repay loans that have been imprudently made by banking institutions.

THE BAKER PLAN

Although debt restructuring has been the major approach to resolving the repayment problems, other actions have been initiated. An effort that requires extensive cooperation and initiative to alleviate debt problems is the Baker Plan—sometimes referred to as the "Program for Sustained Growth." The Baker Plan, proposed by U.S. Secretary of the Treasury James Baker in October of 1985, presumes the cooperative action of creditor commercial banks, the International Bank for Reconstruction and Development (IBRD or World Bank), the Inter-American

Development Bank (IADB), and the governments of the major debtor countries.

The Baker Plan is a U.S. initiative consisting of three "essential and mutually reinforcing" elements:

1. An increase in new lending of $20 billion by the international banking community over a three-year period.
2. A $9 billion increase in lending over a three-year period by the IBRD and the IADB to 15 major debtor countries.
3. Major adjustment policies on the part of debtor countries that would promote economic growth within a market-oriented framework.

The Baker Plan has presumably received the support of the major creditor banks. For example, the Institute for International Finance, which represents over 100 commercial banks from 38 countries, indicates that the Baker Plan has provided a logical solution to the debt problem and that commercial banks expect to remain active in financing developing countries.[9] Within the United States, Paul Volcker, then-Chairman of the Federal Reserve Board, urged U.S. banks to provide an additional $7 billion to comply with the commercial bank contribution to the Plan.[10]

Evidence of the results of the Plan is somewhat less than reassuring. A major obstacle is that overall world economic conditions have not been particularly conducive to debt servicing activities since the inception of the Baker Plan. Deteriorating terms of trade, sluggish economic growth in the creditor countries, and difficulties in creating an appropriate investment climate in some debtor countries have been contributing factors. In addition, there is evidence that, in fact, commercial banks have failed to provide the broad and active support that is needed to ease the debt repayment strain.[11] This concern seems to be directed particularly toward many regional and smaller banks, which have been reluctant to continue lending where doubt arises regarding ultimate repayment.[12]

[9]Horst Schulmann, "Private Banks Urge Debtors and Creditors to Intensify Efforts to Solve the Debt Problem," *IMF Survey* (April 6, 1986), pp. 105-106.

[10]Hang-Sheng Cheng, "The Baker Plan: A New Initiative," *Weekly Letter*, Federal Reserve Bank of San Francisco (November 22, 1985), pp. 1-3. An analysis of various ways of coping with the debt situation, particularly the Baker Plan, is provided in John W. Ingraham, "Global Debt Strategies: Financing Growth in Developing Countries," *The Journal of Commercial Bank Lending* (September 1987), pp. 16-23. See also Jeffrey Sachs, "Managing the LDC Debt Crisis," *Brookings Papers on Economic Activity, Vol. 2,* The Brookings Institution (1986), pp. 397-431.

[11]J. de Larosiere, "Address of the Managing Director of the International Monetary Fund," *Summary Proceedings Annual Meeting 1986* (Washington: International Monetary Fund, 1986), pp. 19-31.

[12]Group of Thirty, *Commercial Banks and the Restructuring of Cross-Border Debt* (New York: 1983), p. 13.

DEBT-TO-EQUITY SWAPS

Another technique that has attracted attention in recent years is the debt-to-equity (or debt-equity) swap. The arrangements vary somewhat from country to country, depending particularly upon the limits or restrictions that debtor countries place on the exchanges.[13] The Philippines, Chile, Venezuela, Argentina, and Mexico have adopted debt-for-equity programs. Several other countries are expected to agree to similar arrangements.

With one approach, banks sell doubtful loans back to the debtor country or other third party buyers at a discount, with the loans converted into equity investments within the debtor country. As a result, banks or other third parties acquire stocks of firms in the debtor country. Rather than receiving repayment in the form of interest and principal, they receive dividends related to the firms' profitability. Manufacturers Hanover Corporation, for example, reportedly participated in an arrangement with Brazil, exchanging debt for equity in a Brazilian paper and pulp company.

With a second type of debt swap, residents of the debtor country purchase the foreign debt at a discount and sell it to the domestic central bank at or near face value for local currency at the prevailing exchange rate. The residents then use the local currency to buy equity interests in domestic firms.

Although debt-to-equity swaps enable creditor commercial banks to dispose of questionable loans, it also means that they must accept a market value on their claims that may be considerably lower than the stated value. As a result, they must absorb short-term losses that might otherwise either be postponed or even avoided should the claims gain in value in the future.

At least initially, regulations restricted the extent to which U.S. banks could participate in some forms of debt-to-equity swaps; the Federal Reserve Board's Regulation K limited bank holding companies and their subsidiaries to 19.9 percent of the voting stock in nonfinancial firms up to a maximum of $15 million in each firm. However, revisions by the Federal Reserve Board in August of 1987 and again in February of 1988 eased the restrictions by giving bank organizations the authority to

---

[13]For an analysis, see Andrew Marton, "The Debate Over Debt-for-Equity Swaps," *Institutional Investor* (February 1987), pp. 177-179; for country experience, see Maxwell Watson, et al, "Debt-to-Equity Conversions," *International Capital Markets: Developments and Prospects* (Washington: International Monetary Fund, December 1986), pp. 62-64. See also Leroy Laney, "The Secondary Market in Developing Country Debt," *Economic Review*, Federal Reserve Bank of Dallas (July 1987), pp. 1-12; and Thomas A. Layman and Timothy F. Kearney, "Debt for Equity: A Solution to the LDC Debt Crisis? Part I," *The Journal of Commercial Bank Lending* (January 1988), pp. 33-46. A summary of the laws of several debtor countries regarding debt-equity conversions is provided in "Direct Conversion Regulations," *Euromoney* (Special Supplement on Global Debt) (January 1988), pp. 38-41.

acquire 40 percent of the stock in private sector, nonfinancial companies in certain specified debtor countries as part of the debt-to-equity swaps arrangements. An important restriction on the new authority is that generally the securities must be held by the parent holding company rather than by the bank itself or its subsidiary; this is designed to insulate the bank in a legal sense from the more risky commercial activities. Long-term possession of holdings is also discouraged; the bank organization must dispose of the securities within two years of the date on which it could repatriate in full the investment in the foreign company, but in any event within 15 years of the initial acquisition.[14]

Debt-equity swaps provide a way for both the creditor banks and debtor countries to partially ease a repayment problem. Yet some disadvantages may arise that would limit their usefulness, at least as a total solution. Creditor banks are able to unload doubtful assets and gain some flexibility in their portfolio management. But if the supply of debt placed in the market increases too rapidly, the discounts may also increase and, as a result, reduce even further the market value of loans still held by banks. The debtor countries eliminate a fixed interest obligation and become responsible for payments only when dividends are actually declared. However, if the market value of debt sold declines significantly, it may be even more difficult for debtor countries to sell new securities at a future date.

Debt-equity swaps have become an important option for U.S. creditor banks to cope with at least part of their Third World debt. The relaxation of regulations by the Board, an increase in the number of debtor countries authorizing such arrangements, and the increased tendency for banks to value their asset position more realistically have contributed to a more widespread use of swaps.

IMF ACTIVITIES

Because of the growth of indebtedness on the part of many of the developing member countries, the International Monetary Fund has become more directly involved in debt management activity in recent years. First, the IMF in 1979 established guidelines on the amount of new borrowing to be undertaken by a country that is having balance of payments problems and is receiving IMF support for a stabilization program.

Second, in instances where it becomes necessary for a member country to renegotiate an existing debt with official lenders, the IMF performs the role of a neutral middleman in an effort to achieve a solution

---

[14]"International Banking Operations," *Federal Register*, February 24, 1988, pp. 5353-5363.

that is acceptable to all parties. During such negotiations, the IMF frequently provides financial assistance to the debtor country to facilitate implementation of the planned debt rescheduling.

The IMF has also established a $3.1 billion lending program to assist the poorest debtor countries in restructuring their economies. The Structural Adjustment Facility (SAF) was established in 1986, in part as a response to the Baker Plan. It is a cooperative effort with the IBRD, in which funds are available in the form of a lending pool to about 60 of the poorest countries; countries with annual per capita incomes of less than $790 are eligible for short-term loans at interest rates of one half of one percent.[15]

A subsequent IMF aid technique—the Extended Structural Adjustment Facility (ESAF)—was created in 1987. The ESAF is a concessional medium-term lending facility also available to about 60 of the poorest countries. The Facility will operate with the equivalent of SDR 6 billion supplied by loans and contributions of IMF countries. Terms of loans are similar to those provided by the SAF. Funds are available to eligible countries experiencing balance of payments strains that are making an effort to resolve their problems.[16]

What is the appropriate role of the Fund regarding the global debt situation? The IMF has been criticized by representatives of some developing countries as having unrealistic expectations regarding their balance of payments conditions and internal austerity programs; adjustment programs are frequently perceived as too severe to be implemented by political authorities. The charge is also made that the avoidance of payments arrears should not be the major short-run goal of developing countries. Instead, the IMF should be strongly supportive of programs of economic growth that would receive first priority on current export earnings.

These charges cannot, of course, be easily countered.[17] The argument is made that the structure and purpose of the IMF would require alteration if it were to deviate significantly from its existing practices; further, developmental aid of a concessional type is more appropriately

---

[15]The Structural Adjustment Facility is described in International Monetary Fund, *Annual Report 1986* (Washington: 1986), pp. 92-98. See also Michel Camdessus, "Camdessus Details SAF Proposal, New Strategy for Poorest Countries," *IMF Survey* (June 29, 1987), pp. 194-198.

[16]Ralph W. Harbison and Aklilu Habte, "New Fund Established," *Finance and Development* (March 1988), p. 27.

[17]See, for example, Bahram Nowzad, "The IMF and Its Critics," *Essays in International Finance* (Princeton, N.J.: Princeton University Press, December 1981). For a history of IMF resource allocation by type of country, see L. H. Officer, "The Differential Use of IMF Resources by Industrial, Other Developed, and Less Developed Countries: A Historical Approach," *Journal of Developing Areas* (April 1982), pp. 401-420. A general statement of the Fund's role is provided in K. Burke Dillon and David Lipton, "External Debt and Economic Management: The Role of the International Monetary Fund," *External Debt Management*, ed. Hassanali Mehran (Washington: International Monetary Fund, 1986), pp. 31-52.

provided by the IBRD or the International Development Association. In general, it is to be expected that the Fund would operate in the direction of efficiency—the best use of scarce world resources. Yet, given the disparities in per capita income throughout the world, there is also a matter of equity—the fairness in the distribution and use of world resources. Particularly in the short run, the goals of efficiency and equity are probably not reconcilable. A judicious use of the Fund's new Extended Structural Adjustment Facility may also blunt some of the criticisms it has received.

Potential balance of payments problems are also recognized by the International Bank for Reconstruction and Development (or World Bank). The World Bank now provides loans for structural adjustment as well as the more traditional project loans. Loans for structural adjustment are to be available and used with minimal delay for financing essential imports. The recipient country must agree to initiate internal structural adjustment; it must alter its trade patterns consistent with a manageable payments deficit—one that can be readily covered with usual capital inflows. Unlike project loans, which are applied to a particular undertaking, the new type of loan involves and calls for broader and more comprehensive alterations in the productive capacity of the borrowing country.

In addition, in early 1983, the IBRD introduced cofinancing instruments to be used with commercial lenders for projects of a long-term nature located in developing countries. The purpose of the technique is to encourage capital flows from the private sector on relatively favorable terms to various low-income countries. Under a cofinancing plan, for example, a commercial bank might provide funding for the first years of a loan with a specified and early maturity date. The World Bank would also provide supplemental funds but would require repayment during the last years of the loan.

OTHER DEBT RELIEF PROPOSALS

Several other debt relief proposals have been advanced. One of the most extreme is an insistence by Cuba's Fidel Castro that creditor countries cancel all debts of Third World countries. However, United Nations Secretary Javier Perez de Cuellar has also asked for government and private forgiveness of Third World debt; the Secretary has argued that protectionism and low commodity prices have increased the seriousness of the debt crisis.

About 30 major Japanese banks have formed a separate company—Japan Bankers Association Investment Inc., a Cayman Islands corporation—to assume part of their loans, especially those made to Mexico and other Latin American countries. The participating banks have sold loans at a discount to the new company, in some instances at about 40 percent below the face value. The company is to either resell the loans to other investors or hold them to maturity.[18]

Proposals have been made for similar types of operations by an organization on an international scale. Such a company would be owned by banks from any country and would buy discounted debts from any creditor bank. As noted in the previous chapter, the U.S. Omnibus Trade and Competitiveness Act of 1988 stipulates that the Treasury Secretary should initiate discussions with other countries to create a special debt facility to acquire Third World debt.[19]

Another proposal (the Wallich Plan) suggests the creation of a bank lending insurance fund to cover loan portfolios of banks (rather than being limited to specific loans). Under one version of this plan, a specified portion of a bank's loan portfolio to developing countries would be insured. This would provide a margin of safety for banks but at the same time encourage bank prudence.

SUMMARY AND CONCLUSIONS

The Third World debt poses a potential threat not only to U.S. commercial banks but also to those of Japan and Western Europe. The possibility of extensive default has serious implications for the international financial system as well as world trade and investment. Accordingly, the IMF, IBRD, and BIS have participated, along with national governments, to alleviate the repayment burden and, in some instances, to augment the flow of capital to debtor countries.

Debt restructuring has been the major approach accepted, especially since 1982, both by governments and commercial banks. Some progress has been made through the Baker Plan, although success has not been as great as expected. To a major extent, of course, the resolution of the debt problem depends upon market conditions for various primary commodities, which at least during the first part of the 1980s were not particularly favorable to the exporting countries.

Commercial banks have assumed a more active role in coping with the situation. In addition to participating in restructuring, many have

---

[18]"Mexican Loans," *Japan Economic Survey* (July 1987), p. 13.

[19]For an analysis of debt facilities, see W. Max Corden, "An International Debt Facility?" *Staff Papers* (Washington: International Monetary Fund, September 1988), pp. 401-421.

increased their loan-loss reserves, and strengthened their capital position; some have participated in debt-for-equity swaps.

United States commercial banks face something of a dilemma in establishing their debt policies. Under the U.S. Treasury's Baker Plan, and as a result of debt restructuring, they are encouraged not only to maintain existing loans, but also to increase the amount of credit for the next several years. The Baker Plan was supported by Paul Volcker, Chairman of the Federal Reserve Board through mid-1987. But the U.S. Congress, as reflected particularly in the International Lending Supervision Act, has taken a more critical position toward what is perceived as imprudent external bank lending. In its approval of additional resources for the IMF, Congress stipulated that funds not be used simply to "bail out" commercial banks.

The Third World debt problem is far from resolved, particularly if a resolution implies the general absence of payments arrears and debt restructuring. Yet recognition of the potential seriousness of the situation, coupled with changes being introduced by banks, governments and international organizations, is an indication that at least some progress is being made.

INTERNATIONAL BANK SUPERVISION AND U.S. PARTICIPATION

Unprecedented growth has occurred in international commercial banking since the mid-1960s despite a continuing element of uncertainty— uncertainty brought on by several factors, including the move to a managed float exchange rate system, widespread inflation and high interest rates, and perhaps most importantly the debt repayment problems of a large number of developing countries.[1] The rapid growth in international banking under such circumstances raises questions pertaining to the adequacy and appropriateness of supervision of foreign banking offices. Historically, banks were chartered in a given country and conducted most of their business in domestic markets, including the establishment of branches and participation in holding companies.

[1]Material in the first part of this chapter is an updated and modified version of Charles W. Hultman, "U.S. International Bank Supervision and the Revised Basle Concordat," *Magazine of Bank Administration* (February 1985), pp. 76-82, published by the Bank Administration Institute.

An extensive analysis of international bank regulation and supervision is provided in Richard Dale, *The Regulation of International Banking* (Englewood Cliffs, N.J.: Prentice-Hall, Inc., 1984).

A good summary of the nature and extent of bank supervision by each of the OECD countries is provided in R. M. Pecchioli, *Prudential Supervision in Banking* (Paris: Organization for Economic Cooperation and Development, 1987).

But the internationalization of commercial banking has resulted in the cross-border establishment of branches, subsidiaries, and joint ventures; it has also raised the basic question of the adequacy and the focus of supervisory authority.

The dimensions of the situation are apparent from the number of international banking institutions that are subject to the supervisory requirement. One study estimated that by the late 1970s, approximately 520 banks from various countries had set up a total of about 6000 offices in other countries throughout the world.[2] The extensiveness of transnational banking organizations is also reflected in the U.S. position in global markets. Over 800 offices have been established by external banks in U.S markets. And U.S. institutions have set up approximately 2000 offices in foreign countries. The cross-border capability of these institutions raises questions regarding responsibility for ultimate supervisory control. For example, is the U.S. government or the British government responsible for supervising the London branch of a U.S.-chartered bank? And which government should supervise the subsidiary of a British bank located in New York? An effort to resolve these questions was made by the Basle Committee—composed of supervisory representatives from the United Kingdom and other major industrial countries— which in 1974 and again in 1983 provided guidelines on supervisory responsibilities. The cross-border activities of international banks also raised questions relating to prudent and equitable bank operations, particularly in terms of capital adequacy standards. Of what importance are capital adequacy standards? And why are they difficult to develop across national boundaries?

This chapter summarizes and analyzes the guidelines of the Basle Concordat, compares them with the U.S. approach, and relates them to the current uncertainties and risks in international finance.[3] It also examines bank capital adequacy guidelines as suggested by the United States and United Kingdom and the final proposals considered by the G-10 countries.

[2]Diane Page and Neal M. Soss, "Some Evidence on Transnational Banking Structure," *Staff Papers* (Washington: Comptroller of the Currency, September 1980).

[3]The text of the revised Basle Concordat is contained in International Monetary Fund, *IMF Survey* (July 11, 1983), pp. 202-204. Countries represented on the Basle Committee included Belgium, Canada, Federal Republic of Germany, France, Italy, Japan, Luxembourg, the Netherlands, Sweden, Switzerland, the United Kingdom, and the United States. Except for Luxembourg and Switzerland, the same group makes up the G-10 countries.

A discussion of the Basle Committee (also known as the Cooke Committee) and the 1975 Concordat is provided in G. G. Johnson and Richard K. Abrams, *Aspects of the International Banking Safety Net* (Washington: International Monetary Fund, March 1983), pp. 24-30.

THE BASLE CONCORDAT

The initial Basle Concordat was established in 1975 following the failures of Herstatt Bank (West Germany) and Franklin National Bank (United States) in 1974. The 1983 statement revises the earlier agreement. It reformulates earlier provisions, takes into account developments in holding companies and consolidated bank supervision, and explicitly notes that the question of lenders of last resort is not considered.

The essence of the Basle Concordat (revised) is in the assignment of supervisory authority to the appropriate government of the different banking offices for certain bank conditions. Supervisory authority is assigned to the government of the host country (where the banking office is located) and/or the parent country (where the parent firm is located). The assignment of supervisory responsibility applies to three types of banking institutions (branches, subsidiaries, and joint ventures) with respect to three factors (solvency, liquidity, and foreign exchange operations and positions). Supervision in this context involves audits, examinations, and other procedures that provide a direct assessment of the degree of safety of a bank's operations.[4]

According to the revised Concordat, the responsibility for the supervision of solvency is with the parent authority for foreign branches. Responsibility is shared jointly in the case of subsidiaries. Responsibility belongs to the country of incorporation in the case of joint ventures. The financial solvency of an office is dependent upon the well-being of an entire bank organization—branches, subsidiaries, affiliates, and the parent company. Logically, supervision of authority is presumed to be with the parent country and relates to the parent company, since this is where basic control and direction regarding solvency conditions rest.

Problems pertaining to liquidity and the needs of depositors are more local in nature and can probably be handled locally more easily. For this reason, supervision of liquidity for both branches and subsidiaries should be with regulatory authorities of the host country. However,

---

[4]A bank's liquidity pertains to the speed and certainty of converting assets into money to satisfy the needs of depositors. A bank's solvency relates to its ability to secure a level of income or receipts over time which exceeds operating costs and provides a normal rate of return to stockholders.

Commercial banks buy and sell foreign exchange for their customers and are able to avoid the risk of exchange rate movements by maintaining a covered position. Generally, it appears that U.S. commercial banks do not limit their activities to that of covering positions that may have developed in dealings with customers; rather, they appear to be willing to take an uncovered position on the basis of expected exchange rate or interest rate movements. However, since 1980, they have been required to follow guidelines set down by the Federal Financial Institutions Examination Council.

the parent authority is responsible for the supervision of the liquidity of entire banking groups.

Authority for supervision of foreign exchange operations and positions is shared jointly by the host and parent regulatory agencies. This principle applies regardless of the type of office. However, an effective monitoring system need not require a complete duplication of efforts. Thus the host country has the primary responsibility for individual institutions; the parent authority, for the entire consolidated system.

The Concordat recognizes the development of multinational banking activity, of banking networks that encompass many countries, and of multibank holding companies that in many cases control hundreds of offices. Thus it emphasizes the importance of consolidated supervision by the parent authority—the need for supervision of the totality of a bank's business wherever conducted. This presumes the likelihood of additional responsibilities for the parent authorities, but is not meant to exclude supervision of individual offices on an unconsolidated basis.

The Basle Concordat does not identify a lender of last resort, although it has been criticized for this reason. A lender of last resort is the institution—government agency or central bank—that assumes responsibility for lending to illiquid but still solvent commercial banks. The approach implicit in the Concordat is preventative rather than corrective—to promote the development of a bank supervisory structure to avoid conditions that might otherwise require the use of a lender of last resort.

The countries with supervisory agencies represented in the Basle Concordat are not bound by its provisions. Nevertheless, there is an expectation that the provisions of the Concordat will serve as a basic and effective guideline for their actions. The need for supervisory cooperation between and among authorities is stressed. The extensiveness of change in international banking is also recognized in a provision that no foreign banking establishment should escape adequate supervision.

UNITED STATES SUPERVISORY POLICIES AND STRUCTURE

The regulatory and supervisory function in the United States is shared by the Office of the Comptroller of the Currency (OCC), the Federal Reserve Board (FRB), the Federal Deposit Insurance Corporation (FDIC), and a regulatory agency in each of the states. The OCC, which is part of the U.S. Treasury, is responsible for chartering and supervising all national banks. The FRB regulates and supervises banks that are members of the Federal Reserve System. The FDIC has supervisory authority over all FDIC-insured banks, which include all but a small percentage of the total. Finally, each state has an agency that charters and supervises all state banks—that is, about two-thirds of all U.S. banks.

Generally, supervision does not apply to the separate aspects of bank operations identified in the Concordat (i.e., liquidity, solvency, or foreign exchange exposure), but rather it encompasses the totality of a bank's operations. Regulatory authorities have power to ensure that banking institutions conduct their business in a prudent manner and in compliance with all laws and regulations. This is accomplished through on-site examinations and analysis of regularly required financial statements and reports. "Problem banks"—those that have a weakness relating to capital adequacy, asset quality, management, earnings, or liquidity—are examined more frequently and closely than those that reflect strength in these areas.

THE UNITED STATES AS HOST AUTHORITY

Supervision of foreign-controlled U.S. banks poses problems because of differences in accounting and legal procedures, and in secrecy and privacy laws. However, foreign-controlled banks located in the United States are subject to the same reporting requirements and regulations as all other U.S. banks.[5] This ensures that local offices of foreign banks are monitored and supervised as closely as domestic banks.

Subsidiaries of foreign banks located in the United States are supervised by the OCC or the FDIC except for those that are state member banks. Foreign bank holding companies are supervised by the FRB.

The supervision of U.S. branches (and agencies) is primarily a responsibility of state regulatory agencies, even since the IBA of 1978, for most of these branch offices are state-chartered or licensed. Branches and agencies that opted for a federal license are regulated by the OCC. By law, these branches and agencies, as well as Edge Act Corporations, must be examined on an annual basis unlike other institutions, which are examined on a need basis.[6] In addition, the Federal Reserve has residual authority over all foreign banking operations. This is an important consideration, primarily in instances where foreign banks have multi-

---

[5] Analyses of supervision of foreign offices of U.S. banks are contained in Comptroller General of the U.S., *Despite Positive Benefits, Further Foreign Acquisitions of U.S. Banks Should Be Limited Until Policy Conflicts are Fully Addressed* (Washington: 1980), pp. 7-1 to 8-24; and John E. Schockey and William B. Glidden, "Foreign-Controlled U.S. Banks: The Legal and Regulatory Environment," *Staff Papers* (Washington: Comptroller of the Currency, 1980).

[6] See Comptroller General of the United States, *Statutory Requirements for Examining International Banking Institutions Need Attention* (Washington: July 11, 1984).

state operations, since a state agency cannot examine an affiliated banking institution in another state.

United States banking laws and supervisory functions center on U.S.-located offices. They encompass the foreign-located organizations and persons that control U.S. banks only to a limited extent—generally focusing on activities and relationships that have a significant effect on U.S. institutions. In an effort to ensure soundness of foreign parent organizations, information is collected on a consolidated basis (that is, for parent and affiliates as a single unit.)

Foreign exchange trading is not regulated in the United States, although exchange transactions are reviewed by examiners as part of the routine supervisory process.[7] Banks are expected to follow prudent practices and usually follow self-imposed internal controls. In 1980, supervisory authorities (the Federal Financial Institutions Examination Council) established general guidelines for bank activity in the exchange markets, which are expected to be followed on a voluntary basis by individual banks.[8] One review of several studies of U.S. banks' participation in the foreign exchange markets drew two major conclusions: **(1)** banks frequently deliberately take a net open position in anticipation of exchange or interest rate movements; **(2)** the positions taken by U.S. banks are not likely to cause serious losses and insolvency.[9]

THE UNITED STATES AS THE PARENT AUTHORITY

United States regulatory agencies have responsibility not only for domestic offices, but also for overseas offices of U.S.-owned banks. Overseas branches and subsidiaries of U.S. banks are generally authorized to engage in the activities usual in connection with the transaction of the business of banking in the host country.[10] However, U.S. supervi-

---

[7]Patricia Revey, "Evaluation and Growth of the United States Foreign Exchange Market," *Quarterly Review*, Federal Reserve Bank of New York (Autumn 1981), pp. 32-44.

[8]For a statement of guidelines on foreign exchange activities, see "Uniform Guideline on Internal Control for Foreign Exchange Activities in Commercial Banks," released by the Federal Financial Institutions Examination Council (May 22, 1980).

A summary of the regulatory approach of each of the OECD countries is provided by R. M. Pecchioli, "Regulations on Banks' Foreign Currency Positions," *The Internationalization of Banking* (Paris: Organization for Economic Cooperation and Development, 1983), pp. 189-192.

[9]H. Randi DeWitty, "Banks and Foreign Exchange Markets," *Weekly Letter*, Federal Reserve Bank of San Francisco (July 22, 1983), pp. 1-3.

[10]For a description of the role of U.S. monetary authorities in the supervision of foreign offices, see "International Banking Operations: Final Rule Revision," *Federal Register* (Washington: June 20, 1979), pp. 36005-36012, and Comptroller General of the U.S., *Despite Positive Benefits, Further Foreign Acquisitions of U.S. Banks Should Be Limited Until Policy Conflicts are Fully Addressed* (Washington: 1980), pp. 10-1 to 10-8.

sory authorities do secure sufficient information to monitor effectively the foreign operations of these institutions. The Federal Reserve Regulation K requires U.S. banks to provide sufficient data on their overseas subsidiaries to permit examination from the home office. Material includes information on risk assets, liquidity management, and conformance to management policies; in some instances, this is the only information available to the U.S. authorities. The Federal Reserve Board relies primarily on information available in the bank's home office on the activities of its overseas offices.

The Office of the Comptroller of the Currency regularly conducts on-site examinations of foreign offices of U.S. banks. Within the OCC, the Multinational Banking Division supervises and examines the major U.S. multinational banks (with assets of $10 billion or more) as well as the international activities of national banks with overseas branches. This approach is particularly consistent with the revised Concordat's emphasis on consolidated supervision.

United States banks are also required to maintain information regarding foreign joint ventures including risk exposure, financial performance, and management policies. This information is to be made available to U.S. bank supervisory agencies. Overseas branches of U.S. national banks are supervised by the OCC; overseas branches of state member banks, by the FRB; and overseas branches of state nonmember banks, by the FDIC and appropriate state agencies.

Generally, foreign regulatory authorities also examine and supervise offices, including branches, of U.S. banks within their respective economies. To an extent, the foreign regulatory systems do not have the same content and objectives as the U.S. system and, accordingly, are not considered a substitute for the U.S. examination.

In the revision of the Concordat, emphasis was placed on coverage of all gaps that might exist in the supervisory process. While full coverage of gaps may pose a problem, the possibility of overlapping authority may also create difficulties. For example, efforts by the Federal Reserve System to secure consolidated information on United States-located offices of foreign banks and the overseas parent company have been considered by the supervisory authorities in other countries as being contrary to the Concordat.[11]

The Federal Reserve also permits U.S. offices of foreign banks along with other U.S. banks to take advantage of discount and advance privileges, that is, to borrow reserves from the Federal Reserve when needed. Accordingly, the liquidity needs of foreign offices, including agencies and branches, are considered by the United States in a relatively concrete fashion.

[11]International Monetary Fund, *International Capital Movements* (Washington: 1980), p. 13.

On an overall basis, it has been concluded that U.S. bank supervision is consistent with Basle Committee guidelines. One difference, and possible concern, is that U.S. regulators may have inadequate knowledge of the nature and degree of supervision of foreign banks. Such information may be important to the extent that a U.S. office of a foreign bank is affected by the prudential operation and degree of supervision of its overseas parent.[12]

Another possible problem is that state chartering and supervisory agencies may be more limited in their ability to secure information on foreign companies and on out-of-state companies following the growth in interstate banking.[13] This particular problem may have been partially resolved as a result of a 1986 recommendation by the Federal Financial Institutions Examination Council that there be a greater sharing of confidential supervisory information between federal and state financial institution regulatory agencies.[14]

Another concern is that while U.S. supervisory efforts are essentially consistent with the Basle Concordat, both U.S. bank supervisory practices and Concordat guidelines are somewhat outmoded. Major changes have occurred both in financial and capital markets, which have become global rather than national in scope. While regulation continues to have a national focus, decisions made by financial institutions are increasingly based on international considerations. The purpose of the Basle Concordat has been to insure the adequacy of supervision; because of major differences in national banking systems, it does not deal with uniformity of regulation and such major issues as capital adequacy and off-balance-sheet activities. However, efforts have continued in this direction, and progress has been made on a bilateral basis by the United States and Great Britain, as well as by other G-10 countries.

REGULATION OF CAPITAL ADEQUACY AND OFF-BALANCE-SHEET ITEMS

The increase in international banking activity and the concern over bank safety have provided the incentive for supervisory coordination in other areas and across national boundaries. One of the most important areas is that of capital adequacy. Banks are expected to maintain a certain amount of capital against the financial assets they hold. A bank's capi-

---

[12]See Comptroller of the Currency, *U.S. Banking Supervision and International Supervisory Principles* (Washington: July 1986), pp. 3–4.

[13]Ibid.

[14]Federal Financial Institutions Examination Council, *Annual Report 1986* (Washington: 1987), pp. 3–5.

tal—essentially its net worth or the difference between assets and liabilities—serves as a safety cushion in event of a decline in the value of
financial assets. In order to monitor the financial position of banks,
monetary authorities have established capital ratios—capital-to-total
assets—as guidelines. These ratios are used to evaluate the financial
strength of individual commercial banks for examination purposes;
they are also used in decisions on applications for bank mergers and
acquisitions. Within the United States, concern has been expressed since
the early 1960s over the downward trend in the capital/asset ratio (from
an average of about 8.2 percent at the end of 1963 to 6.9 percent at the
end of 1978). In view of the large number of bank failures since the early
1980s, regulatory change was considered appropriate. As a result, the
U.S. regulatory agencies moved to establish minimum capital standards
in 1981. In 1985, the minimum primary capital/total asset ratio was set
at 5.5 percent, and the minimum total capital/total asset ratio was set
at 6 percent.[15]

The capital ratio guidelines were also considered to have shortcomings: (a) the ratios did not take into account some types of commitments
made by banks in the form of off-balance-sheet activities; (b) variations
in the degree of risk associated with different types of financial assets
were not considered. Off-balance-sheet activities (described in Chapter
4) are essentially financial services providing a fee income which obligate
banks but do not show up at least initially on balance sheets. In addition,
some bank assets, such as vault cash or deposits at the central bank, are
not likely to deteriorate in value, but other assets such as customer loans
are subject to a decline in value in event of nonrepayment. Accordingly,
because of differences in the degree of risk associated with financial
assets, and because of the risk that off-balance-sheet exposure entails,
guidelines were proposed by the FDIC, FRB, and OCC in 1986 which
classified assets by degree of risk, and which require that off-balance-
sheet activities be supported by capital reserves.

Rather than simply using a 5.5 percent or 6 percent ratio of capital
to assets, and treating all assets as reflecting an equal degree of risk, a
supplementary variable weighting system was proposed. These weights
ranged from 0 to 100 percent, depending upon the risk associated with
the different types of assets. At one extreme, no risk was assigned to
primary bank reserves (vault cash and deposits with the central bank).
At the other extreme, a 100 percent weight was assigned to claims against
private entities and other high-risk claims. An intermediate degree of risk
was associated with other assets, including short-term government obli-

---

[15]Primary capital includes equity and loss allowances. Total capital adds limited life
preferred stock, subordinated debt, and some intangibles.

gations, short-term interbank claims, and general obligations of state and local governments.

Finally, depending upon the type of transaction, certain off-balance-sheet items were assigned a risk category. An appropriate degree of support was required in the capital accounts for each of the risk categories.

THE UNITED STATES-BRITISH PLAN FOR UNIFORM BANK REQUIREMENTS

The reevaluation of capital adequacy guidelines, coupled with the increased integration of world money and capital markets, focused attention on inequities and shortcomings of regulation across national boundaries. Banks that are permitted by their governments to maintain a relatively low capital-to-asset ratio may be able to function in a less prudent fashion and also at a competitive advantage as compared with banks operating in a more conservative framework. Accordingly, representatives of two of the major banking countries, the United States and the United Kingdom, developed and in early 1987 proposed a set of capital adequacy guidelines for commercial banks in their respective economies. Provisions of the agreement between the Bank of England and U.S. regulatory agencies (the FRB, the FDIC, and the OCC) are similar to guidelines proposed by the three U.S. regulatory agencies in 1986.

The agreement between the United States and the United Kingdom established a minimum capital standard for all banks. The proposed set of risk-based capital requirements provided a common definition of capital, including one for base primary capital and one for limited primary capital. It included a method of weighting bank assets based on risk similar to the one proposed by the U.S. regulatory agencies in 1986. And it provided a method for the inclusion of off-balance-sheet bank commitments in risk assessment by converting them to on-balance-sheet credit equivalents.[16]

The ultimate convergence of U.S.-U.K. policies would create greater uniformity in the regulatory process as well as equity of operations among major international banks. It was anticipated that successful implementation of the proposed guidelines would require inclusion and adherence on the part of regulatory authorities of other major banking

---

[16]The U.S.-U.K. proposal is examined in Federal Reserve Board, "Proposed Action," *Federal Reserve Bulletin* (Washington: May 1987), p. 350 and Federal Reserve Board, "Capital Maintenance: Revision to Capital Adequacy Guidelines," *Federal Register* (Washington: February 19, 1987), pp. 5119-5139.

countries, especially Japan and Germany. Adherence to the guidelines would be particularly important for countries in which actual capital/asset ratios of banks are relatively low compared with those of other countries.[17] According to one study, the capital/asset ratio for Japanese banks was about 3.4 percent in 1984, as compared with 6 percent for U.S. banks and 6.6 percent for West German banks.[18]

Implications of the U.S.-British proposal are significant in a number of respects. First, the guidelines would create uniformity of policy among regulatory authorities of the different participating countries. As a result, they would reduce the inequities faced by banks based on the nature and operations of national regulators. Second, they direct regulatory attention to off-balance-sheet activities of commercial banks. Third, the proposal at least implies a need for greater uniformity of bank accounting practices among countries. Fourth, the proposal is consistent with the Basle Concordat philosophy of covering gaps in bank regulatory procedures. Finally, it is in keeping with the Congressional mandate embodied in the International Lending Supervision Act of 1983 that U.S. regulatory agencies cooperate with regulatory bodies of other countries to establish a more effective approach to the supervision of international banking.

G-10 PROPOSALS

The proposed U.S.-U.K. guidelines also served as a model for an even broader arrangement to accommodate capital adequacy standards. In late 1987, representatives of the United States and United Kingdom, along with other G-10 countries (France, West Germany, Italy, Belgium, Sweden, Netherlands, Canada, and Japan) plus Switzerland and Luxembourg, under the direction of the Bank for International Settlements (the Basle Committee), made public an even more extensive set of capital standards for commercial banks.[19] The major objective of the G-10 (or Basle Committee) proposal is to establish a convergence in the supervision and regulation of capital adequacy primarily for the inter-

---

[17]For an analysis of the implications of variations in capital ratios, see Raj Aggarwal, "Variations in Capital Ratios of the World's Largest Banks," *Management International Review*, Vol. 22, (1982/4), pp. 45-54.

[18]Randall Jones, "Japan's Role in World Financial Markets," *JEI Report* (November 14, 1986), p. 6.

[19]Committee on Banking Regulations and Supervisory Practices, "Proposals for International Convergence of Capital Measurement and Capital Standards" (Basle, Switzerland: Bank for International Settlements, December 1987).

The guidelines as modified slightly and adopted by the Committee are presented in Committee on Banking Regulations and Supervisory Practices, "International Convergence of Capital Measurement and Capital Standards," (Basle, Switzerland: Bank for International Settlements, July 1988).

national banks of the major industrialized countries. In view of the G-10 proposals, action on the earlier U.S.-U.K. agreement was deferred in the hope of securing agreement on the part of a larger number of countries.

The G-10 proposals reflect a recognition of differences among countries in commercial bank accounting practices and terminology as well as the regulatory structure within which banks operate. Accordingly, the proposals provide definitions of capital to include core and supplementary capital that are similar to but more flexible than the U.S.-U.K. definitions. Various categories of assets and off-balance-sheet commitments are weighted on the basis of degree of risk. Although the focus is on credit risk, the need to consider interest rate risk, exchange rate risk, country risk, and concentration risk is also recognized, primarily because the proposals relate to international banks and international financial activities. The country risk, for example, is reflected in the weighting scheme, which places a heavier weight on foreign claims than on domestic claims. In addition, the G-10 proposals give national regulatory agencies more discretion in the choice of an appropriate weighting system for their own banks. Finally, unlike the U.S.-U.K. agreement, the G-10 proposals establish a specific capital ratio—7.25 percent by 1990 and 8 percent by 1992.

Essentially, the G-10 guidelines are more comprehensive than the U.S.-U.K. agreement in terms of country coverage, type of risk, and specification of ratio guidelines and target dates. Yet the guidelines appear to afford greater flexibility with regard to discretionary decisions for national regulators primarily to accommodate the needs of individual banking and regulatory systems. In mid-1988, the central bankers of the 12 countries agreed in principle to the guidelines.

It was anticipated that the United States, the United Kingdom, and the remaining industrial countries would adopt a national version of the proposals tailored to the specific structure of the respective economies. The G-10 proposals were modified somewhat in early 1988 by the U.S. regulatory agencies to reflect existing national regulations and accounting practices; subsequently they were offered for public comment. Under the U.S. version, the guidelines apply to all U.S. banks and holding companies rather than only to the large, international institutions. In addition, there are some differences in the definition of capital designed to reflect the particular accounting system and regulatory structure of this country. Finally, the U.S. version initially placed some assets in a different risk category; individual mortgages held by banks were included in the 100 percent risk weight category, unlike the G-10's assignment to the 50 percent category. (An overall summary of the U.S. guidelines as adapted to the G-10 proposals is presented in Appendix A14.1.)

The guidelines finally adopted by U.S. monetary authorities in late 1988 are similar to those proposed earlier in the year with certain exceptions. First, it was decided to include home mortgages in the 50 percent risk weight category. Second, for purposes of assigning risk, a distinction is made between claims held against OECD countries and those held against nonOECD countries. The effect of both changes is to make it easier for banks to meet capital guidelines.

IMPLICATIONS OF CAPITAL GUIDELINES

The adoption of a national version of the G-10 capital guidelines will require significant changes in the financial and capital markets. Banks in many countries will find it necessary to improve their capital position in order to raise their capital ratios. Japanese banks may have to make the greatest adjustment, but the Ministry of Finance indicated a willingness to participate in the arrangement. Several Japanese banks have sold additional common stock in anticipation of the need to improve their capital positions.

The establishment of risk-weighted asset categories may also cause banks to readjust their asset portfolios to reflect new cost-income opportunities. Assets with a high risk weight require a larger amount of capital and accordingly may come to be either a smaller portion of bank assets or may be tied to a higher interest rate return. For example, loans to governments and banks of OECD countries carry a lower risk weight than loans to nonOECD countries. This is likely to reduce the incentive for U.S. banks to provide credit to the developing countries.

Banks in some countries, such as the United States, may also find it more difficult to compete against other financial institutions, especially investment banks and insurance companies. A shifting in off-balance-sheet commitments may also occur depending upon the assigned risk category, fee and interest returns, and degree of risk perceived by banks. In general, the G-10 guidelines may result in a redirection of the "securitization" process in which banks have expanded their income through fee-based activities while holding external loans at a relatively constant level.

A possible advantage of the widespread adoption of capital adequacy guidelines is that with a major component of bank supervision conducted in a uniform manner, the basis for allegations that external banks operate from a favored position may be minimized. As major international banks develop uniform standards of capital adequacy, national regulators may also be more comfortable with the financial position of external banks operating under their jurisdiction. In connection, the likelihood of a more open policy on the part of national governments to external banks may also be improved.

Successful implementation of the G-10 proposals, particularly if they are adopted by all major banking countries, may provide the basis for an updating of the Basle Concordat and even the stimulus for the development of some type of international regulatory or supervisory institution for commercial banks. Although national banking systems and supervisory approaches differ significantly from country to country, given the rapid growth and importance of commercial banks in both national and international commerce, there are at least some indications of a need for such an agency.[20]

BUSH TASK GROUP PROPOSALS

As noted previously, U.S. banks may be regulated by the FRB, the FDIC, the OCC, and state agencies. The Securities and Exchange Commission and the Justice Department are also involved on occasion. Despite major changes in bank legislation in the United States during the last decade, considerable dissatisfaction remains regarding the complexity of the regulatory and supervisory framework. In practice the various U.S. supervisory agencies have established arrangements that eliminate most of the duplication, yet there remain policy inconsistencies and unneccesary costs ultimately borne by the bank user. In an effort to streamline the system, the Reagan Administration created the Task Group on Regulation of Financial Services under Vice-President George Bush in 1982 to review the federal system of regulating financial services and to propose any desirable legislative changes.

The report of the Task Group (Bush Committee) was released in 1984.[21] Although recommendations focus on the regulation of U.S.-owned banks, some of the major proposals would affect offices of foreign banks. These include the establishment of a Federal Banking Agency (FBA) to replace the Office of the Comptroller of the Currency (OCC) and to assume some of the responsibilities of the FDIC, the possible certifica-

---

[20]For a discussion of some of the implications of an international bank regulatory institution, see Serge Bellanger, "Regulating International Banking," *The Bankers Magazine* (November-December 1987), pp. 44–49.

[21]*Blueprint for Reform*: The Report of the Task Group on Regulation of Financial Services (Washington: July 2, 1984). Summaries of *Blueprint* are provided by Sandra Pianalto, "Reorganizing the U.S. Banking Regulatory Structure," *Economic Commentary*, Federal Reserve Bank of Cleveland (April 9, 1984); Verle B. Johnston, "Reorganization," *Weekly Letter*, Federal Reserve Bank of San Francisco (March 2, 1984).

tion of state bank agencies to examine and supervise state-chartered banks, and the identification of an "international class" of bank holding companies.

Perhaps the most important change recommended by the Task Group would be the creation of a Federal Banking Agency to assume the responsibilities of the Comptroller of the Currency. The FBA would supervise, examine, and regulate all federally chartered banks. Although this provision may not alter substantially the nature of the supervisory and regulatory impact, since the agency would remain under the Treasury Department, it would apply to a large number of foreign banking offices in the United States that now have federal charters or licenses.

The source of the charter of foreign banking organizations varies in part depending upon the type of office. Over one-half of the approximately 230 subsidiaries with some foreign ownership are federally chartered. Agencies and branches of foreign banks were given the option of being licensed by the federal government as a result of the IBA. Slightly more than one-third of the U.S. branches of foreign banks have selected a federal rather than a state license. Only about five percent of all agencies have selected a federal license.

All state-chartered (licensed) banks (both members and nonmembers of the Federal Reserve System) would come under the control of the FRB or a certified state agency. Regulatory-supervisory authority over insured nonmember banks would initially be held by the FRB and the qualified state regulatory agencies; it could eventually be transferred back to a state agency certified to demonstrate capability of conducting effective examination and supervision.

Under existing law, offices of foreign banks with state charters are examined by state agencies and the FDIC if insured by that institution. The FDIC would no longer examine all insured institutions; instead, it would focus efforts on troubled institutions that pose a risk to the system. Eventually, all state banks could be under a single state agency, rather than some banks being under the direction of one agency and another group under a second.

Another important Task Force proposal would place individual banking organizations (banks and their holding companies) under a single regulatory agency. However, this consolidated approach would not apply to an "international" class of BHCs, a group which is defined to include foreign-owned BHCs. The international class of BHCs would remain under the authority of the FRB. Banks controlled by these holding companies could be under the direction of the FBA, the FRB, or a state agency.

POLITICAL FACTORS AND INTERNATIONAL BANKING

Although banks throughout the world are subject to a continuing and relatively constant set of laws and regulations, they are also occasionally caught up in and experience restrictions and also losses associated with political and military conflict. Generally, this occurs as a result of governments imposing economic sanctions and the blocking or "freezing" of foreign assets in domestic banks.

Sanctions were imposed against Argentina in 1982 by Britain and several other European Economic Community members as a result of the Falkland Islands dispute. The sanctions included a freeze on Argentine assets in London banks and an embargo on Argentine exports into the United Kingdom. A side effect of this action was that it further jeopordized Argentina's ability to export and to service an estimated $34 billion in external debt, a substantial share of which was held by U.S. banks and their branches.

The U.S. government, through the Treasury Department, has used various legislative authorities to freeze the claims or assets of foreigners in U.S. banks. As a result, hostile countries are denied the use of such claims until political differences are resolved. The Trading With the Enemy Act of 1917 was used in recent years to freeze bank assets held by Cuba, East Germany, and Vietnam.

Iranian seizure of U.S. hostages in 1979 led to the blocking of Iranian deposits both in U.S. banks and in the overseas branches of U.S. banks. Under the authority provided by the International Emergency Economic Powers Act (IEEPA of 1977), President Carter signed an executive order that blocked or deprived Iran of the use of deposits in U.S. banks (about $2 billion) and in U.S.-owned branches abroad (about $5.6 billion), a large share of which was located in the United Kingdom. The decision to invoke jurisdiction over deposits held by U.S. banks in other countries raised important legal questions both in terms of presidential authority and in terms of the commercial banks' rights and responsibilities; these legal questions were eased at the time with the freeing of the hostages.[22]

In 1986, the U.S. government froze Libyan assets that were held in New York banks and in branches of U.S. banks located in London. The

---

[22]An analysis of the implications of the freezing of Iranian deposits is provided in "Emergency Economic Powers: Iran," *Hearings Before the Subcommittee on International Economic Policy and Trade*, House of Representatives, 97th Congress (Washington: March 5, 1981).

See also Comptroller General of the United States, "Treasury Should Keep Better Track of Blocked Foreign Assets," *Report to The Congress* (Washington: November 1980) and John Marcum, Jr., "U.K. Court Says U.S. Bank Owes Money to Libya," *The Wall Street Journal* (September 3, 1987), p. 12.

Libyan government challenged U.S. action by bringing suit in the British judicial system. A key question centered on the right of the U.S. government to institute such measures against offshore deposits. Britain's High Court, in effect, ruled in 1987 that the U.S. freeze on Libyan assets did not apply to branch banks in London. Further appeals are expected in the case. The ultimate judgment rendered by British courts has important implications not only for international banks, and London as a financial center, but also for the blocking of bank claims as a type of economic sanction.

The ultimate merits of freezing of bank claims involve many of the same arguments used for and against a more general use of economic sanctions. Short-term gains and objectives may on occasion be achieved by the imposing country. Yet such advantages must be weighed against the long-term costs of uncertainty in interbank relationships, extensive judicial litigation, disruption of various forms of commercial activities between countries, and the implication of such actions on other friendly countries.

Because of political and military considerations, questions have also been raised in the United States regarding the desirability of commercial bank loans to communist countries. For example, the proposed International Financial Security Act of 1987 would have granted the U.S. President authority to prohibit bank loans to the Soviet Union and other Eastern bloc countries. The presumption, of course, is that "untied" loans could be used for the purpose of financing military aggression. Opponents of the proposed legislation argue that controls on capital are not always effective and that there is no agreement among allied countries on the desirability of such restrictions.

Lending by home offices of U.S. banks and their European offices to communist bloc countries was previously restricted and has been relatively unimportant, although new opportunities may arise as a result of major economic and political changes occurring in the Soviet economy. For example, as a result of the growing volume of trade with the West, the Soviet banking system introduced a mechanism in 1988 that would permit Russian exporters to hedge their foreign exchange exposures.[23] United States bank transactions with the bloc countries is minimal; by early 1988, cross-border claims of U.S. banks against the Eastern European countries amounted to about $3.2 billion, less than two percent of all cross-border claims of U.S. banks.

The political dimension of international banking also takes other forms. For example, Peru's decision to nationalize (bring under public

---

[23]See John J. Duffy, "Soviets Test Linking the Ruble to Foreign Currencies," *American Banker* (August 12, 1988), p. 2. See also David Fairlamb, "Financing Perestroika," *Institutional Investor* (May 1988), pp. 95-102.

control) a segment of the locally owned financial sector in 1987 has caused some retrenchment on the part of foreign bankers. Several, including Citibank and BankAmerica, have reduced the size of their staff as part of efforts to scale back operations in Peru. South Africa represents a different type of case. Standard Chartered PLC (British), the last remaining foreign bank in South Africa, finally sold its ownership shares to local interests in 1987. This action followed the divestiture by other foreign banks, including Citicorp.

SUMMARY AND CONCLUSIONS

The U.S. banking system is undergoing a profound change from several directions. Part of the change is the trend toward deregulation, from what is termed overregulation to competitive self-regulation, as reflected in the Depository Institutions Deregulation and Monetary Control Act of 1980. But another development relating to both the internationalization of banking and to deregulation is that of increased supervision of bank activities. The International Banking Act, among other things, placed more of the control over U.S. branches and agencies of foreign banks under the federal government.

The emphasis on a more comprehensive system of supervision of international banking is partially a result of efforts of the Basle Committee. The original Basle Concordat of 1975 and the revised version of 1983 represent an attempt on the part of the major industrial countries to ensure that the supervision of commercial banks is adequate and comprehensive. The designation of supervisory control by the appropriate government is essential, given the trend toward internationalization of commercial bank operations. Although the Basle Concordat has been perceived as deficient for its failure to assign responsibility for the lender of last resort, it does contribute to an essential aspect of commercial banking in assigning supervisory authority and stressing its importance.[24]

Although many agencies are involved in supervisory efforts and proposals have been made to centralize the process, the U.S. system is among the most comprehensive in the world. It also appears to correspond relatively closely with the guidelines of the Basle Concordat, although supervision is generally undertaken on the entirety of a bank's operations rather than separately for liquidity, solvency, or foreign exchange exposure.

---

[24]See, for example, M. S. Murdelsohn, "New Bank Concordat: Main Deficiency is Intact," *The American Banker* (June 16, 1983), p. 2.

The U.S. supervisory system, in terms of reflecting the role of both the host authority and the parent authority, is quite extensive. In fact, although the system may not provide the depth of analysis that would be desired under ideal circumstances, it does appear to be quite inclusive in nature.

A national version of the G-10 guidelines for capital adequacy standards has been accepted by regulatory authorities of the United States and other industrial countries. The actual implementation by participating countries, even if only approximating existing provisions, would represent a major development in the supervision of international commercial banking. The guidelines not only provide a basis for monitoring safety and prudence in bank operations, but also provide a framework for greater equity of regulatory treatment across national lines.

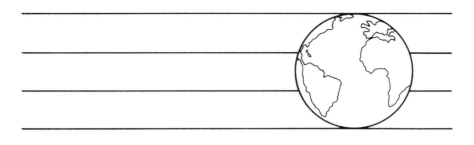

APPENDIX A14.1
SUMMARY OF REVISED
RISK-BASED CAPITAL
ADEQUACY GUIDELINES
FOR U.S. BANKING
ORGANIZATIONS*

Risk-based capital adequacy guidelines are provided by the U.S. regulatory agencies for state and national banks and for bank holding companies. Essentially, all banks are required to hold a specified amount of capital (stated in the form of a ratio) against financial assets (weighted on the basis of degree of risk) and against off-balance-sheet commitments (weighted on the basis of degree of risk). The guidelines:

A. Define core capital elements (tier 1) and supplementary capital elements (tier 2).
B. Categorize balance sheet assets by degree of risk.
C. Categorize off-balance-sheet items by degree of risk.
D. Specify ratios to determine capital adequacy.

---

*The risk based capital adequacy guidelines are contained in Federal Reserve System, *12 Code of Federal Regulations*, Parts 208 and 225, Regulation H, Regulation Y; Docket No. R-0628, *Capital; Risk-Based Capital Guidelines*. Guidelines issued by the Comptroller of the Currency for national banks, and guidelines issued by the Federal Reserve Board for state banks and holding companies are contained in *Federal Register* (Washington: January 27, 1989), pp. 4168-4221.

The following provides a summary of the guidelines adopted by the Federal Reserve Board for state member banks in December of 1988 effective March 15, 1989. Similar guidelines apply to national banks and bank holding companies.[1]

A. Core capital elements (tier 1). Defined to include common stockholders' equity (including common stock, surplus, and retained earnings), minority interest in the equity accounts of consolidated subsidiaries, and noncumulative perpetual preferred stock.

   Supplementary capital elements (tier 2). Includes allowances for loan and lease losses, perpetual preferred stock, hybrid capital instruments, subordinated debt, and intermediate-term preferred stock, all of which are subject to certain specified limitations.

   In addition, supplementary capital elements are limited to 100 percent of core capital elements; subordinated debt and intermediate-term preferred stock are limited to 50 percent of core capital.

   Goodwill and other disallowed intangibles are deducted from tier 1; investments in unconsolidated subsidiaries are deducted from tiers 1 and 2; reciprocal holdings of capital instruments of banking organizations are deducted from tiers 1 and 2.

B. On-balance-sheet items weighted on the basis of risk include:
   i. 0 percent weight. Cash (domestic and foreign); balances due from Federal Reserve Banks and central banks of OECD countries; claims on, or guaranteed by, the U.S. government or Treasury or an OECD government or its agencies; local currency claims on, or guaranteed by, nonOECD countries.
   ii. 20 percent weight. Cash items in the process of collection; all claims on, and the portion of claims that are guaranteed by, U.S. depository institutions and OECD banks; claims on, and the portion of claims that are guaranteed by, official multilateral lending institutions or regional development banks; claims on, and the portion of claims that are guaranteed by, U.S. government sponsored agencies.
   iii. 50 percent weight. Revenue bonds or similar obligations of U.S. state or local governments and other local OECD governments; loans fully secured by first liens on 1-4 family residential properties.

[1]Guidelines for bank holding companies are similar. Major differences include:

   a. Bank holding companies are allowed to include cumulative preferred stock in tier 1 capital.

   b. Bank holding companies are allowed to grandfather existing goodwill for the transition period as part of tier 1 capital. But all new goodwill must be deducted from tier 1 capital, and all goodwill must be deducted from tier 1 capital at the end of the transition period.

   c. Parent company investment in unconsolidated subsidiaries is excluded from its total capital components.

   d. Small bank holding companies (less than $150 million in consolidated assets) are exempt from calculation and analysis of risk based ratios on a consolidated holding company basis.

   Guidelines for national banks are similar to those for state banks. For example, cumulative perpetual stock is included in tier 2 capital for both national and state banks.

iv. 100 percent weight. All other claims on private obligors; claims on, or guaranteed by, nonOECD foreign banks with a remaining maturity exceeding one year; claims on commercial firms owned by a government; premises, plant, equipment, and other fixed assets.

C. Off-balance-sheet items are included in a two-step process. First, the face value of the off-balance-sheet item is multiplied by a credit conversion factor to establish a balance sheet credit equivalent amount. The credit equivalent amount is then assigned to the appropriate risk category in the same way as on-balance-sheet items.

C1. Establishment of credit equivalent factor.

   i. 100 percent conversion factor. Includes any direct credit substitutes or general guarantees of indebtedness, such as standby letters of credit, sale and repurchase agreements and assets sold with recourse, and forward agreements to purchase assets.

  ii. 50 percent conversion factor. Includes contingencies related to transactions, unused portions of commitments with original maturity exceeding one year, revolving underwriting facilities, and note issuance facilities.

 iii. 20 percent conversion factor. Includes short-term, self-liquidating trade-related contingencies, such as commercial letters of credit.

  iv. 0 percent conversion factor. Includes unused commitments with an original maturity of one year or less which can be cancelled at any time.

C2. Assignment of credit risk category. After the face value of an off-balance-sheet item is adjusted by multiplying it by the credit conversion factor, it is assigned a risk category according to the obligor, or, if relevant, the guarantor or nature of the collateral.

D. Key capital to weighted risk asset ratio guidelines:

   i. Total capital to weighted risk assets, 7.25 percent by year-end 1990; 8.0 percent by year-end 1992.

  ii. Tier 1 capital to weighted risk assets, 3.625 percent by year-end 1990; 4.0 percent by year-end 1992.

 iii. Common stockholders' equity to weighted risk assets, 3.25 percent by 1990; 4.0 percent by year-end 1992.

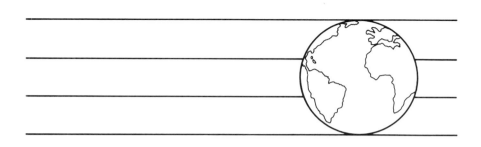

EPILOGUE

One of the more dynamic areas of economic activity in recent years and in all likelihood in the years ahead is that of international finance and banking. Changes in world finance are reflected in the continuing growth in the Eurocurrency market, the collapse of the Bretton-Woods system of pegged exchange rates, and the adoption of a system of floating rates. The action of the OPEC countries, unprecedented inflation, high interest rates, balance of payments difficulties, payments arrears, and debt restructuring are also part of the changing environment.

Major U.S. banks remain important creditors to low-income countries, yet the United States has experienced a large current account deficit and a net capital inflow since the early 1980s and is now the major debtor country. The volume of international lending and borrowing in the private sector evidenced ongoing expansion at least through 1982 and financial crisis sometimes appeared imminent. Yet the international financial system for the most part has escaped the serious disorder that could have easily developed; as a result, world trade has not been seriously affected. In the United States, commercial banks have lost their uniqueness as the only institutions able to accept transactions deposits and to create deposits through loans. The question of what constitutes a commercial bank is being reappraised, and the definitions of the broad monetary aggregates (M1, M2, and M3) continue to change. Off-balance-sheet activities are becoming increasingly important for banks as a way to escape restrictive regulations and to enhance profits. IBFs first became operational in late 1981; the assets booked by these facilties amounted to over $250 billion by mid-1988, and facilities had been established by banks in over half of the states.[1]

Changes within U.S. financial markets are partially the result of new legislation and regulations designed to permit greater competition among different types of financial institutions. They are the result of changing economic conditions, especially the inflation of the 1970s and 1980s. They are also the result of industrial, commercial, and population shifts within the country.[2] Florida and, at least for a time, Texas, and other areas of the sunbelt have emerged as important banking centers both through local banks and Edge Act Corporations.

Many small banks have failed as a result of loan losses to domestic agriculture, real estate, and the energy sectors. Yet the United States remains an attractive market for foreign banks. Not only have the traditional banking countries increased their penetration of American markets, but also banks in Japan and other countries in the Far and Middle East have greatly expanded operations in recent years. Japanese banks have come to be a dominant power in international finance.[3]

GENERAL NATURE OF CHANGES IN THE UNITED STATES

What lies ahead for the remainder of the 1980s and for the 1990s? Projections in any area of economic and social activity are hazardous. Yet such projections are essential if only to prepare for potential problems that may arise. Several areas of certainty include the continued development and usage of communications technology, the improved

[1]Federal Reserve Board, "Monthly Report of Assets and Liabilities of International Banking Facilities as of March 31, 1988," *Statistical Release* (Washington: April 1988).

[2]A useful survey of current developments in U.S. commercial banking is provided in *Bank Performance Annual*, ed. Edwin B. Cox (Boston: Warren, Gorham & Lamont). The Seventh Annual Yearbook was published in 1987.

[3]Changes in the financial structure of three major countries are described in Charles Freedman, "Financial Restructuring: The Canadian Experience," pp. 63-79; Anthony Loehnis, "Financial Restructuring: The United Kingdom Experience," pp. 81-102; and Yoshio Suzuki, "Financial Restructuring: The Japanese Experience," pp. 103-119, in Federal Reserve Bank of Kansas City, *Restructuring the Financial System* (Kansas City: 1987). See also Randall Jones, "Japan's Role in World Financial Markets," *Japan Economic Institute Report* (November 14, 1986), p. 6.

flow of information across political boundaries, the integration of money and capital markets, the intensity of "nonlocal" competition in financial markets, and changes in the regulatory-legislative framework in part to keep up with changes in the financial services sector.

Developments regarding interstate banking remain transitory, although all but about a half-dozen of the states authorize some form of banking across state lines. Many U.S. banks, especially those of a medium size, have restructured their operations, particularly through bank holding companies, in order to position themselves for opportunities that arise as new legislation is enacted in this area. The Reagan Administration advocated interstate banking as a way of strengthening the U.S. banking system.[4] And the Chairman of the Federal Reserve Board, Alan Greenspan, has indicated support for additional bank deregulation. The trend toward interstate banking is certain to continue, although legislative, regulatory, and judicial change is expected to take place gradually over an extended period of time.

Reduced regulation of domestic financial activity is likely to be accompanied by increased supervision.[5] Extensive supervision is consistent with the need for greater amounts of information and policy guidelines, especially as bank activity expands globally. Although it may be difficult and probably impossible to achieve uniformity of laws and regulations, it is possible to provide timely and comprehensive information on developments in the financial marketplace.

Regulatory concern has also developed as an increasing number of U.S. and foreign-owned banks become involved in lending to finance leveraged buy-outs (LBOs) among American commercial and industrial companies. In an LBO, a company finances the purchase of a second company largely by borrowing, in part, from banks. Bank financing of LBOs is recognized as a legitimate activity; the concern is that LBO activity and bank participation have expanded rapidly in recent years. As a result, banks are being requested by regulatory authorities to establish written policies regarding this type of lending.

Deregulation was clearly a trademark of the Reagan Administration, but the philosophy had earlier support as reflected, for example, in the Monetary Control Act of 1980. Regulatory changes permitting the establishment of the IBFs were another sign of a continuing trend toward

---

[4]*Economic Report of the President Transmitted to the Congress, February 1986* (Washington: 1986), pp. 209-212.

[5]Although bank "supervision" and "regulation" are sometimes used synonomously, the terms are generally intended to be distinct and different. Regulation pertains to the formulation and issuance of rules and regulations to provide a framework for bank behavior. Supervision involves continuing oversight to ensure that banks are operated in accordance with laws and regulations. See Federal Reserve Board, *The Federal Reserve System, Purposes and Functions* (Washington: 1984), p. 88.

deregulation. A major justification of the IBFs was that a greater volume of international banking activity would take place on American soil rather than at an offshore center. Indeed, it has been argued that competition among bank regulators of different countries to attract indigent bank activity may in fact lead to reduced financial regulation.[6]

Within the United States, the regulatory structure is perceived as inefficient, inconsistent, and, as indicated in the Bush Task Force report, in need of streamlining. National regulatory structures have also been characterized as arrangements established years ago that are not designed for a marketplace of worldwide dimensions.

Appropriately, one might expect future U.S. bank legislation to be similar in nature to the Monetary Control Act—that is, to contain some provisions that reduce regulation and some provisions that increase regulation. In specific terms, it might be expected that United States-located banks (and/or their holding companies) will gain the authority to expand from both a product and a geographic perspective. But, in addition, banks will find their off-balance-sheet commitments an important object of the supervisory/evaluation process; in fact, regulations are being implemented by the Federal Reserve Board and Comptroller of the Currency, and banks have started to make the necessary adjustments.

In the past, foreign banks have been most competitive in the United States in wholesale functions with emphasis on transactions at the corporate level. The 1990s will probably see more emphasis directed toward opportunities at the retail level, in part because of a growing familiarity with American markets. Some of the objections regarding foreign takeovers of U.S. domestic banks appear to have diminished. Yet some changes may be made in policies regarding outright acquisitions. To achieve an acceptable degree of competitive equality, restrictions on U.S. banks are likely to be dropped rather than subjecting foreign banks to increased restrictions. There is also support for granting additional authority to U.S.-owned banks to provide a broader foundation for increased competition in world markets.[7] Although Congress has been unwilling to establish new policies on securities underwriting, bank regulatory agencies at both the federal and state level are likely to move toward an easing of restrictions in this area. The significant decline in the

---

[6]Deborah Allen and Ian Giddy, "Towards a Theory of Interdependence in Global Banking Regulation," *Eastern Economic Journal* (December 1979), pp. 445-452.

See also D. B. Crane and S. L. Hayes, III, "The Evolution of International Banking Competition and its Implications for Regulations," *Journal of Bank Research* (Spring 1983), pp. 39-53.

[7]An analysis of bank involvement in the securities business is provided in John Cranford, "Expanded Powers: The View From Three Banks," *Congressional Quarterly* (May 7, 1988), pp. 1195-1199.

relative importance of U.S. banks in international financial activity is certain to provide a strong incentive for changes that might enhance the competitiveness of U.S. institutions.

Although regulation of domestic activity may be diminished, it is not likely that a similar change will occur with respect to international lending and banking. The revision of the Basle Concordat in early 1983 is one indication of strengthened interest in comprehensive supervision; this trend was confirmed in the G-10 guidelines for uniform risk-adjusted capital requirements for banks.

The increased frequency with which debtor countries have sought the renegotiation of external obligations caused concern on the part of members of Congress that banks have not followed prudent lending policies toward the developing countries. The seriousness of the situation became even more apparent with the Congressional decision (the International Lending Supervision Act of 1983) to provide additional funds to the IMF to support its efforts with the debtor developing countries. As a result, greater control on loans has been exerted through restrictive regulatory and supervisory action introduced by U.S. bank regulatory authorities.

The volume of new international bank lending declined during the early 1980s, according to data estimates from both the Bank for International Settlements and the International Monetary Fund.[8] Many U.S. banks experienced a profit squeeze on their overseas activities as a growing number of financial institutions, both domestic and foreign, became competitive in the market.[9] Declining profits, payments arrears, and indications of default by debtor countries are likely to cause many medium-sized regional banks to continue to reassess their positions and possibly curtail their international transactions.

The securitization of financial markets may also have entered a transitory phase. Empirical evidence suggests a renewed growth in international bank lending since about 1986, particularly among the industrialized countries. Despite the concern over inflation and the managed float, the U.S. Gold Commission study and conclusions reduce the likelihood that a gold standard will be promoted by the United States. Yet some proposals have developed that the exchange market be tied to a "commodity basket" that includes gold. Although there may be some merit in a return to a form of the gold standard, other control measures

[8]Comptroller of the Currency, *Annual Report 1979* (Washington: 1980), pp. 315-316; Maxwell Watson, et al., *International Capital Markets* (Washington: International Monetary Fund, December 1986), pp. 2-5.

[9]See, for example, Joseph Pinola, "Gateway to the New Frontiers in Banking," *The Journal of Commercial Bank Lending* (January 1981), pp. 8-16.

are sufficiently effective and efficient in the control of money and price levels. The real problem is principally the will to use existing control measures, especially when there is a possible conflict with other national goals.

CHANGES AT THE INTERNATIONAL LEVEL

Changes in bank activity at the international level are closely related to and cannot be separated from national developments. Perhaps the most important considerations in international commercial banking in the near future relate to the ultimate resolution of Third World debt problems vis-a-vis commercial banks, to financial innovation and off-balance-sheet bank activities, and to regulatory-supervisory policies at both the national and international levels.

The external debt of Latin American countries to U.S. and other commercial banks is likely to affect lending attitudes and practices, to lead to the use of alternative sources of capital by developing countries, and to create valuation problems for creditor commercial banks for the forseeable future. Banks have already introduced changes and are better equipped to cope with the uncertainty associated with repayment strains than they were in 1982. To a great extent, however, alleviation of the debt problems is beyond the control of banks, and rather depends upon market conditions—the demand, supply, and price of items exported by debtor countries.

Financial innovation of various types, including technological improvements and the use and development of off-balance-sheet activities, have received less public attention than the Third World debt, yet may prove to be equally important. Innovation also relates to regulation and/or deregulation at both the national and international level. Several countries, including the United States, have removed some of the restrictions on the activity of financial institutions. Yet the use of modern technology has facilitated the internationalization of financial markets. And off-balance-sheet endeavors frequently include a degree of risk that was not incorporated into traditional capital ratios and standard supervisory methods until late 1988.

Another important set of considerations centers largely on political considerations, epecially with regard to the centrally planned economies. A modest revival of interest in bank lending to Eastern European countries has been criticized by some Congressional leaders. In the Soviet Union, *perestroika* and major domestic reforms have led to efforts to improve foreign economic relationships. The Soviet consideration of a forward currency market, gradual currency convertibility, and accession to the General Agreement on Tariffs and Trade are an indication of the strength of the reform movement.[10]

There is also a possibility of new banking opportunities in mainland China (PRC). Chinese leaders have permitted an inflow of external investment in the form of joint ventures; foreign banks have been authorized to establish branches in order to serve existing Chinese entrepreneurs. United States bank opportunities in the PRC depend at least as much on political considerations as on economic requirements—particularly the nature of relationships between the United States and Taiwan.

The possible use of economic sanctions and the blocking or "freezing" of assets of unfriendly countries in U.S. banks and their overseas offices add another element of uncertainty stemming from political considerations. Events relating to terrorism, taking of hostages, the Persian Gulf situation, Panama, and other developments of a political nature suggest that economic sanctions and freezing of assets of foreigners may not diminish in importance. In addition to the uncertainty created for international banking, the possibility of ensuing litigation suggests complex problems that may be difficult to resolve.

The growth of Islamic banking is another interesting facet of change in the international banking community. The first contemporary Islamic banks were established in the mid-1970s, but the number increased significantly thereafter, in part as a result of OPEC cash balances. Islamic banking principles, if fully implemented, involve the payment of funds to investors on an equity capital and profit and loss sharing basis, since they proscribe interest payments or receipts. An estimated 45 countries have some form of Islamic banking, including Bahrain, United Arab Emirates, Sudan, Egypt, Saudi Arabia, Jordan, Kuwait, and Qatar, which competes with conventional banking. Pakistan and Iraq have made the most extensive changes to transform to such a system.[11]

The European Economic Community's decision to implement a single market may have an important impact on U.S. commercial relations with the member countries, which include most of Western Europe. Not only will a single banking market come into existense, but commercial banks may become universal banks in the sense that they are able to perform various securities transactions as well as other related financial functions.

---

[10]See Abel Aganbegyan and Timor Timofeyev, *The New Stage of Perestroika* (New York: Institute for East-West Security Studies, 1988).

[11]See Mohsin S. Khan and Abbas Mirakhor, "The Framework and Practice of Islamic Banking," *Finance & Development* (September 1986), pp. 32-36; and Shahrukh Rafi Kahn, "Profit and Loss Sharing as a Substitute for Interest in Islamic Banking," *Savings and Development Quarterly Review* (No. 3, 1987), pp. 317-327.

There are indications that foreign direct investment will assume a more important channel for the flow of capital in the years ahead.[12] Historically, direct investment has been a predominant form of resource transfer. Because it does not create an overhang of debt and because it is more likely to facilitate technology transfers and the generation of productive capacity, private direct investment could partially alleviate the payments problems of some of the large debtor countries.

Whether or not a phenomenon such as the Eurocurrency market as an international system can be or should be regulated by an international agency remains open to question. The Eurocurrency market has facilitated the cross-border flow of funds and thus has promoted an efficient use of resources on an international level. Yet the possibility remains that because of its structure the market may contribute to financial instability if weaknesses were to develop in the international system. In the meantime, some regulation, perhaps on an occasional basis, along with continued monitoring and supervision can be expected from national governments. Furthermore, should the Eurocurrency market ever exhibit the characteristics that suggest a threat to international or national financial structures, it is quite likely that appropriate regulatory measures would be introduced on a coordinated basis. The Eurocurrency market is central to the international banking system and provides important advantages and efficiencies that accrue to the world financial community. Given that neither specific objectives nor an easy method of control has been enunciated, extensive regulation of the market is not likely to occur in the near future.

What role will the IMF and World Bank play in the future? The agreement to expand IMF lending facilities is an indication that this institution and the World Bank will regain some of their importance in the area of international capital flows. Some studies have concluded that commercial bank lending will not meet the needs of developing countries and that a larger financing role will be placed on the official institutions.[13] Although the IMF's lending role is likely to expand somewhat in the future, its most important responsibility is likely to be the surveillance of foreign exchange markets. This implies a continuation of IMF efforts to insure that exchange rate and related policies of member countries are consistent with domestic and international growth and stability.[14]

[12]Group of Thirty, *Foreign Direct Investment, 1973-87* (New York: 1984).

[13]David Roberts and Eli Remolova, *Finance for Developing Countries: Alternative Sources of Finance Debt Swaps* (New York: Group of Thirty, 1987).

[14]A projected evolution of the international monetary system is provided in Per Jacobsson Foundation, *The International Monetary System: The Next Twenty-five Years* (Washington: International Monetary Fund, 1988).

Continued disagreement can be expected among the various groups of countries regarding the role of the IMF and the World Bank in their contribution toward world monetary stability and economic development of the low-income countries; the concern is that IMF-imposed austerity measures are unrealistic. The basic conflict regarding equity in the use of world resources as compared to the more conventional standard of efficiency is not likely to be diminished in the forseeable future. Unilateral transfers by national governments and assistance on concessional terms generally conform to perceptions of equity. Conventional loans with interest and principal repayment at competitive rates as provided by international banks are more in line with the principle of efficiency.

Coordinated regulation of international banking is more likely to proceed in another area relating to bank safety and equity of operations—that of capital adequacy. The G-10 guidelines are important not only because of the concern with emerging financial problems, but also because of the recognition of the need for regulatory action that transcends national boundaries. As has been the case historically, new institutional arrangements will continue to be created to cope with new problems that have arisen.

CONCLUSIONS

A major theme of this overview of international commercial banking is that the financial and capital markets of individual countries and the world economy remain in a transitory phase and that the nature of an equilibrium state of affairs cannot be predicted. Interestingly enough, as these markets become more closely integrated, increased competition appears to be developing not only in financial markets across geographic areas but also between and among even larger types of financial institutions. The blurring of prerogatives of the various financial activities, the increased merger activity among savings and loan institutions, the new authority given to Edges, the establishment of the IBFs and a financial futures market, and the continuing strong interests of the larger banks in international activities attest to the dynamic nature of this environment within the United States.

The growth in international commercial bank activity in future years will depend upon the leadership role assumed by the U.S. government in matters of trade liberalization, exchange rate intervention, resource transfers both through concessional finance and private international investments, and coordination of regulatory efforts.[15] With an appropriate framework for activity and an expansive, liberal approach in official U.S. foreign economic policy, commercial bank activity is likely to continue to expand in future years; not necessarily in terms of lending, but rather in terms of interest rate swaps, note issuance facilities, standby letters of credit, options, and futures. This will be particularly true if there were to be a decline in international political tensions, terrorism, and cold war rhetoric. Much will also depend upon the attitude and role of the Japanese government and banking community as they come to occupy a dominant position in the world economy.

Perhaps the most important factors to be considered in assessing the nature of the financial markets are the strength, resiliency, and the willingness to adapt to change that has been demonstrated in these markets. Despite the major shocks that have occurred, particularly regarding exchange rate regimes, petroleum prices, and sources of capital, the U.S. current account deficit, and the sharp appreciation and then depreciation of the dollar since 1980, and despite the serious financial problems that many individual countries have encountered, the system has been able to adjust, and widespread financial crises of serious magnitude have been avoided. Perhaps the major reason is that at least the most important element of the Bretton-Woods system—that of cooperation among governments of the major trading nations—appears to have remained intact.

---

[15]The nature of an expansive foreign economic policy is examined in G. M. Meier, "U.S. Foreign Economic Policies," *The United States in the 1980s*, Peter Duignan and Alvin Rabushka, eds. (Stanford, California: Hoover Institution Press, 1980), pp. 585-611.

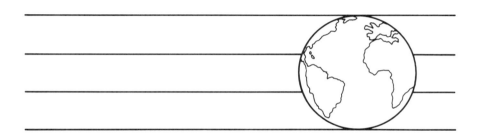

GENERAL BIBLIOGRAPHY

ABRAMS, RICHARD, "The Role of Regional Banks in International Banking." *Columbia Journal of World Business* (Summer 1981), pp. 62-72.

AGGARWAL, RAJ, *The Literature of International Business Finance.* New York: Praeger Publishers, 1984.

AHARONI, Y., *The Emerging International Monetary Order and the Banking System.* Tel Aviv: University Publishing Projects, 1976.

American Banker, *American Banker Yearbook.* New York: published annually.

American Bankers Association, *Statistical Information on the Financial Services Industry*, 4th ed. Washington, D.C.: 1987.

American Bankers Association, *Banking Terminology.* Washington, D.C.: 1981.

American Bankers Association, *International Banking: U.S. Laws and Regulations.* Washington, D.C.: 1984.

ANDO, ALBERT, RICHARD HERRING, AND RICHARD MARSTON, *International Aspects of Stabilization Policies* (Proceedings of a Conference Held at Williamstown, Mass.), Federal Reserve Bank of Boston, June 1974.

ANGELINI, ANTHONY, MAXIMO ENG, AND FRANCIS LEES, *International Lending, Risk, and the Euromarkets.* New York: John Wiley & Sons, Inc., 1979.

ARONSON, JONATHAN D., *Money and Power: Banks and the World Monetary System.* Beverly Hills, Cal.: Sage Publications, 1977.

ARONSON, JONATHAN D., "Politics and the International Consortium Banks," *Stanford Journal of International Studies* (Spring 1976), pp. 42-69.

BAIRD, JANE, AND DARRELL DELAMAIDE, "The Lesson of Poland," *Institutional Investor* (January 1982), pp. 223-228.

BAKER, JAMES C., *International Bank Regulation.* New York: Holt, Rinehart and Winston, 1978.

BAKER, JAMES C., AND M. GERALD BRADFORD, *American Banks Abroad* (Edge Act Companies and Multinational Banking). New York: Praeger Publishers, 1974.

BAUGHN, WILLIAM H., AND DONALD MANDICH, *The International Banking Handbook.* Homewood, Ill.: Dow Jones-Irwin, 1983.

BECKER, JOSEPH D., "International Insolvency: The Case of Herstatt," *American Bar Association Journal* (October 1976), pp. 1290-1295.

BEIM, DAVID O., "Rescuing the LDCs," *Foreign Affairs* (July 1977), pp. 717-731.

BERGER, FREDERICK E., "U.S. Banking Regulations: On the Brink of Sweeping Proposals," *American Import Export Management* (January 1982), pp. 80-84.

BERGSTEN, C. FRED, WILLIAM CLINE, AND JOHN WILLIAMSON, *Bank Lending to Developing Countries.* Cambridge, Mass.: Institute for International Economics, April 1985.

BHATTACHARYA, A. K., "Offshore Banking in the Caribbean by U.S. Commercial Banks: Implications for Government-Business Interaction," *Journal of International Business Studies* (Winter 1980), pp. 37-46.

BHATTACHARYA, ANINDYA, *The Asian Dollar Market: International Offshore Financing.* New York: Praeger Publishers, 1977.

BLACK, JOHN, AND JOHN H. DUNNING, *International Capital Movements.* New York: Holmes and Meier Publishers, Inc., 1982.

BRENNER, LYNN, "How to Insure Against Political Risks," *Institutional Investor* (April 1981), pp. 211-220.

BRIMMER, ANDREW F., "Commercial Bank Lending Abroad and the U.S. Balance of Payments," *The International Monetary System in Transition.* Federal Reserve Board of Chicago (March 1972), pp. 76-91.

BRIMMER, ANDREW F., AND FREDERICK DAHL, "Growth of American International Banking: Implications for Public Policy," *Journal of Finance* (May 1975), pp. 341-363.

BROWN, BRENDAN, *The Forward Market in Foreign Exchange: A Study in Market-Market Arbitrage and Speculation.* New York: St. Martin's Press, 1983.

BRYANT, RALPH C., *International Financial Intermediation.* Washington, D.C.: The Brookings Institution, 1987.

BUTERA, M. LEE, ED., *Fourth Annual Foreign Banking Conference.* Washington, D.C.: Foreign Bank Focus, March 1985.

CARLSON, ROBERT S., ET AL., *International Finance* (Cases and Simulation). Reading, Mass.: Addison-Wesley Publishing Company, 1980.

CARMICHAEL, EDWARD, *Foreign Exchange Risk Management in Canadian Companies.* Ottawa: Conference Board of Canada, 1980.

CARVOUNIS, CHRIS, "The LDC Debt Problem: Trends in Country Risk Analysis and Rescheduling Exercises," *Columbia Journal of World Business* (Spring 1982), pp. 15-19.

CLINE, WILLIAM R., *Mobilizing Bank Lending to Debtor Countries.* Washington, D.C., Institute for International Economics, June 1987.

COHEN, BENJAMIN, *Banks and the Balance of Payments* (Private Lending in the International Adjustment Process). Montclair, N.J.: Allanheld, Osmun and Company, Publisher, Inc., 1981.

COMPTON, ERIC N., *The New World of Commercial Banking*, Lexington, Mass.: D. C. Heath and Company, 1987.

CONNOLLY, MICHAEL B. ED., *The International Monetary System: Choices for the Future.* New York: Praeger Publishers, 1982.

DALE, RICHARD, *The Regulation of International Banking.* Englewood Cliffs, N.J.: Prentice-Hall, Inc., 1985.

DAS, DILIP K., *Migration of Financial Resources to Developing Countries.* New York: St. Martin's Press, 1986.

DAVIDSON, PAUL, *International Money and the Real World.* New York: John Wiley & Sons, 1982.

DAVIS, R. R., "Alternative Techniques for Country Risk Evaluation," *Business Economics* (May 1981), pp. 34-41.

DAVIS, STEVEN I., "How Risky is International Lending?" *Harvard Business Review* (January-February 1977), pp. 135-143.

DEAK, NICHOLAS, AND JO ANNE CELUSAK, *International Banking.* New York: New York Institute of Finance, 1984.

DEAN, JAMES W., AND IAN H. GIDDY, *Averting International Banking Crises.* New York: New York University, Salomon Brothers Center for the Study of Financial Institutions, 1981.

DEAN, JAMES W., AND RICHARD SCHWINDT, *International Banking and Finance* (Business Administration Readings Lists and Course Outlines). Durham, N.C.: Eno River Press, 1981.

DENNIS, GEOFFREY E. J., *International Financial Flows.* Lexington, Mass.: Lexington Books, 1984.

DICKENS, ENGLEBERT, "International Banking Abroad," *The International Monetary System in Transition.* Federal Reserve Board of Chicago (March 1972), pp. 114-120.

DICKS, G. R., ED., *Sources of World Financial and Banking Information.* Westport, Col.: Greenwood Press, 1981.

DOD, DAVID, "Bank Lending to Developing Countries," *Federal Reserve Bulletin,* Washington, D.C. (September 1981), pp. 647-656.

DONALDSON, T. H., *Lending in International Commercial Banking.* New York: Halstead Press, 1979.

DOOLEY, M. P., "The Implications of the Internationalization of Banking for the Definition and Measurement of U.S. Credit and Monetary Aggregates," *Economic Forum* (Winter 1980), pp. 54-68.

DORNBUSCH, RUDIGER, *Dollars, Debts, and Deficits.* Cambridge, Mass.: The MIT Press, 1986.

DUFEY, GUNTER, AND IAN GIDDY, *The International Money Market.* Englewood Cliffs, N.J.: Prentice-Hall, 1978.

DUFEY, GUNTER, AND ROLF MIRUS, "Forecasting Foreign Exchange Rates: A Pedagogical Note," *Columbia Journal of World Business* (Summer 1981), pp. 53-61.

Edge Corporation Branching: Foreign Bank Takeovers and International Banking Facilities (Hearing Before the Committee on Banking, Housing and Urban Affairs), U.S. Senate (July 16 and 20, 1979), Washington: 1979.

EITEMAN, DAVID K., AND ARTHUR I. STONEHILL, *Multinational Business Finance,* 3rd ed., Reading, Mass.: Addison-Wesley Publishing Company, 1982.

ERBE, RAINER, "Indicator Systems for the Assessment of the External Debt Situation of Developing Countries," *Intereconomics* (November-December 1980), pp. 285-289.

FAHMG, SAMIZ B., "Foreign Exchange Accounting," *Review of Business* (Spring 1983), pp. 5-8.

Federal Reserve Bank of Boston, *Key Issues in International Banking.* Proceedings of a Conference Held at Melvin Village, N.H. Boston: October 1977.

Federal Reserve Bank of Kansas City, *Restructuring the Financial System.* Kansas City, Mo.: 1987.

FEIGER, GEORGE, AND BERTRAND JACQUILLAT, *International Finance* (Text and Cases). Boston: Allyn and Bacon, Inc., 1982.

FENNEMA, M., *International Network of Banks and Industry.* The Hague: Martinus Nijhoff Publishers, 1982.

FIELEKE, NORMAN S., "The Growth of U.S. Banking Abroad: An Analytical Survey," *Key Issues in International Banking.* Federal Reserve Board of Boston (October 1977), pp. 9-40.

FISHLOW, ALBERT, "Latin America's Debt," *Columbia Journal of World Business* (Spring 1982), pp. 35-46.

FRENKEL, JACOB A., ED., *Exchange Rates and International Macroeconomics.* Chicago: University of Chicago Press, 1983.

FRIEDER, LARRY A., ED., *Commercial Banking and Interstate Expansion.* Ann Arbor, Mich.: UMI Research Press, 1985.

General Accounting Office, *Bank Examination for Country Risk and International Lending.* Washington, D.C.: September 2, 1982.

General Accounting Office, *Lending to Troubled Sectors.* Washington, D.C.: September 1988.

GEORGE, ABRAHAM M., AND IAN H. GIDDY, *International Finance Handbook,* Vols. I and II. New York: John Wiley & Sons, 1983.

GERAKIS, A. S., AND O. RONCESVALLES, "Bahrain's Offshore Banking Center," *Finance and Development* (June 1980), pp. 29-31.

GIDDY, IAN, "International Banking," *Handbook of Financial Markets and Institutions*, 6th ed., Edward Altman, ed. New York: John Wiley & Sons, 1987, pp. 19.3-19.61.

GOLDBERG, LAWRENCE G., "The Causes of U.S. Bank Expansion Overseas: The Case of Great Britain," *Journal of Money, Credit and Banking* (November 1980), pp. 630-643.

GOLEMBE, CARTER H., AND DAVID S. HOLLAND, *Federal Regulations of Banking*. Washington, D.C.: Golembe Associates, 1981.

GOODMAN, LAURIE S., "An Alternative to Rescheduling LDC Debt in an Inflationary Environment." *Columbia Journal of World Business* (Spring 1982), pp. 20-27.

GOODMAN, STEPHEN H., *Financing and Risk in Developing Countries*. New York: Praeger Publishers, 1978.

GOODMAN, STEPHEN, "How the Big U.S. Banks Really Evaluate Sovereign Risks," *Euromoney* (February 1977), pp. 105-110.

GRABBE, J. ORLIN, *International Financial Markets*. New York: Elsevier Science Publishing Company, 1986.

GRADY, JOHN, AND MARTIN WEALE, *British Banking, 1960-85*. New York: St. Martin's Press, 1986.

GRIFFITH-JONES, S., "The Growth of Multinational Banking, the Euro-currency Market and Their Effects on Developing Countries," *Journal of Development Studies* (January 1980), pp. 204-223.

Group of Thirty, *Balance-of-Payments Problem of Developing Countries*. New York: 1981.

Group of Thirty, *How Bankers See World Financial Markets*. New York: 1982.

Group of Thirty, *Risks in International Bank Lending*. New York: 1982.

Group of Thirty, *The Outlook for International Bank Lending*. New York: 1981.

HEFFERNAN, SHELAGH, *Sovereign Risk Analysis*. London: Allen & Unwin, 1986.

HELLER, H. ROBERT, and Emmanuel Frankel, "Determinants of LDC Indebtedness," *Columbia Journal of World Business* (Spring 1982), pp. 28-34.

HENNING, CHARLES N., WILLIAM PIGOTT AND ROBERT H. SCOTT, *International Financial Management*. New York: McGraw-Hill Book Company, 1978.

HUGHES, HELEN, "The External Debt of Developing Countries," *Finance and Development* (December 1977), pp. 22-25.

International Banking. Committee on Banking, Currency and Housing, Washington, D.C.: May 1976.

International Monetary Fund, *World Economic Outlook*. Washington, D.C.: annual.

KAHLEY, WILLIAM J. "Assessing Economic Country Risk." *Economic Review*, Federal Reserve Bank of Atlanta (June 1981), pp. 32-36.

KAMMERT, JAMES L., *International Commercial Banking Management*. New York: AMACOM, 1981.

KATZ, JEFFRY, *Capital Flows and Developing Country Debt*. Washington, D.C.: International Bank for Reconstruction and Development, August 1979.

KELLY, JANET, *Banker and Borders: The Case of American Banks in Britain*. Cambridge, Mass: Ballinger Publishing Company, 1977.

KENEN, PETER, *The Role of the Dollar as an International Currency*. New York: Group of Thirty, 1981.

KESSLER, G. A., "The Need to Control International Bank Lending," *Banca Nazionale Del Lavoro Quarterly Review* (March 1980), pp. 57-81.

KETTELL, BRIAN, AND GEORGE MAGNUS, *The International Debt Game*. Cambridge, Mass.: Ballinger Publishing Company, 1986.

KEY, SYDNEY J., AND JAMES BRUNDY, "Implementation of the International Banking Act," *Federal Reserve Bulletin* (October 1979), pp. 785-796.

KHOURY, SARKIS, *Dynamics of International Banking*. New York: Praeger, 1980.

KIM, SEUNG, AND STEPHEN W. MILLER, *Competitive Structure of the International Banking Industry*. Lexington, Mass.: Lexington Books, 1983.

KRAYENBUEHL, THOMAS, *Country Risk*. Lexington, Mass.: Lexington Books, 1985.

KVASNICKA, JOSEPH G., *Readings in International Finance*, 3rd ed. Chicago: Federal Reserve Bank of Chicago, no date.

LEES, FRANCIS A., *Foreign Banking and Investment in the United States*. New York: Halsted Press, 1976.

LEES, FRANCIS A., *International Banking and Finance*. New York: John Wiley & Sons, 1974.

LESSARD, DONALD, AND JOHN WILLIAMSON, *Financial Intermediation Beyond the Debt Crisis*. Washington, D.C.: Institute for International Economics, 1985.

LEWIS, M. K., AND K. T. DAVIS, *Domestic and International Banking*. Cambridge, Mass.: The MIT Press, 1987.

LEWIS, W. ARTHUR, *The Evolution of the International Economic Order*. Princeton, N.J.: Princeton University Press, 1978.

LONG, M., AND F. VENEVOSA, "The Debt-related Problems of the Non-Oil Less Developed Countries," *Economic Development and Cultural Change* (April 1981), pp. 501-516.

MACDONALD, DUNCAN A., AND ROBERT L. GELTZER, *Federal Banking Laws*, rev. ed. Boston: Warren, Gorham and Lamont, 1979.

MATHIS, F. JOHN, "International Banking: An Outlook for the 1980s," *Journal of Commercial Bank Lending* (July 1980), pp. 25-32.

MATHIS, F. JOHN, ED., *Offshore Lending By U.S. Commercial Banks*, 2nd ed. Washington, D.C.: Bankers' Association for Foreign Trade and Robert Morris Associates, 1981.

McKINNON, RONALD I., *Money in International Exchange*. New York: Oxford University Press, 1979.

MEHRAN, HASSANALI, ED., *External Debt Management*. Washington, D.C.: International Monetary Fund, 1985.

MELOE, T., "Oil and the Transfer Problem," *Journal of Energy Development* (Autumn 1981), pp. 17-25.

MENDELSOHN, M. S., *Money on the Move*. New York: McGraw-Hill Book Co., 1980.

MERRILL, JAMES, "Country Risk Analysis," *Columbia Journal of World Business* (Spring 1982), pp. 88-91.

MEZNEZICS, I., *Law of Banking in East-West Trade*. Dobbs Ferry, N.Y.: Oceana Publications, 1973.

MIKESELL, RAYMOND F., AND J. HERBERT FURTH, *Foreign Dollar Balances and the International Role of the Dollar*. Washington, D.C.: National Bureau of Economic Research, 1974.

MONROE, WILBUR, *The New Internationalism*. Lexington, Mass.: Lexington Books, 1976.

MOYA, HENRI, "Euro-yen Bond Issues: A Growing Market?" *Finance and Development* (December 1978), pp. 42-44.

NAGY, PANCRAS, "Country Risk: A Quality Indicator for the International Loan Portfolio," *Euromoney* (April 1980), pp. 165-169.

NEHRT, L.C., *International Finance for Multinational Business*. Scranton, Pa.: International Textbook Co., 1973.

NOWZAD, BAHRAM, "Managing External Debt in Developing Countries," *Finance and Development* (September 1980), pp. 24-27.

ODLE, MAURICE, *Multinational Banks and Underdevelopment*. New York: Pergamon Press, 1981.

OGILVIE, NIGEL, "Foreign Banks in the U.S. and Geographic Restrictions on Banking," *Journal of Bank Research* (Summer 1980), pp. 72-79.

OH, JOHN S., *International Financial Management: Problems, Issues and Experience*. Greenwich, Conn.: Jai Press Inc., 1983.

OSINGHER, R., *Banks of the World*. New York: Walker and Company, 1967.

PARK, YOON S., AND JACK ZWICK, *International Banking in Theory and Practice*. Reading, Mass.: Addison-Wesley Publishing Company, 1985.

PEAT, MARWICK, MITCHELL & CO., *Banking in the United States* (A Guide for Foreign Bankers). New York: 1980.

PECCHIOLI, R. M., *Prudential Supervision in Banking*. Paris: Organization for Economic Cooperation and Development, 1987.

PECCHIOLI, R. M., *The Internationalisation of Banking* (The Policy Issues). Paris: Organization for Economic Cooperation and Development, 1983.

PHELPS, CLYDE W., *The Foreign Expansion of American Banks*. New York: Arno Press, 1976.

POLLARD, ALFRED M., ET AL., *Banking Law in the United States*. London: Butterworth Legal Publishers, 1988.

RIEHL, HEINZ, AND RITA M. RODRIGUEZ, *Foreign Exchange and Money Markets*. New York: McGraw-Hill Book Company, 1983.

ROBINSON, STUART W., *Multinational Banking*. Leiden: A.W. Sijthoff, 1972.
RODRIGUEZ, RITA M. AND E. EUGENE CARTER, *International Financial Management*. Englewood Cliffs, N.J.: Prentice-Hall, Inc., 1976.
ROOT, FRANKLIN, *International Trade and Investment*, 3rd ed., Cincinnati: South-Western Publishing Company, 1973.
ROSENBERG, JERRY, *Dictionary of Banking and Finance*. New York: John Wiley & Sons, 1982.
ROUSSAKIS, EMMANUEL, *International Banking: Principles and Practices*. New York: Praeger Publishers, 1983.
RUDING, H. O., "Country Risk: Lenders Ought to Consult the IMF," *Euromoney* (February 1980), pp. 34, 36, 38.
SAMPSON, ANTHONY, *The Money Lenders: Bankers and a World in Turmoil*. New York: Viking Press, 1982.
SAVAGE, DONALD T., "Developments in Banking Structure, 1970-81," *Federal Reserve Bulletin* (February 1982), pp. 79-89.
SCHULER, HAROLD D., "Evaluation of Risk in International Lending: A Bank Examiner's Perspective," *Key Issues in International Banking*. Federal Reserve Board of Boston (October 1977), pp. 137-153.
SHAPIRO, ALAN, *Foreign Exchange Risk and Management*. New York: American Management Association, 1978.
SHORT, GENIE DUDDING, AND BETSY BATTRILL WHITE, "International Bank Lending: A Guided Tour Through the Data," *Quarterly Review*, Federal Reserve Bank of New York (Autumn 1978), pp. 39-46.
SKULLY, MICHAEL T., *Financial Institutions and Markets in the Far East*. New York: St. Martin's Press, 1982.
SNOWDEN, P. N., *Emerging Risk in International Banking*. London: George Allen & Unwin, 1985.
SPERO, JOAN EDELMAN, *The Failure of the Franklin National Bank: Challenge to the International Banking System*. New York: Columbia University Press, 1980.
STERLING, J. F., "A New Look at International Lending by American Banks," *Columbia Journal of World Business* (Fall 1979), pp. 40-48.
STERN, RICHARD, "Insurance for Third World Currency Inconvertibility Protection." *Harvard Business Review* (May-June 1982), pp. 62-64.
STERN, SIEGFRIED, *The United States in International Banking*. New York: Columbia University Press, 1951.
STIGUM, MARCIA, AND RENE O. BRANCH, JR., *Managing Bank Assets and Liabilities*. Homewood, Ill.: Dow-Jones-Irwin, 1983.
SWANSON, P. E., "How Important Are OPEC Deposits in U.S. Banks?" *The Bankers Magazine* (September-October 1982), pp. 16-24.
TERRELL, HENRY S., AND SYDNEY J. KEY, "The Growth of Foreign Banking in the United States: An Analytical Survey." *Key Issues in International Banking*, Federal Reserve Bank of Boston (October 1977), pp. 54-86.
The Eurocurrency Market Control Act of 1979. Committee on Banking, Finance and Urban Affairs, U.S. House of Representatives, June 26 and 27 and July 12, 1979. Washington, D.C.: 1979.
The International Monetary System in Transition (A Symposium). Federal Reserve Bank of Chicago, March 1972.
The Rand McNally Bankers Directory. Chicago: Rand McNally & Company (published annually).
Trading in Foreign Exchange Markets. Hearings Before the Committee on Banking, Housing and Urban Affairs, U.S. Congress, December 20, 1978. Washington, D.C.: 1978.
TSCHOEGL, ADRIAN, *The Regulation of Foreign Banks: Policy Formation in Countries Outside the United States*. New York: Salomon Brothers Center for the Study of Financial Institutions, 1981.
U.S. Department of Treasury, *Report to Congress on Foreign Government Treatment of U.S. Commercial Banking Organizations*. Washington, D.C.: 1979.
WALLICH, HENRY C., "Why the Euromarkets Need Restraint," *Columbia Journal of World Business* (Fall 1977), pp. 17-24.

WALMSLEY, JULIAN, *The Foreign Exchange Handbook (A User's Guide)*. New York: John Wiley & Sons, Inc., 1983.

WASSERMAN, MAX J., ANDREAS PRINDL, AND CHARLES TOWNSEND, JR., *International Money Management*. New York: American Management Association, 1972.

WELLONS, PHILIP A., *World Money and Credit (The Crisis and Its Causes)*. Boston: Harvard Business School, 1983.

WELLONS, PHILIP A., *Passing the Buck*. Boston: Harvard Business School Press, 1987.

WILLETT, THOMAS D., *Floating Exchange Rates and International Monetary Reform*. Washington, D.C.: American Enterprise Institute, 1977.

WILLIAMS, ALEX O., *International Trade and Investment: A Managerial Approach*. New York: John Wiley & Sons, 1982.

WILLIAMS, DAVID, "Opportunities and Constraints in International Lending," *Finance and Development* (March 1983), pp. 24-27.

WOOD, GEOFFREY E., AND DOUGLAS R. MUDD, "Do Foreigners Control the U.S. Money Supply?" *Monthly Review*. Federal Reserve Bank of St. Louis (December 1977), pp. 8-11.

ZLOCH-CHRISTY, ILIANA, *Debt Problems of Eastern Europe*. Cambridge: Cambridge University Press, 1987.

INDEX

SUBJECT INDEX

NAME INDEX

(f= footnote; b = bibliography)